RENAISSANCE

DRAMA IN ENGLAND & SPAIN

Renaissance
Drama in England & Spain

TOPICAL ALLUSION AND

HISTORY PLAYS

JOHN LOFTIS

PRINCETON, NEW JERSEY

PRINCETON UNIVERSITY PRESS

MCM · LXXXVII

ISBN 0-691-06706-6

PUBLICATION OF THIS BOOK HAS BEEN AIDED BY
A GRANT FROM THE PAUL MELLON FUND
OF PRINCETON UNIVERSITY PRESS

CLOTHBOUND EDITIONS OF
PRINCETON UNIVERSITY PRESS BOOKS
ARE PRINTED ON ACID-FREE PAPER, AND
BINDING MATERIALS ARE CHOSEN FOR
STRENGTH AND DURABILITY. PAPER-
BACKS, ALTHOUGH SATISFACTORY FOR
PERSONAL COLLECTIONS, ARE NOT
USUALLY SUITABLE FOR
LIBRARY REBINDING

★

PRINTED IN THE UNITED STATES OF
AMERICA BY PRINCETON UNIVERSITY PRESS
PRINCETON, NEW JERSEY

THIS BOOK IS
FOR MY GRANDCHILDREN
SAFIA BENAOUDA, MATTHEW &
REBECCA CRAVEN &
ANDREW TULLER

Contents

List of Illustrations

Preface

IN THE long span of years between Lope de Vega's death in
1635 and the beginning of the twentieth century, Spain's
fortunes were declining, while England's—after the trauma of
the Great Civil War—were rising. Images used in Golden Age
drama to describe the Spanish empire became commonplace in
descriptions of the British empire. Espínola in Calderón's *El
sitio de Bredá* anticipates a familiar English boast (II.i):

> *a su dilatado imperio*
> *sirva de testigo el sol,*
> *sin que le falte un momento.*   (Ed. Valbuena Briones, I, 84a)

> the sun serves as a witness to his [Philip IV's] vast empire, never
> leaving it for a moment.

England became very rich, as Habsburg Spain had been. English
became an international language, rivaling Spanish in its
geographical dispersion and in the number of its speakers.

   The altered roles of the two nations had consequences in the
attention devoted to their national dramas outside Spain and
England and their former colonies. This is one reason—but
only one and probably not the most important—why Golden
Age drama is not more widely studied in Britain and the
United States. "Of all the notable achievements in European
literature," Clifford Leech wrote in 1950, "the Spanish drama
of the sixteenth and seventeenth centuries is the least known to
English readers." I would alter Leech's final phrase to "English-speaking
readers" and add that little has changed in the
thirty-six years since he wrote this.

   To be sure, a distinguished company of English and American
men and women of letters have admired the *comedia*, and,
particularly in the twentieth century, English-speaking Hispanists
have been among the leaders in critical, bibliographical,
biographical, and editorial studies devoted to Golden Age
drama. But the number of Hispanists in Britain and the United

States is small; the number of serious students of English literature is much larger. Apart from my thematic preoccupations in this book, I attempt to demonstrate that the *comedia* can contribute to our understanding of English Renaissance drama.

Because the calendar in use in England in the later sixteenth and the seventeenth centuries differed from that used in Spain and most other Continental nations, I must explain my practice in dating events. The Julian or Old Style calendar of the English differed in two major respects from the Gregorian or New Style calendar of the Continent: in England a new year began on March 25, on the Continent on January 1; in the period with which I am concerned, dates of the months in England were ten days behind those on the Continent. When referring to events on the Continent, I use the New Style calendar; when referring to events in England, I follow customary modern practice in considering a year to begin on January 1 but otherwise using the dates of the Old Style calendar. In my accounts of Prince Charles's residence in Madrid in 1623 and the English attack on Cádiz in 1625, I provide double dates.

I am pleased to have an opportunity to acknowledge assistance given me by institutions as well as by individuals in writing this book. Among the institutions, I thank my university, Stanford, for sabbatical leave in addition to much else; the National Endowment for the Humanities for a fellowship for independent study and research; the Ford Foundation, not only for recent grants administered by Stanford that assisted me in research travel and the preparation of my manuscript for publication, but also for a fellowship thirty years ago from its subsidiary, the Fund for the Advancement of Education, that enabled me to begin the study of Spanish Golden Age drama.

Among the individuals, I must first thank Mrs. Carol B. Pearson, who has provided skilled assistance with this book as with most of my writing and editorial projects since 1961. I thank the editors in whose journals articles, portions of which I reprint here, were published in somewhat different form: Professors Thomas R. Hart and Steven F. Rendall, respectively editor and associate editor of *Comparative Literature* ("*Henry VIII* and Calderón's *La cisma de Inglaterra*," *CL* 34 [1982]: 208–22); and Professors Arthur F. Kinney and Kirby Farrell, respectively editor and co-editor of *English Literary Renaissance* ("English Renaissance Plays from the Spanish *Comedia*," *ELR* 14 [1984]: 230–48).

Because this book has led to areas of study that for me were new, I have sought assistance from a group of scholars who have responded generously: Professors Willard F. King and Shirley B. Whitaker in Spanish; Professors Leland H. Carlson and Paul H. Hardacre in History; Professors W. B. Carnochan, J. Kent Clark, and Herbert Lindenberger in English. Most of them read a preliminary draft of my manuscript in the summer of 1984 and collectively they gave me substantive and organizational recommendations that enabled me, during the following year, to make comprehensive revisions. The final draft, including possible error, is mine.

In three conversations in consecutive summers, Willard King answered bibliographical questions and made suggestions that proved to be fruitful: about the writings of Francis Bacon and several Spanish theologians on the doctrine of "just war"; about Spanish political theorists' assertions of the right of Catholic rulers to "dissimulate" in dealing with Protestants; about the significance of Cervantes' *La Numancia*. Shirley Whitaker made suggestions that led me to two Spanish plays which include reference to Prince Charles's courtship of the infanta María, gave me copies of relevant passages from documents she had transcribed in the Tuscan archives, and called my attention to recently published work. Leland Carlson gave me useful transcripts of passages from Tudor documents, corrected errors I had made, and wisely advised me to shorten my manuscript. Paul Hardacre provided references to the work of historians who in the past twenty-five years have clarified our understanding of King James I, and he explained the role of Maximilian, duke of Bavaria, in the first phases of the Thirty Years' War. My colleagues at Stanford, Bliss Carnochan and Herbert Lindenberger, gave help from the beginning, and they provided indispensable guidance in recent developments in the theory of literary scholarship.

My debt to Kent Clark is unique. With a generosity of time I have experienced only once before (from my dissertation director, Louis A. Landa), he wrote critiques of the preliminary drafts of my chapters, providing detailed recommendations for revision. I am grateful indeed.

Stanford, California
JUNE 27, 1986

List of Abbreviations

A.S.F.   Archivo di Stato di Firenze

B.A.E.   Biblioteca de Autores Españoles

BH   *Bulletin Hispanique*

BHS   *Bulletin of Hispanic Studies*

B.L.   British Library

CODOIN   *Colección de documentos inéditos para la historia de España*, 103 vols. (Madrid: 1842–95)

C.S.P.   *Calendar of State Papers*

DIE   *Documentos inéditos para la historia de España* (Madrid: Tipografía de Archivos, 1936–   )

Ed. Acad.   *Obras de Lope de Vega*, 15 vols. (The Royal Academy of Spain: 1890–1913)

ELH   *A Journal of English Literary History*

ELR   *English Literary Renaissance*

ESR   *European Studies Review*

H.M.C.   Historical Manuscripts Commission

JEGP   *Journal of English and Germanic Philology*

Historia *Historia de España*, founder Ramón Menéndez Pidal (Madrid: Espasa-Calpe, 1935–   )

            Manuel Fernández Álvarez, *La España del Emperador Carlos V*, 2nd edn., 20 (Madrid: Espasa-Calpe, 1979)

            Luis Fernández y Fernández de Retana, *España en Tiempo de Felipe II*, 3rd edn., 22 (Madrid: Espasa-Calpe, 1976)

            Ciriaco Pérez Bustamente, *La España de Felipe III*, 24 (Madrid: Espasa-Calpe, 1979)

            Francisco Tomás y Valiente et al., *La España de Felipe IV*, 25 (Madrid: Espasa-Calpe, 1982)

MLN   *Modern Language Notes*

MLR   *Modern Language Review*

PMLA   *Publications of the Modern Language Association of America*

PQ   *Philological Quarterly*

P.R.O.   Public Record Office

RD   *Renaissance Drama*

RES   *Review of English Studies*

RQ   *Renaissance Quarterly*

SEL   *Studies in English Literature*

STC   Alfred W. Pollard and Gilbert R. Redgrave, *A Short-Title Catalogue of Books Printed in England, Scotland, and Ireland, and of English Books Printed Abroad, 1475–1640*, 2 vols. (London: Bibliographical Society, 1926)

BLACK KNIGHT [*representing the count of Gondomar*]:
But let me a little solace my designs
With the remembrance of some brave ones past
To cherish the futurity of project
Whose motion must be restless till that great work
Called the possession of the world be ours.

  THOMAS MIDDLETON, *A Game at Chess* (1624)

SERGEANT:
¡Bredá por el Rey de España!
Breda for [has yielded to] the King of Spain!

AMBROSIO SPÍNOLA, *marquis of the Balbases:*
¡Y plegue al cielo que llegue
a serlo el mundo, rendido
desde levante a poniente!

And may heaven grant the whole world may
come to be under his sovereignty!

  CALDERÓN DE LA BARCA, *El sitio de Bredá* (1625)

Chapter One

INTRODUCTION: THE REFORMATION
IN ENGLAND

The place of the royal divorce in the history of the Reformation will always remain a subject for argument. Protestant writers have tended to dismiss it as a mere "occasion" rather than a genuine cause; Catholics have sometimes regarded the divorce as the chief cause of the cataclysm and supposed that, had it not been pressed, England might well have remained a Catholic nation.

> A. G. DICKENS, *The English Reformation* (1964)

WRITING IN 1734, Voltaire called attention to the early appearance in England and Spain of preeminent dramatists: "The English as well as the Spanish already had a theatre when the French had only stages made of trestles. Shakespeare, whom the English regard as a Sophocles, flourished at about the same time as Lope de Vega: he created their theatre."[1] Of course, Shakespeare did not create the English theatre. But Voltaire isolated the essential facts: Shakespeare and Lope (1562–1635), close contemporaries whose careers reveal similarities, began to write plays several decades before the first of the great French dramatists, Pierre Corneille, did so—before the formulations of dramatic theorists became as influential as they were in French classical drama and in English Restoration drama.

Even Voltaire's prejudices are informative. In a letter of 1776 to the French Academy, he attributed what he regarded as barbarisms in Shakespeare's tragedies to the influence of Spain:

> Yes, gentlemen, in this dark chaos [of Shakespeare], made up of murders and ludicrous behavior, of heroism and of vice, of dia-

---

[1] Voltaire, *Lettres philosophiques* in *Oeuvres complètes*, ed. Louis Moland, 22 (Paris: Garnier Frères, 1879), 148–49. All translations are mine unless otherwise noted.

logue sometimes fit for the marketplace and sometimes of great interest, there are striking insights into human nature. Tragedy was similar in Spain under Philip II, during the lifetime of Shakespeare. At that time the temper of Spain, as you know, dominated Europe, even Italy. Lope de Vega is a great example of it. . . . [Lope's] contemporaries and even more his predecessors made Spanish drama a monster to please the public.

It was impossible, Voltaire added, that the example of the Spanish stage should not have an impact in England; it corrupted the plays of English dramatists long before the time of Shakespeare.[2] Voltaire's dramatic history will not sustain close scrutiny. He articulated an assumption about the relationship of English to Spanish drama that in modified form continued to haunt study of the subject into the twentieth century.

We now know that the similarities between the Spanish and English dramas are the consequence of independent development from medieval literature. The two nations were at war from 1585 until 1604, crucial years in the histories of their dramas; and travel between the countries was all but impossible. Because of England's alliance with the Dutch, who had spent many years under Spanish rule, Englishmen had opportunities to read Spanish plays and perhaps to see them in performance in Amsterdam.[3] Nevertheless, the direct influence of Spanish drama was slight.[4] As for the influence of English plays upon Spanish dramatists, it was nonexistent. No Spanish Golden Age play of any consequence has been traced to an English one.

Voltaire overstates Lope's and Shakespeare's indifference to Classical and Renaissance dramatic theory. Both dramatists were familiar with neoclassical precepts, though they observed them selectively. Shakespeare wrote no critical statement com-

---

[2] Ibid., 30 (1880), 364.

[3] See John Loftis, *The Spanish Plays of Neoclassical England* (New Haven: Yale University Press, 1973), pp. 36–37; and Henry W. Sullivan, *Calderón in the German Lands and the Low Countries: His Reception and Influence, 1654–1980* (Cambridge: Cambridge University Press, 1983), pp. 45–47.

[4] On the English plays based on Spanish ones, see the Appendix, below.

parable to Lope's *El arte nuevo de hacer comedias in este tiempo*[5] or Cervantes' prologue to Act II of *El rufián dichoso*. Yet, as Leo Salingar puts it, "The Spanish dramatists make explicit a conscious choice in face of the rules which is implicit in Shakespeare."[6] Attention to Lope's and Shakespeare's refusal to discriminate consistently between matters appropriate to comedy and to tragedy and their indifference to the unities of time and place has obscured their concern for other aspects of neoclassical theory: for example, those pertaining to dramatic action and to decorum in characterization. In their attitudes toward neoclassicism, the two men are representative of most of their important contemporary dramatists.

This conscious refusal to be limited by neoclassical theory made possible the development of history plays that are representations—with varying degrees of fidelity to historical or semihistorical records or legends (including in Spain the record preserved in the ballads)—of coherent sequences of events, usually of national significance. Although the dramatists sometimes turned for their subjects to the Rome or Greece of antiquity or to the histories of foreign countries, they wrote most frequently about their own countries. Spain and England alone in the Renaissance produced important dramas of national history.[7]

[5] See Lope's *El arte nuevo* in the edition, with a preliminary study, by Juana de José Prades (Madrid: Consejo Superior de Investigaciones Científicas, 1971). See also, on Lope's classical learning, Duncan Moir, "The Classical Tradition in Spanish Dramatic Theory and Practice in the Seventeenth Century," in M. J. Anderson, ed., *Classical Drama and Its Influence* (New York: Barnes and Noble, 1965), pp. 193–228.

[6] Salingar, *Shakespeare and the Traditions of Comedy* (Cambridge: Cambridge University Press, 1974), p. 80.

On Shakespeare's training in classical literature and in rhetoric, see "Shakespeare's Grammar-School Training": Chapter 2 in Virgil K. Whitaker, *Shakespeare's Use of Learning: An Inquiry into the Growth of his Mind & Art* (San Marino: The Huntington Library, 1953), pp. 14–44.

[7] The history play, as the term is applied to Spanish and English drama, is incompatible with French seventeenth-century classicism. The focus of Corneille and even more of Racine on the interrelationships of a few historical characters at a decisive time in their lives produced history plays remarkable for emotional intensity and insight into motives for behavior. But attention to

By the late sixteenth century, drama in Spain and England had reached a level of maturity that enabled men of genius to examine the fundamental issues of their time, including those related to Spain's military power and aggressiveness. Spain "hath an ambition to the whole empire of Christendom," Francis Bacon wrote;[8] Lope de Vega and Thomas Middleton alike would have endorsed this assertion. Lope's plays reveal his allegiance to the Spanish imperial tradition and his acceptance of the premise on which it was based: that it was Spain's destiny to rule the world. Dramatists of both nations wrote plays about Spain's efforts to achieve that destiny; in doing so they provided alternative versions of European history in the sixteenth and early seventeenth centuries.

To examine the differences in historical interpretation in Spanish and English plays is to be reminded that history in any form in which we encounter it is culture-bound, not objective, not immutable. Historical drama and narrative history alike are conditioned by the time at which they are written, by social and institutional constraints, by the nature of available sources, by literary theory and convention, and—in the Spain and England of the Renaissance—by myth: in Spain, by the myth of the nation's imperial destiny; in England, by the myth known in the twentieth century as the "Black Legend."[9]

In a recent essay portraying what he calls "a new history in

---

the unity of time precluded the representation of historical process.

On the French history play, see Herbert Lindenberger, *Historical Drama: The Relation of Literature and Reality* (Chicago: University of Chicago Press, 1975), pp. 4–5.

[8] "A Short View to be taken of Great Britain and Spain" (1619), *Works*, ed. James Spedding et al., 14 (London: Longmans, Green, 1874), 26.

[9] Although the term "Black Legend" is of twentieth-century origin, the phenomenon to which it refers had its beginnings in the sixteenth century, in denunciations of the conquistadores' alleged inhumanity to the Indians of America. The Legend gained force during the Revolt of the Netherlands, in the course of which Spanish imperial policy became a subject of Dutch and English propaganda. Philip Wayne Powell describes "The Basic Premise of the Black Legend": "Spaniards have shown themselves, historically, to be *uniquely* cruel, bigoted, tyrannical, obscurantist, lazy, fanatical, greedy, and treacherous" (*Tree of Hate: Propaganda and Prejudices Affecting United States Relations with the Hispanic World* [New York: Basic Books, 1971], p. 11).

literary study," Herbert Lindenberger writes that to many scholars history has sometimes come to seem "no more than just another fiction."[10] Certainly the existence of a fictional dimension in history is suggested by differences between a Spanish and an English play on the Reformation in England.

★

In May 1527, troops of the Holy Roman Emperor Charles V captured Rome and took Pope Clement VII prisoner. Charles, not in Italy at the time, learned of all this after it happened. His commander in Italy, the duke of Bourbon, had been forced to take the offensive by a league of Italian princes led by Clement VII in his temporal role as ruler of the papal domains. Unpaid and hungry, the imperial troops, many of them German Lutherans, were not to be held back. In the attack on Rome, May 6, the duke of Bourbon was killed; his death intensified the ferocity of the imperial troops, who for eight days plundered the city. The pope found refuge in the Castle Saint Angelo, where he was confined[11] until December, when Charles arranged for his release.

At about the time these events occurred, Henry VIII of England made known his desire to dissolve his marriage to Katherine, the emperor's aunt. Had there not been cause for hostility between Clement and Charles, Henry could scarcely have expected the pope to antagonize so powerful a person as the emperor by an act that would humiliate a member of the emperor's family. Both Henry and Cardinal Wolsey, acting independently, attempted unsuccessfully to make use of the pope's captivity to gain an annulment of the king's marriage. After releasing Clement, Charles could not relinquish his military power over the pope lest Clement again—in his secular

---

[10] Lindenberger, "Toward a New History in Literary Study," in *Profession 84* (New York: Modern Language Association, 1984), p. 16. A recent book with a focus on eighteenth-century France provides a valuable analysis of the subject described in its first title: Suzanne Gearhart, *The Open Boundary of History and Fiction: A Critical Approach to the French Enlightenment* (Princeton: Princeton University Press, 1984).

[11] Manuel Fernández Álvarez, *Emperador Carlos V: Historia*, 20: 407–12.

role—make war on Charles's own territories. By 1529 Henry understood that he could expect nothing from Rome and that Wolsey was useless to him. He dismissed Wolsey and looked for a solution to his problem in England.[12]

To Charles V, the Reformation in England meant the loss of a useful ally. To his son, Philip II, it meant—after the death of his wife Queen Mary I—the transformation of a useful ally into a dangerous enemy.

To Shakespeare and Calderón, the English Reformation provided the subject of plays—*Henry VIII* and *La cisma de Inglaterra*—plays that reveal characteristic Protestant and Catholic interpretations of the cause of the religious revolution. Writing in 1613 about a performance of *Henry VIII*, Sir Henry Wotton calls the play "All is True," presumably using its second or alternate title. Shakespeare's prologue reiterates the claim to "truth."[13] Yet such an assertion in the title of a play about the English Reformation—a controversial and emotionally charged subject—would seem to invite contradiction. Some external and public facts about the momentous event can be determined with assurance, but not the motives and private actions of persons who had leading roles in bringing it about.

If it is impossible to say what is the truth about the English Reformation, it is at least possible to say that more Catholics than Protestants have believed that they knew the cause of it. From Shakespeare's time to our own, Catholics have often as-

---

[12] A. G. Dickens, *The English Reformation* (London: B. T. Batsford, 1964), pp. 106–07; J. J. Scarisbrick, *Henry VIII* (Berkeley: University of California Press, 1968), pp. 198–235.

[13] Shakespeare, *King Henry VIII*, ed. R. A. Foakes, New Arden, corrected edn. (London: Methuen, 1964), pp. 180, xxviii–xxix. (All citations of Shakespeare follow the New Arden editions.) Foakes notes that the alternate title might have been directed against Samuel Rowley's play about Henry VIII, *When You See Me, You Know Me*.

In a later study, Foakes returns to the subject of "truth" in *Henry VIII*: "The truth is not simple, or easily arrived at, and the nature of 'truth' is as central an issue in the action as is the business of 'rule' " (*Shakespeare, the Dark Comedies to the Last Plays: From Satire to Celebration* [London: Routledge & Kegan Paul, 1971], p. 175).

sumed that Henry's divorce of Katherine determined England's break with Rome; Protestants, on the other hand, have ordinarily considered the divorce to be an important event in complex developments that would, in time, have led to the Reformation even if the king had remained faithful to his first wife.[14]

La cisma de Inglaterra and *Henry VIII* illustrate Catholic and Protestant attitudes on the subject: the former, tightly organized, with a focus from beginning to end on the divorce; the latter, loosely organized, with the divorce and its consequences portrayed in the context of thirteen years of Henry's reign. Most of Shakespeare's first act is taken up with the arrest and trial of the duke of Buckingham on a charge of high treason. Henry does not meet Anne Boleyn until late in the first act (I.iv), after his concern with perpetuating his dynasty has been revealed. *La cisma* opens with a scene in which Henry, asleep, has a dream that prefigures the divorce.[15]

★

For nearly a hundred years, from the mid-nineteenth until almost the mid-twentieth century, criticism of *Henry VIII* was

[14] See Dickens, *The English Reformation*, p. 107.

[15] In an important and influential article of 1948 on Shakespeare's and Calderón's plays, Alexander A. Parker justly asserted the excellence of *La cisma de Inglaterra* ("Henry VIII in Shakespeare and Calderón: An Appreciation of *La cisma de Ingalaterra*," *MLR* 43 (1948): 327–52; reprinted in J. E. Varey, ed., *Critical Studies of Calderón's Comedias* [London: Gregg International Publishers, 1973], pp. 47–83. Subsequent references are to the reprint). Parker is severe indeed, however, in his criticism of *Henry VIII*, excessively so in my opinion. At the time he wrote—on the eve of a resurgence of interest in *Henry VIII*—he could have found precedent for much, though not all, of his criticism of the English play in the works of Shakespearean scholars.

Parker's criticism of *Henry VIII* in comparison with *La cisma* seemingly does not take into account differences in the English and Spanish dramatic traditions. Shakespeare wrote an English history play (in which some obligation to recorded history is recognized); Calderón wrote a *comedia* (in which historical accuracy is subordinated to thematic and structural concerns). ". . . despite its impressive action," Parker writes about *La cisma*, "the subtle pattern of its structure and its artistic unity, *La cisma de Ingalaterra* is a travesty of history. Must a historical play that is a successful example of dramatic art be none the

preempted by consideration of its authorship. Although earlier critics had noted metrical irregularities in the play and
questioned Shakespeare's sole authorship of it, James Spedding, the distinguished editor of Francis Bacon's works, gave
impetus to consideration of the subject: in 1850 he published a
study in which he assigned certain scenes to Shakespeare and
others to Fletcher as collaborator, largely on the basis of an examination of language and versification.[16] The subject of authorship is related to critical analysis: the most frequent criti-

---

less condemned if it alters historical fact?" Like Parker, I would answer that
question with a negative. But is it just to compare and contrast the structure
of a play that wears its history so lightly with the structure of one, such as
Henry VIII, that follows the chronicles except in minor details?

Parker finds grounds for criticism of *Henry VIII* in the principle of poetic
justice as it is observed or not observed in the portrayal of Queen Katherine by
Calderón and Shakespeare. It should be noted that Katherine is not the protagonist of either drama but the victim, culpable or not, of events having national importance, interpreted differently by the two dramatists.

Parker contrasts their depiction of the queen's fate. First, Shakespeare's:
"She is an innocent victim, and the fullest demand is made on our sympathy
for her. Everything possible is done to enhance her moral stature, to make her,
in Henry's own words, 'the queen of earthly queens' " (p. 51). Whatever the
conventions of the *comedia*, English Renaissance dramatists portray, repeatedly
and poignantly, innocent victims suffering and sometimes dying through no
fault of their own. If the victim is a protagonist—Cleopatra, for example—
moral responsibility often becomes relevant, but it is not consistently so in
English drama and criticism written before the Restoration.

Parker prefers Calderón's portrayal of the queen because the Spanish playwright, unlike Shakespeare, depicts her as responsible for her misfortunes:
". . . she is not, as in Shakespeare's play, an innocent victim; for she has
brought her own disaster upon herself. This departure from his source [in Ri-
vadeneira] is further evidence of Calderón's dramatic skill, of his impressive
transformation of this theme into moving art" (p. 70).

Many Hispanists disagree with the conception of poetic justice implicit in
this passage. (For an informed and well-reasoned rebuttal to Parker's arguments concerning poetic justice in the *comedia*, see Willard F. King, "*El caballero de Olmedo*: Poetic Justice or Destiny?" in *Homenaje a William L. Fichter*, ed.
A. David Kossoff and José Amor y Vázquez [Madrid: Editorial Castalia,
1971], pp. 367–79.) Anglicists will find the conception alien to their experience
of drama.

[16] J[ames] S[pedding], "Who Wrote Shakspere's *Henry VIII*?" *Gentleman's
Magazine*, n.s., 34 (1850): 115–23, 381–82.

cism of *Henry VIII* concerns alleged lack of continuity between episodes and inconsistency of tone—qualities that could be attributed to collaboration. The controversy initiated by Spedding has not been terminated and perhaps never can be, but the subject has ceased to have major importance in assessments of a play that is included in the First Folio and that has always been regarded as part of the Shakespeare canon.

The opinions about the play expressed by early critics contrast with those of some of the leading Shakespeareans of the twentieth century, though the difference is attributable partially to the circumstance that in the earlier era, which was one of repertory theatres, the play was often seen in performance. In 1691 Gerard Langbaine emphasized its popularity with audiences: "This Play frequently appears on the present Stage; the part of *Henry* being extreamly well acted by Mr. *Betterton*."[17]

Nearly a century later, in 1783, Samuel Johnson and Sarah Siddons agreed in conversation that "Queen Catharine, in *Henry the Eighth*" was "the most natural" of Shakespeare's characters, and Johnson complimented the actress with the remark that "whenever you perform it, I will once more hobble out to the theatre myself."[18] Earlier, Johnson had not been uncritical of *Henry VIII*, but he had described the death scene of the queen (IV.ii) as "above any other part of Shakespeare's tragedies, and perhaps above any scene of any other poet, tender and pathetick, without gods, or furies, or poisons, or precipices, without the help of romantick circumstances, without improbable sallies of poetical lamentation, and without any throes of tumultuous misery."[19]

The conception of the play conveyed by these remarks differs sharply from the opinion expressed by J. Dover Wilson (1881–1969) in a prefatory note to J. C. Maxwell's 1962 edition that he, Wilson, finds the play "less interesting than any other

[17] *An Account of the English Dramatick Poets* (Oxford, 1691), p. 457.
[18] James Boswell, *Life of Johnson*, ed. R. W. Chapman; new edn. corr. J. D. Fleeman (London, New York: Oxford University Press, 1970), p. 1251.
[19] *Johnson on Shakespeare*, ed. Arthur Sherbo, 8 (New Haven, Conn.: Yale University Press, 1968), 653.

in the Folio," adding that "its chief interest to me is the question of authorship."[20] Wilson wrote late in his career. Few Shakespeareans now active would share his opinion.

★

A brief account of Calderón's dramatic action will reveal how neatly structured it is, as well as how different the action is from Shakespeare's. Shakespeare and Calderón wrote different kinds of plays, both of them remarkable achievements, within the different dramatic patterns of their countries.

Calderón opens with a scene that provides, in its revelation of the conflicts in Henry's mind, a foreshadowing of the momentous events to come. Seated at a writing table in his private chamber, Henry, sleeping lightly, perceives the beautiful figure of a woman, which he subsequently learns is that of Anne Boleyn.[21] He awakens as Wolsey enters and, strangely troubled, tells his minister about the dream that had come to him as he dozed while trying to write a refutation of Luther's arguments about the sacrament of marriage. Wolsey has brought the king letters from both the pope and Luther, and unwittingly Henry opens Luther's first.

Several short scenes follow. In the first, Wolsey in soliloquy makes known his ambition to become pope, with the support of Henry and also of either King Francis I of France or the emperor Charles V. In another scene, we learn that the French ambassador loves Anne Boleyn, who had recently been in France with her father (Sir Thomas, Earl of Wiltshire and Or-

---

[20] Maxwell, ed., *King Henry the Eighth* (Cambridge: Cambridge University Press, 1962), p. vii. Maxwell himself in his Introduction is notably more severe in his criticism of the play than R. A. Foakes had been in his New Arden edition of 1957.

For a compact review of the history of the criticism of *Henry VIII*, see H. M. Richmond, "Shakespeare's *Henry VIII*: Romance Redeemed by History," *Shakespeare Studies* 4 (1968): 334–49.

[21] For a study of the role of the unconscious in the play, see Ludwig Pfandl, "Ausdrucksformen des archaischen Denkens und des Unbewussten bei Calderón," in Heinrich Finke, ed., *Gesammelte Aufsätze zur Kulturgeschichte Spaniens*, 6 (Münster, Westphalia: Verlag der Aschendorffschen Verlagsbuchhandlung, 1937), 366–89.

mond), the English ambassador to that country. In another, Anne is received as a lady in waiting by Queen Katherine in a large assembly that includes the French ambassador. In a portentous scene, Wolsey angers Queen Katherine by his lack of tact in refusing to allow her to enter the king's chamber, the king having instructed him to admit no one. In a display of emotion, the queen denounces Wolsey, reminding him of his humble birth. Wolsey foresees danger for himself in the queen's anger and recalls a warning by his nurse that a woman would be the cause of his destruction.

Wolsey's fear of the queen leads him to plan her disgrace. He finds a ready instrument in Anne Boleyn, who has captivated the king as lady in waiting and is eager to employ her charms in the manner Wolsey counsels. At an opportune moment, Wolsey tells the king that his marriage to Katherine, the widow of his older brother, was illegal and that hence the king is a bachelor: "Tú estás, señor, soltero: / no fué tu matrimonio verdadero."[22] Although the king, as he later admits in soliloquy, believes that Wolsey has not advised him truthfully, he accepts Wolsey's judgment and orders him to summon the royal counselors. They come and are assembled before the king and queen seated in state. The king, after reminding them of his diligence in maintaining the purity of the Catholic faith, announces with feigned grief that his marriage is unlawful and that the queen must leave him, although Princess Mary is to remain the acknowledged successor to his throne. To the queen's dignified though tearful expostulation, Henry turns his back and leaves, accompanied by Wolsey.

We learn of the king's marriage to Anne in a conversation between the French ambassador, who had hoped to marry her himself, and his friend and confidant. Wolsey appears in his pride, disdainfully refusing to accept the petitions of poor soldiers. When he asks the new queen for a position for himself, "la presidencia del reino," she refuses, having already given

[22] Pedro Calderón de la Barca, *Obras completas: Vol. 1, Dramas,* ed. Ángel Valbuena Briones, 1 (Madrid: Aguilar, 1959), 574a. (All quotations from Calderón follow this edition.)

that position to her father. She expresses in soliloquy the irritation she feels in having an obligation to Wolsey. Soon she finds opportunity, in the king's fatuous love for her, to dispose not only of the cardinal but of Katherine as well. To the latter she sends poison; to the former she brings dismissal and disgrace by telling Henry that Wolsey has spoken to her without respect. Katherine and Wolsey appear in their sorrows, first separately and then together, the queen compassionate and forgiving, the cardinal despairing. He dies a suicide. Soldiers escort Princess Mary to Queen Katherine, with whom she is to reside. But the queen has only a short while to live: a captain brings her a letter from the king in which Anne Boleyn has secretly placed poison.

Meanwhile the king reveals in soliloquy his troubled mind, his suspicions of all around him. In an effort to learn the true feelings of his courtiers, he listens secretly from an enclosed room to conversations—and soon hears Anne Boleyn incriminate herself in a private meeting with the French ambassador. The king acts swiftly and terribly, ordering the arrest and imprisonment in the Tower of Anne and the Frenchman. Anne's pleas do not save her from death. Henry determines that Katherine should return. Princess Mary tells him of her mother's death and begs justice for herself. This the king grants in a final scene of stately ceremony, in which, not without hesitation, the princess promises to uphold the laws—with a reservation, spoken in an aside, that she will restore and protect Catholicism—and is proclaimed her father's rightful successor.

★

A summary account such as this one, based on a literal reading of the play, would be misleading without closer attention to Calderón's final scene. The birth of Queen Elizabeth (on September 7, 1533) has not been mentioned. The play closes with the execution of her mother, Anne Boleyn, followed by the ceremonial induction of Mary as "Princesa de Walia." Mary's perjury, in taking the oath required of her with a secret resolution to violate its conditions, raises interpretative problems for a modern audience. When her reluctance to swear to

uphold the Protestant settlement in the English church becomes apparent, Thomas Boleyn asks the king to intercede
with her, saying that the leaders of the kingdom will not swear
allegiance unless she takes the oath. Mary replies defiantly, in
lines that look forward to the historical queen's reign. The
leaders act judiciously, she says, because they believe that those
who swear allegiance to her, and fail to comply with what her
law requires, will be burned alive if they do not repent. The
king speaks, attributing Mary's intransigence to her age: she is
prudent and will know how to moderate her conduct.

> *El reino puede jurarla,*
> *y si, cuando llegue a Reina,*
> *no fuere del reino a gusto,*
> *depóngala Ingalaterra.*

The kingdom can swear allegiance to her, and if, when she becomes
queen, she is displeasing to the kingdom, England can depose her.

He then speaks in an aside to Mary:

> *Callad y disimulad,*
> *que tiempo vendrá en que pueda*
> *ese celo ejecutarse,*
> *ser incendio esa centella.*

Keep quiet and dissimulate; the time will come
when you can reveal your zeal, and the smoldering
fire of your passion can burst into flame.

After brief hesitation, she speaks, referring to the provisions of
the Protestant religious settlement in England:

> *Yo la recibo.* Ap. *Sin ellas.*[23]

I accept. *Aside.* Without them.

After cheering and ceremonies of rejoicing, the play closes.

    How are we to interpret the princess's action: taking a sol-
emn oath with intent to violate it? Mario Ford Bacigalupo argues that Calderón employs the episode to prefigure Mary's

----

[23] Ibid., 1:588b.

failure to reestablish Catholicism when she became queen.[24] At the time the play was written and first performed, Bacigalupo writes, the dramatist and his audiences knew that Mary had attempted and failed to reestablish Catholicism in England. Calderón chose to explain the failure—the argument goes—by attributing it to moral weakness in Mary, who is portrayed in the play as committing an act of deception said to be contrary to natural law and to the Catholic religion. In support of his argument, Bacigalupo quotes a passage from Pedro de Rivadeneira (with whose writings we may assume Calderón was familiar),[25] in which Rivadeneira asserts the importance of a person's keeping his promises, particularly those made under oath.

Bacigalupo quotes from Rivadeneira's *Tratado de la religión y virtudes que debe tener un príncipe cristiano* (1595);[26] other sections of the *Tratado* have more relevance to the difficult position of Calderón's Princess Mary in the final scene of *La cisma*. Rivadeneira recognizes that the duties and responsibilities of princes sometimes require a wide latitude in conduct. Although careful to avoid the amoral expedience of Machiavelli's "reason of state," he would allow the prince to "dissimulate" in certain circumstances, among them when dealing with heretics.[27] He provides an example that has application to Princess Mary's declared intention to use cruel measures in the future and her decision to use deception in the present:

> With his own example and other mild measures the prince will try to banish from his kingdom infectious doctrines. He should also distinguish between those who are deceived and those who maliciously embrace false doctrines. But if conciliation fails he must use harsh and vigorous measures. Before applying them, however, he

[24] Bacigalupo, "Calderón's *La cisma de Ingalaterra* and Spanish Seventeenth-Century Thought," *Symposium* 28 (1974): 212–26.

[25] Calderón's source for *La cisma* was a tract written by Rivadeneira.

[26] Pedro de Rivadeneira, S.J., *Tratado*, in *Obras escogidas*, ed. Vicente de la Fuente, B.A.E. 60 (Madrid: M. Rivadeneyra, 1868), 542.

[27] For an informed discussion of the subject, see J. A. Fernández-Santamaría, *Reason of State and Statecraft in Spanish Political Thought, 1595–1640* (Lanham, Md.: University Press of America, 1983), pp. 89–93.

should be very attentive to the conditions prevailing in the realm and find out whether the heretics are many or few. Because if the entire kingdom, or a large part thereof, is heretical and it is impossible to uproot the tares without damaging the wheat or without serious danger of revolution or war, Christian prudence teaches the need to *disimular*.[28]

The King Henry of the play whispers to his daughter: "Callad y disimulad."[29]

We are left with an interpretative problem: why did Calderón close the play with a scene that seems to point unhistorically to the reestablishment of Catholicism in England? Attention to some historical facts may suggest a tentative answer.

Apart from plays based on semi-mythological or Roman history, *La cisma* is Calderón's only major history play with a "foreign" subject. This play about English history impinges so closely on Spanish history, however, that it can be considered foreign only with qualifications. The title refers to the Reformation in England at a time when the emperor Charles V was attempting to suppress the Reformation in Europe; and it was performed, in 1626 or early in 1627, before March 31,[30] when Spain, though less powerful, remained a principal force in the opposition to Protestantism and was at war with England.

We may reasonably ask why Calderón in 1626 or early in 1627 should have written a play about religious conflict in

---

[28] Rivadeneira, *Tratado*, B.A.E. 60: 499. Trans. Fernández-Santamaría, in his *Reason of State*, p. 91.

[29] Calderón need not have turned to Rivadeneira; he could have found recommendations of "Christian prudence" in the writings of other Spanish theorists of the period. See, for example, Juan de Mariana, S.J., *De Rege et Regis Institutione* (1599), Book I (trans. George Albert Moore as *The King and the Education of the King* [Washington, D.C.: The Country Dollar Press, 1948], p. 344): "Then, the Prince ought not to oppose the multitude when it is upset; it is like a torrent which destroys everything in its path. . . . By some sort of art the floods must be calmed. Meanwhile dissimulation should be practiced; even some concession, in my judgment, must sometimes be made to the requests." See also Pedro de Vega, ed., *Antología de escritores políticos del Siglo de Oro* (Madrid: Taurus Ediciones, n.d.), passim.

[30] See N. D. Shergold and J. E. Varey, "Some Early Calderón Dates," *BHS* 38 (1961): 277.

England that is patently unhistorical, in which departures
from recorded history accentuate—from the Catholic perspective—the religious tragedy of England. In the essay to which I
have referred, Bacigalupo comments that "a very brief summary of Anglo-Spanish relations at the time of the play's composition would be appropriate."[31] When Calderón wrote the
play, he states, "the English schism still had not been resolved
and there were no signs that a solution would be reached in the
near future."[32] This latter statement requires, in my opinion, a
major qualification: all historical evidence suggests that by the
1620s Catholicism could have been restored in England only
by an invading foreign army. But in 1626 the prospect of a successful Spanish invasion would not have seemed implausible to
Calderón. Spain was then under the vigorous and militant
leadership of the count-duke of Olivares: in 1625 Spanish
forces had won a series of spectacular victories, including, in
early November (N.S.), the repulse (with heavy enemy losses)
of an attack on Cádiz by a large English fleet supported by a
contingent of Dutch ships. Not long before news of the English attack reached Madrid, Calderón's El sitio de Bredá, celebrating the Spanish capture of that Dutch city on June 5, 1625,
was performed at court, in late October or early November of
that year. In writing El sitio, Calderón drew on information
made available to him by Olivares, who sponsored the court
performance.[33] After the unsuccessful attack on Cádiz, Olivares and his aides made plans for an invasion of England,[34]
and in London King Charles and his ministers made plans for
defense. On June 9, 1626, Charles warned the House of Commons of the nation's danger: he was, he said, "daily advertised
from all parts of the great preparations of the enemy ready to
assail us."[35] But nothing happened. All these are verifiable

[31] "Calderón's La cisma," p. 226 n. 2.

[32] Ibid., p. 212.

[33] Shirley B. Whitaker, "The First Performance of Calderón's El sitio de
Bredá," RQ 31 (1978): 515–31.

[34] John Lynch, Spain Under the Habsburgs, 2nd edn., 2 (New York: New
York University Press, 1981), p. 80.

[35] Quoted from Roger Lockyer, Buckingham: The Life and Political Career of

facts, and they suggest the political temper of Spain at the time Calderón wrote *La cisma*. It is possible to interpret Mary's final promise in the play to restore Catholicism as a foreshadowing of what might happen again in England.

Calderón's liberties with the historical record raise problems in literary theory that should be confronted. His departure from conventional practice in his era again suggests that he may have had a political objective in writing *La cisma*. Aristotle's distinction between the truth of history and the truth of poetry, frequently paraphrased in the Renaissance, has limited application with reference to a play about events in the recent past. Torquato Tasso addressed the relevant issue in his *Discourses on the Heroic Poem* (published in 1594):

> Modern stories offer a great advantage and convenience in this matter of custom and usage, but almost entirely remove the freedom to invent and imitate, which is essential to poets, particularly epic poets. Moreover, for yet another reason, Aristotle apparently denies the tragic poet arguments drawn from contemporary events: tragedy is an imitation of men more excellent than ourselves; on the same ground the present or the recent past should not be the subject of a heroic poem. But with the action of Charles V, the first reason or reasons ought rather be considered: he would seem too daring who chose to describe them otherwise than many know them to have been, either directly or from the positive accounts of their fathers and grandfathers.[36]

If not all this is applicable to *La cisma*, the thrust of the passage is: the events that provided Calderón's subject were arguably too recent to allow him "freedom to invent."

In assessing Renaissance dramatists' and theorists' attitudes toward historical accuracy in drama, one must take into account the nature of the history that provides the subject: in instances involving great national issues, the proximity or remoteness in time and locale to the dramatist and his audience.

George Villiers, First Duke of Buckingham, 1592–1628 (London: Longman, 1981), p. 339.

[36] Tasso, *Discourses on the Heroic Poem*, trans. with notes, Mariella Cavalchini and Irene Samuel (Oxford: Clarendon Press, 1973), pp. 40–41.

Sidney defended poetic license in drama with historical subjects, but the play he chose to praise, *Gorboduc*, was based on
mythological history. Bacon also defended poetic license, but
elsewhere wrote of government that it was a "part of knowledge secret and retired"—and drama about national issues in
the recent past impinged on "government." In *Cigarrales de Toledo*, Tirso satirized a pedant who objected to the introduction
of an historical character into a play with fictional action. But
when Tirso wrote an historical drama, *La prudencia en la mujer*,
in the manner of Shakespeare's histories, he used his historical
sources much as Shakespeare used his. When Calderón in *El
sitio de Bredá* wrote on the war in the Netherlands, he wrote not
merely with patriotic zeal but also with remarkably close attention to accuracy. Let us remember that Heminges and Con-
dell in the First Folio grouped not only *Macbeth* and *King Lear*,
based on mythological history, but also the Roman plays, with
Shakespeare's tragedies rather than his histories.

   Henry VIII and *La cisma* differ from one another profoundly. Yet the differences are not attributable to the sources
used by the two dramatists: by Shakespeare, Raphael Holinshed's *Chronicles of England, Scotland, and Ireland* (in the edition of 1587) and, for the episode of the attempted entrapment
of Archbishop Cranmer, John Foxe's *Actes and Monuments* (in
the edition of 1583);[37] by Calderón, Rivadeneira's *Historia ecle-
siástica del cisma del reino de Inglaterra*, Book One (1588).[38] Although Rivadeneira and Holinshed differ in details and—much
more widely—in the portrayal of persons, they are both faithful to the essential historical facts. Calderón's fictional revision
of history is his own.

★

Shakespeare wrote *Henry VIII* in 1612 or in the early months
of 1613, perhaps intending it for performance during the mar-

[37] Geoffrey Bullough, ed., *Narrative and Dramatic Sources of Shakespeare*, 4
(London: Routledge and Kegan Paul, 1966), 443–44.

[38] Max Cabantous, "Le Schisme d'Angleterre vu par Calderón," *Les Lan-
gues Néo-Latines* 62 (1968): 43–44. On Rivadeneira's sources, see Eusebio Rey,
S.J., ed., *Historias de la Contrarreforma* (Madrid: [Editorial Cathólica], 1945),
pp. 855–73.

riage celebrations of King James's daughter, Elizabeth, to Frederick V, the elector Palatine, a leader of the Protestant Union of German princes. Whatever the political overtones of that marriage, Shakespeare, unlike Calderón, wrote his play during a time of peace—though it was an uneasy peace.[39] Shakespeare is extraordinarily sympathetic in his portrayal of Queen Katherine, for whom he provides the principal female role, and he displays little more anti-Spanish bias than is implicit in his subject.

That subject, the accomplishment of the Reformation in England, is of epic proportions, and Shakespeare treats it in epic fashion, with rises and falls in intensity, employing fewer closely joined episodes than are required in tragedy, in which cumulative intensity is necessary. Our view of Henry as an individual remains distant and external; our attention is directed to his actions. He is fallible; he does not foresee the result of his break with Rome. Rather, he fulfills a providential role as king,[40] leading the nation to the greatness, prophesied by Cranmer, that will come during the reign of his younger daughter.

Of no character is it more difficult to arrive at a just understanding than of Henry himself. Although he is the character whose decisions determine the nature and outcome of the successive episodes by which the play is given structure, he remains a remote figure into whose thoughts we are given only fleeting glimpses. Shakespeare could not provide any such self-revelation as we encounter in the introspective Henry IV. Henry VIII embodied the Tudor settlement, to which James I owed his English throne. Discretion was required. To the spectator or the reader, the execution of Buckingham is likely to seem a judicial murder. Yet to Henry, misled by the self-serving but able Wolsey, the duke represented a potential threat to his dynasty—and all the king's major decisions, including that to divorce Katherine, may be related to his desire

[39] *King Henry VIII*, ed. Foakes, pp. xxx–xxxv. See also Graham Parry, *The Golden Age restor'd: The Culture of the Stuart Court, 1603–42* (Manchester: Manchester University Press, 1981), pp. 103–05.

[40] On his "providential role," see Frank V. Cespedes, " 'We are one in fortunes': The Sense of History in *Henry VIII*," *ELR* 10 (1980): 418–19.

to perpetuate the dynasty founded by his father. Wolsey, it must be remembered, fulfilled the double role of trusted priest to a king troubled in conscience and of chief minister of state. When documentary evidence of Wolsey's falsehood reaches the king, he is prompt to act appropriately, and thereafter asserts his royal will. The double motive that drives Henry to divorce Katherine—his long-held doubts of the legitimacy of his marriage to his brother's widow and his desire for Anne Boleyn, who offers not only her person but the promise of a male heir—are honestly portrayed. So, too, is the king's disappointment that her child is a girl. Henry perceives and aborts the plot set for Cranmer, who as archbishop of Canterbury christens the infant Elizabeth, prophesying her greatness to come.

The historical Henry VIII, as portrayed in the twentieth century, was a cruel man, and the end of his life may reasonably be considered "tragic." He was portrayed more ambiguously by the Tudor chroniclers, the most important of whom wrote during the reign of Elizabeth. Yet the chief significance of Henry's reign lies not in his begetting of Elizabeth—though she was to become the great queen of Archbishop Cranmer's oracular pronouncement—but in the accomplishment of the Reformation in England. Whether the Reformation was ultimately morally good or bad is an unanswerable question. Henry's motives in divorcing Katherine, the precipitating event in the English Reformation, were ambiguous as both Shakespeare and Calderón portray them. Writing about the English play, Madeleine Doran aptly refers to "the fundamental moral ambiguity in Henry's motives and in the attitudes toward the divorce, an ambiguity inherent in the chronicles."[41]

Henry VIII differs from Shakespeare's earlier histories, among other ways in its failure to explore serious political problems.[42] *King John* portrays a usurping king, ruling in place of the legitimate king, Arthur, who is too young to rule. John is a wicked man, whose criminal acts strain the loyalty of his subjects. In *King Richard II*, the king's close relation, Henry,

[41] Review of R. A. Foakes, ed., *King Henry VIII*, in *JEGP* 59 (1960): 291.

[42] Howard Felperin, "Shakespeare's *Henry VIII*: History as Myth," *SEL* 6 (1966): 246.

who has valid grievances, deposes Richard; but Henry's illegitimacy as king and that of his descendants plague England in the period from 1399 to 1485. In *Henry VIII* Shakespeare keeps his distance from the problems of political life, partly, perhaps, because that sovereign was the father of Queen Elizabeth; more probably because King James, the reigning sovereign when Shakespeare wrote the play, believed in the divine right of kings.

Some of the distinctive qualities that separate *Henry VIII* from Shakespeare's earlier history plays may be attributed to the introduction of political values and theatrical techniques and resources derived from the masques prepared by Ben Jonson and Inigo Jones.[43] Spectacle and pageantry, prominent in the play, contributed to its popularity in the era of repertory theatres. In the opening scene, the duke of Norfolk describes to the duke of Buckingham a famous English display of royal wealth, the Field of the Cloth of Gold. Royal ceremonies appear several times in the play: at the execution of Buckingham, the trial of Katherine, the coronation of Anne Boleyn, and the christening of Elizabeth.[44]

The values of the court masques, which embody the political assumptions of their patron, King James, have their reflection in *Henry VIII*, notably in the stage monarch's ability to restore order and dispense justice. His godlike role appears in his detection and frustration of the plot against Archbishop Cranmer. When Dr. William Butts alerts him to the discourtesy shown Cranmer by the council, Henry refers to his position as arbiter:

> Is this the honour they do one another?
> 'Tis well there's one above 'em yet. (v.ii.25–26)

After he dismisses Wolsey, Henry reveals his royal wisdom, but he remains a masquelike figure, though one whose emotions occasionally intrude.

Emotions are muted in *Henry VIII*, even in those characters

---

[43] Among other works on the subject, see John D. Cox, "*Henry VIII* and the Masque," *ELH* 45 (1978): 390–409. See also Stephen Orgel, *The Jonsonian Masque* (Cambridge, Mass.: Harvard University Press, 1965).

[44] Cox, "*Henry VIII*," p. 390.

who fall from high place. Queen Katherine is saintlike in her sorrows. The duke of Buckingham acquires humanity as he faces death. Cardinal Wolsey accepts humiliation without bitterness. The English play moves to its fulfillment in the christening of Elizabeth I, whose birth symbolized the Reformation. *La cisma de Inglaterra* also closes with a focus on a future queen, Mary I, though one whose reign the Spaniards remembered with frustration.

★

The historical Princess Mary succeeded to the throne after her brother's death in 1553, and as Calderón's character resolves in the final scene, Queen Mary I undertook to restore and protect Catholicism. Her first cousin, the emperor Charles V, saw at once the opportunity her accession presented for enhancing his dynasty; less than a month after Mary became queen, he proposed that she, then thirty-seven, marry his twenty-six-year-old heir, Prince Philip. The daughter of Katherine of Aragon accepted. The prospective marital alliance with England came at an auspicious time for father and son, both of whom had recently suffered a severe disappointment in the negotiations concerning the succession to Charles's imperial title. England would provide compensation for the loss of Germany, and furthermore the English alliance would enable Philip to protect his future sovereignty in the Netherlands. He and Mary were married in Winchester Cathedral, July 25, 1554; Philip became titular king of England. Mary's sterility frustrated the hope of adding England to his inheritance. On Mary's death, November 17, 1558, he lost his English title and with it the best hope of returning England to Catholicism.[45]

But he did not at once give up hope of winning England by marriage. Knowing that Elizabeth would attract many suitors, he instructed his ambassador, the count of Feria, to determine if she would be receptive to him and to learn what her religious

---

[45] Fernand Braudel, *The Mediterranean and the Mediterranean World in the Age of Philip II*, trans. Siân Reynolds, 2 (London: Collins, 1973), 913–18; Luis Fernández y Fernández de Retana, *Felipe II: Historia*, 22:323–54, 472–76.

policy would be. Elizabeth received Feria cautiously: she needed Philip's friendship. On January 10, Philip sent Feria more specific instructions: to convey a conditional proposal of marriage that would require Elizabeth, among other things, to practice Catholicism and to preserve it as the religion of her country.[46] Although the queen knew her own mind, she avoided a categorical refusal. Philip had his answer as she revealed her Protestant convictions.

★

In the following chapters, I turn to a group of Spanish and English plays arranged chronologically according to their subjects or to their thematic relevance to the successive phases of Anglo-Spanish relations in their European setting. The prolonged though intermittent hostilities between England and Spain are inseparable from the Revolt of the Netherlands and the civil wars of France. Lope's plays about campaigns fought by the Spanish Army of Flanders are relevant; so are Marlowe's and Chapman's plays about French history from 1572 to 1602.

The pace of English affairs related to Spain quickens after James I's accession, gathering speed throughout his reign. James made peace with Philip III in 1604; he later attempted, unsuccessfully, to arrange a marriage for his heir with the Spanish king's daughter. In 1620 Spanish troops, who had fought in the Thirty Years' War almost from the beginning, made that war an English concern by invading the Palatinate in Germany, the inherited domain of Frederick, the son-in-law of King James. In the early years of the Thirty Years' War, English and Spanish dramatists unknowingly carried on a dialogue that is audible to us: Massinger and Middleton sounding warnings of danger from Spain; Lope, Tirso de Molina (Gabriel Téllez), and Calderón providing assurances that their English counterparts were not alarmists.

Except in three instances, I have for prudential reasons lim-

---

[46] Sir John E. Neale, *Queen Elizabeth* (New York: Jonathan Cape, 1934), pp. 68–71.

ited myself on the Spanish side to plays by Lope, Tirso, and Calderón.[47] The exceptions are Antonio Coello's *El Conde de Sex*, a version of the Elizabeth and Essex story, and two plays that refer to Prince Charles's courtship of the infanta María, Luis Vélez de Guevara's *El caballero del sol* and Francisco de Quevedo's *Cómo ha de ser el privado*. No such principle of selection was practicable for the English plays. In choosing them, I have given attention to the need for coherence in my chapters as well as to dramatic merit.

Of the principal Spanish and English dramatists, Lope alone wrote a large number of histories about events that occurred in his own lifetime. His history plays about his own era provide a Spanish commentary on the prolonged conflict between Catholics and Protestants for which no English counterpart exists. Neither Calderón nor Tirso wrote extensively and literally about contemporary European affairs. Tirso, the boldest of the three in addressing issues relevant to the domestic politics of Spain, includes occasional allusions to his country's foreign wars, but these appear in comedies of intrigue. Calderón wrote only one contemporary history, *El sitio de Bredá*, a dramatization of successive phases in the siege of that Dutch fortified city by a Spanish army.[48] English dramatists rarely wrote about their recent national history. Shakespeare wrote about no period later than the Reformation, though his plays with medieval subjects include situations and passages that invite topical interpretation. Other English dramatists found subjects in the recent history of foreign countries that could be directed to English concerns. Marlowe and Chapman, for ex-

---

[47] The copiousness of the three Spanish dramatists is well known. The total number of *comedias* each of them wrote cannot be determined; many have been lost. In a recent authoritative work of reference, Lope is credited with 316 surviving *comedias*; Calderón, with 114; and Tirso, with 51: Richard W. Tyler and Sergio D. Elizondo, *The Characters, Plots and Settings of Calderón's Comedias* (Lincoln, Nebraska: Society of Spanish and Spanish-American Studies, 1981), p. 7.

[48] I refer solely to extant plays. In collaboration with Antonio Coello, Calderón wrote a play about the Imperial general Wallenstein, which was performed in Madrid early in 1634. The play has been lost but contemporary accounts of it survive. See Václav Černý, "Wallenstein, héros d'un drame de Calderón," *Revue de Littérature Comparée* 36 (1962): 179–90.

ample, turned to French history. Fletcher and Massinger, in collaboration, wrote a play (*Sir John van Oldenbarnevelt*) about a controversial episode in the history of England's Dutch ally.[49]

Some of the plays to which I refer address problems of government at the time they were written as well as problems of the historical periods that provide their subjects. In *King John*, Shakespeare, remaining within the expected limits of fidelity to historical sources, wrote about a sovereign who ruled England from 1199 to 1216. Yet he included situations suggesting the England of the 1590s, when Elizabeth and her ministers feared that another armada might reach its destination. In *La prudencia en la mujer*, Tirso wrote about the regency of Queen María of Molina (1295–1302) during the minority of her son, Fernando IV of Castile. While remaining faithful to his historical sources, Tirso made of the play a "mirror for princes," more precisely, an admonition in dramatic form directed to the young King Philip IV.[50]

In both Spain and England, censorship—and the anticipation of it—qualified the dramatists' portrayal of the European conflict. The need for the approval of a censor led all but a few dramatists to avoid politically sensitive subjects—Tirso was an exception in Spain; Chapman, Massinger, and Middleton were in England. The administrative arrangements for censorship in the two countries had some resemblances: a high official had responsibility for the theatres, the actors, and the plays presented. In Spain, the official, a member of the Council of Castile called the "protector," also supervised the hospitals (institutions that were beneficiaries of the theatres' earnings).[51] In

---

[49] On other plays of the era relevant to Anglo-Spanish relations, see Richard V. Lindabury, *A Study of Patriotism in the Elizabethan Drama* (Princeton: Princeton University Press, 1931); David Bevington, *Tudor Drama and Politics: A Critical Approach to Topical Meaning* (Cambridge, Mass.: Harvard University Press, 1968); Margot Heinemann, *Puritanism and Theatre: Thomas Middleton and Opposition Drama under the Early Stuarts* (Cambridge: Cambridge University Press, 1980).

[50] Ruth L. Kennedy, "*La prudencia en la mujer* and the Ambient that Brought It Forth," *PMLA* 63 (1948): 1131–90.

[51] N. D. Shergold, *A History of the Spanish Stage from Medieval Times to the End of the Seventeenth Century* (Oxford: Clarendon Press, 1967), pp. 386, 517–

England, a member of the Royal Household, the lord chamberlain, had duties at court as well as responsibility for the theatres. The lord chamberlain and the protector appointed persons to pass judgment on the manuscripts submitted for licensing. In England, the Master of the Revels, who sometimes had a deputy, read them;[52] in Spain, a group of persons did so.[53] With predictable differences in emphasis, the objectives of censorship in the two countries were similar: to prevent performance of plays that were morally or theologically offensive, that made reference to persons in high places (including recent sovereigns of foreign countries), or that included critical comment on the governance of church or state.[54] In Spain, there was more attention to theological orthodoxy;[55] in England, where the parliamentary system permitted debate on foreign policy, there was more attention to political comment.

Lope and Calderón seem to have had no major or lasting trouble with the censors or other governmental officials because of their plays. With Tirso, matters were otherwise. In March 1625, a reform committee of high authority, the *Junta*

---

18. See also J. E. Varey and N. D. Shergold, *Teatros y comedias en Madrid, 1600–1650* (London: Tamesis Books, 1971), pp. 13–19.

[52] See Virginia C. Gildersleeve, *Government Regulation of the Elizabethan Drama* (New York: Columbia University Press, 1908; rpt. New York: Burt Franklin, 1961); Joseph Quincy Adams, ed., *The Dramatic Records of Sir Henry Herbert, Master of the Revels, 1623–1673* (New Haven: Yale University Press, 1917); G. E. Bentley, "Regulation and Censorship," in his *The Profession of Dramatist in Shakespeare's Time, 1590–1642* (Princeton: Princeton University Press, 1971), pp. 145–96.

[53] A report to the king on theatrical matters in 1600 specifies merely that the censorship be performed by "learned and responsible persons": Shergold, *The Spanish Stage*, p. 518. See also Edward M. Wilson, "Calderón and the Stage-censor in the Seventeenth Century. A Provisional Study," *Symposium* 15 (1961): 165–84.

[54] The Master of the Revels' "concern was, in general, not a moral, but a practical political one,—the suppression of anything tending to cause disorder or contempt of authority": Gildersleeve, *Government Regulation*, pp. 89–90.

[55] Deletions were made even in Calderón's plays, apparently because of moral or theological improprieties. See Edward M. Wilson, "Calderón and the Stage-censor."

de Reformación, judged his plays to be "irreligious dramas that offer examples and encouragement of bad behavior" and ruled that he should stop writing them and that furthermore he should be sent away from Madrid by his religious order, the Mercedarian, to one of its most remote monasteries.[56] This severe judgment seems not to have been enforced, though it altered Tirso's life. He continued to write for the theatre, but apparently less frequently. (Some of his plays include topical references to events later than March 1625.)[57] Increasingly, he devoted himself to tasks associated with his order.[58]

No important English dramatist suffered a rebuke comparable in severity to that of Tirso by the junta, though several were imprisoned for short periods.[59] Four plays that gave of-

[56] For a short but comprehensive biography of Tirso, see the Introduction by A.K.G. Paterson to his edition of Tirso's *La venganza de Tamar* (Cambridge: Cambridge University Press, 1969), pp. 1–4. Paterson includes the text of the Junta's ruling, p. 2 n. 1.

[57] See Tirso de Molina, *Obras dramáticas completas*, ed. Blanca de los Ríos, 3 (Madrid: Aguilar, 1958): *Desde Toledo a Madrid*, pp. 825b–826a; *No hay peor sordo*, pp. 1055b–1056a; and *Habladme en entrando*, p. 1222b.

[58] Was the junta's censure of Tirso, a friar who was a prolific and successful dramatist, an expression of the reform movement led by the count-duke of Olivares in the early years of Philip IV's reign? Or was it a reprisal for specifically political offenses committed in one or more plays? No firm answer can be given to these questions. Yet Ruth L. Kennedy has advanced strong—I believe convincing—arguments that *La prudencia en la mujer* was written about 1622 as an admonition to Philip IV to free himself from advisors such as Olivares and assume the duties of kingship (Kennedy, "*La prudencia en la mujer* and the Ambient that Brought It Forth"). See also Kennedy, "La perspectiva política de Tirso en *Privar contra su gusto*, de 1621, y la de sus comedias políticas posteriores," in *Homenaje a Tirso* (Madrid: Revista "Estudios," 1981), pp. 199–238.

J.C.J. Metford argues, with good supporting evidence, that the junta's condemnation of Tirso was directed by Olivares in retaliation for criticism of himself included in Tirso's *Tanto es lo de más como lo de menos*. However, Metford concludes his argument with the wise admonition that "at this distance in time, it is impossible to be dogmatic about the elucidation of political references in the *comedias* of the seventeenth century" (Metford, "Tirso de Molina and the Conde-Duque de Olivares," *BHS* 36 [1959]: 15–27).

[59] Yet the English authorities could be savage in dealing with offenses related to the stage, as the Star Chamber's punishment of William Prynne in

Chapter Two

THE DUKE OF AERSCHOT:

Ya vuelven los españoles,	Now the Spaniards return, those who
Los que haciendo tantos robos,	robbing much are smelters of our silver
Son de nuestra sangre lobos,	plate, wolves who suck our blood.
De nuestra plata crisoles.	

LOPE DE VEGA, *Los españoles en Flandes* (c. 1597–1606)

THE SPANISH empire of King Philip II developed from the Holy Roman Empire of Philip's father, the emperor Charles V. Charles's inheritance of large domains from each of his four grandparents had resulted in a European realm larger than that of any of his predecessors since Charlemagne, the first of the Holy Roman emperors from the North. His Spanish inheritance brought him America, the scope of which only gradually became known. Hernán Cortés wrote to him in 1530 about its size and wealth—of such immensity, in the opinion of Cortés, that Charles could style himself emperor of the Indies with a title no less justified than that he possessed as emperor of Germany.[1] To the domains he inherited he added more through the wars he fought. He did not rule the world and insisted he did not wish to do so by conquest;[2] but his territories were of an extent to put men in mind of a universal rule of peace under the secular leadership of the emperor and the spiritual leadership of the pope.

Charles talked about world unity and the means to achieve

---

[1] "Carta segunda" (October 30, 1530). In Cortés, *Cartas de relación de la conquista de Méjico* (Buenos Aires: Espasa-Calpe Argentina, 1945), p. 39. See John H. Elliott, *Imperial Spain, 1469–1716* (New York: St. Martin's Press, 1964), p. 162.

[2] Ramón Menéndez Pidal, *Idea Imperial de Carlos V* (1937); reprinted Buenos Aires: Espasa Calpe Argentina, 1946), pp. 11–36.

[31]

it:[3] by a crusade against the Ottoman Turks and by peaceful conciliation of Protestants. The hostility of Francis I of France, so intense as to lead him to form an alliance with the Turks against Charles, offered a formidable obstacle. Another obstacle was the intermittent hostility of popes, who regarded Charles's dominions in Italy as a threat to the papal states, which they considered a safeguard of papal supremacy in spiritual matters. The opposition forced Charles to a truce with the Turks and to a war against the Protestants of Germany. Paradoxically, his greatest victory, against a league of Protestant princes at Mühlberg, April 20, 1547, led to further frustration. The scale of his victory frightened not only his German enemies but other rulers throughout western Europe.

As an elected emperor, Charles could influence but not control the choice of his successor. Despite his desire that Philip inherit his imperial title, Charles could not prevail with the German electoral princes, who chose his brother Ferdinand instead. Ferdinand (to whom Charles had ceded his inherited Austrian dominions in 1522) and Ferdinand's son Maximilian had spent most of their lives in central Europe. They could rely on German opposition, Catholic and Protestant alike, to the candidacy of the Spanish Philip as successor to the imperial title.[4]

With his abdication, Charles's territories were divided. But the remembrance of his empire became a force in political thought. It was not as a reality, Frances A. Yates wrote, but "as a phantom that Charles's empire was of importance, because it raised again the imperial idea and spread it through Europe in the symbolism of its propaganda. . . ."[5] The emperor's son and many of his subjects found the idea congenial.

[3] On Charles V's conception of empire, see José Antonio Maravall, *Carlos V y el pensamiento político del Renacimiento* (Madrid: Instituto de Estudios Políticos, 1960), pp. 61–161; Manuel Fernández Álvarez, *Emperador Carlos V: Historia*, 20:15–18; John M. Headley, *The Emperor and His Chancellor: A Study of the Imperial Chancellery under Gattinara* (Cambridge: Cambridge University Press, 1983), passim.

[4] Braudel, *The Mediterranean*, 2:913–18.

[5] Yates, "Charles V and the Idea of the Empire," in her *Astraea: The Imperial*

The larger part of Charles's territories passed to Philip rather than to Ferdinand. In dividing his dominions, Charles interpreted the empire in its most restricted sense. He separated from it the Netherlands and Milan, both of which passed to Philip.[6] Spain, rather than the empire (now diminished and confined to Germany), gained hegemony in Europe. Except for Portugal, annexed by Philip II in 1580, Spain in the sixteenth century had no effective rival in either North or South America. In acquiring Portugal, Spain gained control of her colonies in Brazil, in Asia, and in Africa. Insofar as the term "empire" retained connotations of universality, it could most accurately be applied to Philip's domains. He was, in the opinion of most of the statesmen in Europe, the most powerful monarch in the world.

But Philip was not an emperor; until the 1590s Spaniards did not call his domains an empire despite their extent, wealth, and diversity.[7] It would appear, however, that Philip wished to have an imperial title. There were rumors in 1563 and the following year that he would be proclaimed "Emperor of the Indies." In 1583 there was again talk of an imperial title for him.[8] By the later date, at least, Philip acted as though he were an emperor.

Unlike his father, he ruled, so far as is known, without a systematic program or clearly defined objective.[9] If he aimed at universal monarchy, neither he nor any of his ministers left a

---

Theme in the Sixteenth Century (London and Boston: Routledge & Kegan Paul, 1975), pp. 1–28; quotation, p. 1.

[6] Antonio Domínguez Ortiz, *La sociedad española en el siglo XVII* (Madrid: Consejo Superior de Investigaciones Científicas, 1963), p. 10. Domínguez Ortiz points out that the geographical locations of the Netherlands and Milan, widely separated by territories of the empire, would suggest that in dividing his domains Charles V envisaged a continuing bond between those inherited by Ferdinand and Philip.

[7] H. G. Koenigsberger, "The Statecraft of Philip II," *ESR* 1 (1971): 10.

[8] Braudel, *The Mediterranean*, 2:675–76.

[9] Koenigsberger, "Philip II," pp. 1–21. See also Geoffrey Parker, "Spain, Her Enemies and the Revolt of the Netherlands, 1559–1648," in his *Spain and the Netherlands, 1559–1659: Ten Studies* (Short Hills, N.J.: Enslow Publishers, 1979), pp. 17–43.

record of a plan to achieve it. In his earlier years, his wars—in the Mediterranean against the Turks and in the Netherlands against his rebellious subjects—were fought to protect his dominions and his sovereignty in them.

In 1580, conditions changed for him: his war with the Turks came to an end; with the annexation of Portugal, he gained additional wealth; his American possessions began to yield more treasure. He found himself in a position to confront dangers posed by the turn of events in France, England, and the Netherlands. The death of the duke of Anjou in 1584 left the Protestant Henry of Navarre as heir presumptive to the French throne. In 1585, Queen Elizabeth sent an English army to the Netherlands in support of the rebels. In the summer of 1588, Philip sent the Invincible Armada to provide a shield behind which the prince of Parma in the Netherlands could transport his troops to England as an invading army. After Henry IV became the legitimate king of France in 1589, Philip sent Spanish armies to support the French Catholic League against him. With the stated purpose of preserving Catholicism in the country, Philip put forward the claim of his daughter Isabel Clara Eugenia, grandchild of Henry II, to be queen of France.[10] He continued the war in the Netherlands. In all this he saw himself as the defender of the Catholic faith, the only Catholic sovereign with sufficient power to confront the Protestant leaders. At a time when he aimed at the conquest of England, France, and the Netherlands, when he could count on the support of the Austrian Habsburgs, when he ruled the entire Iberian Peninsula and the combined overseas empires of Spain and Portugal, when his influence at the Vatican was strong enough (as it was from 1590 to 1592) to determine the election of popes[11]—at this time, in these closing years of his reign, it seemed to many observers that he had universal rule in view.

He failed in England, France, and the Netherlands. When he died in 1598, he left Spain impoverished and with a king, his

---

[10] Koenigsberger, "Philip II," p. 19.

[11] Ibid., p. 17. Throughout this paragraph I am indebted to Koenigsberger.

son Philip III, whose competence to rule he had with good reason doubted. Spain was weaker, but she retained the empire,
and Spaniards retained their pride in it.

★

Many years earlier Charles V, in planning Prince Philip's marriage with Queen Mary, had foreseen his son's need for a close
alliance with England if he were to maintain his sovereignty in
the Netherlands without challenge. Lacking such an alliance, a
Spanish governor in Brussels would be distant from his base of
power. The friendship, or at the least the neutrality, of England might be required if the sea lanes between Spain and the
Netherlands were to be kept open. With Mary's death in 1558,
and Elizabeth's refusal of his conditional offer of marriage,
Philip lost the alliance. Less than nine years later, in 1567, he
sent the duke of Alba at the head of an army to the Netherlands
in an attempt to suppress the Dutch Revolt.

Queen Elizabeth and her ministers perceived the danger to
England inherent in the proximity of a large army led by
Spain's most able general. Although she disliked the idea of
subjects rebelling against their sovereign, she faced Catholic
opposition not unlike that confronted by Prince William of
Orange: some from fellow countrymen, some from Rome and
France, more from Spain. In the early years of the Revolt, she
did not want open war, but she did not avoid provocative acts.
She allowed English and Netherlands privateers, who greatly
restricted Alba's sea transport, to use English ports as a base.[12]
In November 1568, her government seized four Spanish ships
carrying money intended to pay Alba's army, which had entered the harbors at Southampton and Plymouth to escape
from privateers and Channel storms.[13] On their side, King
Philip and the duke of Alba wanted no less than Elizabeth's
life. They were informed of attempts to assassinate her, and in

[12] R. B. Wernham, *Before the Armada: The Growth of English Foreign Policy,
1485–1588* (London: Jonathan Cape, 1966), pp. 302, 317.
[13] Ibid., pp. 296–97.

some instances, such as the Ridolfi-duke of Norfolk conspiracy in 1570–1571, they gave active encouragement.[14]

For eighty years the Revolt of the Netherlands affected the security and prosperity of England. In Spain the English and the Netherlanders had a common enemy. The defense of England became more difficult when harbors in the Netherlands were controlled by a strong, hostile power, whether Spain or, potentially, France, for the Revolt provided an opportunity for France, a traditional enemy of Spain as well as of England, to invade the small country on its northwestern border. English trade required access to Continental ports, of which Antwerp was the most important. Queen Elizabeth could not afford to allow England to be isolated from the Continent, as could happen if either France or Spain gained undisputed control of the Netherlands.

In the decade of the 1570s, Prince William and his fellow leaders of the Revolt expected more aid than they received from Queen Elizabeth, who was more liberal in words of support than in the supply of troops; but she encouraged English volunteers to join them, she sent them money, and she provided subsidies for German mercenaries to aid them.[15] The rebels began to recruit Scots for military service in 1572.[16] In 1585, at a time when it seemed likely that the prince of Parma would succeed in suppressing the Revolt, she sent an army to the Netherlands,[17] and she kept troops there as long as she lived.

★

[14] Neale, *Elizabeth*, pp. 197–200; Wernham, *Before the Armada*, pp. 312–14.

[15] See Charles H. Wilson, *Queen Elizabeth and the Revolt of the Netherlands* (London: Macmillan, 1970), for a critical analysis of the Queen's policy. On the English volunteers, see Clements R. Markham, *"The Fighting Veres": Lives of Sir Francis Vere . . . and of Sir Horace Vere . . .* (Boston and New York: Houghton Mifflin, 1888), pp. 41–52; and Wernham, *Before the Armada*, p. 321.

[16] *Papers Illustrating the History of the Scots Brigade in the Service of the United Netherlands, 1572–1782*, ed. James Ferguson, 3 vols. (Edinburgh: Scottish History Society, 1899-1901).

[17] On Queen Elizabeth's reasons for entering the Netherlands war in 1585, see R. B. Wernham, "Elizabethan War Aims and Strategy," in S. T. Bindoff et

Even before he went to the Netherlands in 1576, Don Juan of Austria, Philip II's half-brother, believed that the source of Spain's troubles there lay in England.[18] Others in high place shared his opinion. Long before 1585, the English had given aid to the rebels at crucial times, as in 1572, the year in which the Dutch first captured strongholds that proved to be defensible against Alba's army.

In May of that year, Count Louis of Nassau, leading Huguenot and Netherlands troops, captured the fortified city of Mons, the capital of the southern province of Hainault. The duke of Alba—knowing that Count Louis's brother, the prince of Orange, had raised an army in Germany and knowing also that French reenforcements for Mons were expected—concentrated his forces in the South. After a summer-long siege, Alba captured Mons, and by his skillful leadership of troops in the field, he frustrated Orange's attempt to attack him. But during the months he was in the southern provinces, Netherlands privateers, whom Queen Elizabeth had forced to leave English ports in March of that year, captured towns in the northern maritime provinces, Holland and Zeeland, beyond the natural defenses provided by the great rivers. English volunteers went to the support of the rebels.[19] By the time Alba turned to the North, he found the Dutch firmly entrenched. Despite savage fighting, with heavy losses on both sides, he was unable to dislodge them. The Dutch, holding towns of their own, had become more formidable opponents.[20] When King Philip perceived the consequences of Al-

---

al., *Elizabethan Government and Society: Essays Presented to Sir John Neale* (London: The Athlone Press, 1961), pp. 344–45.

[18] See Garrett Mattingly, *The Defeat of the Spanish Armada* (London: Jonathan Cape, 1959), p. 57.

[19] The contemporary Spanish historian Bernardino de Mendoza describes the arrival of the English: "At this time [1572] the rebels were being reenforced with the aid and assistance of the English, who were of great usefulness to the Dutch, because troops sent by the English could arrive in a few days. . . ." *Comentarios de lo sucedido en las guerras de los Países-Bajos, desde el año de 1567 hasta el de 1577* (1592), in B.A.E. 28 (Madrid: M. Rivadeneyra, 1853), 464a.

[20] Geoffrey Parker provides a map of "towns in revolt against Philip, 1572," in his *The Dutch Revolt* (Ithaca: Cornell University Press, 1977), p. 139.

ba's strategy, he lost confidence in his general, who returned to Spain late in 1573.

Control of the Low Countries was important to the entire edifice of Philip's empire—for the access they provided to the territories of the Austrian Habsburgs, among other reasons. The provinces were industrialized as Spain was not, and they imported Spanish wool and other raw materials. Holland and Zeeland had prospered through international trade. Antwerp was the commercial and banking center of western Europe. The Netherlands were too rich a prize to be lost without a struggle; and even when the struggle became more costly than they were worth, Philip could not give them up. To lose them through inability to crush the Revolt would destroy his reputation as the most powerful sovereign in the world. Reputation was itself, in the sixteenth as in the twentieth century, a source of military strength. To Philip and his ministers an acknowledgment of defeat by a group numerically so small as the rebellious Netherlanders was an unacceptable alternative, no matter what the cost in men and treasure.

The king replaced Alba with Don Luis de Requesens, who attempted with little success to bring peace by softer methods. Requesens's sudden death in March 1576 precipitated a crisis— a series of mutinies by long-unpaid soldiers—that plagued his successor, Don Juan of Austria. A character representing Don Juan is one of the two protagonists of Lope de Vega's *Los españoles en Flandes*.

★

In the edition of Lope's works published by the Royal Academy of Spain, Menéndez y Pelayo included three plays, now considered "authentic," that dramatize phases of Spain's war in the Low Countries in the late sixteenth century. In the chronological order of their subjects, they are: *Los españoles en Flandes, El asalto de Mastrique por el Príncipe de Parma*, and *Pobreza no es vileza*.[21] Differences in attitudes toward the war ex-

---

[21] He included two others now regarded as of "doubtful authenticity": *La aldehuela y el gran prior*, in part fictional, about the duke of Alba and his ille-

pressed in the plays may plausibly be associated with the times at which Lope wrote them: *Los españoles en Flandes* and *El asalto de Mastrique* between 1595 and 1607, *El asalto* probably between 1600 and 1606;[22] and *Pobreza no es vileza* between 1613 and 1622, probably between 1620 and 1622.[23] Passages in *Los españoles* and *El asalto* reveal an awareness of the suffering the long war has caused as well as of the cost of the war to Spain. A character in *Los españoles* comments on its drain of the nation's resources:

> . . . el patrimonio disipe
> Con los que vienen y van.   (Ed. Acad. 12:382b)

> . . . [the king] squanders his patrimony on the comings and goings [to the Netherlands].

The plays suggest the frame of mind that led to the negotiation of a ceasefire in 1607 and of a twelve-year truce in 1609.

If the date of *Pobreza no es vileza* is indeed between 1620 and 1622, Lope wrote the play just before or not long after the expiration of the truce in April 1621, at a time when Don Baltasar de Zúñiga was either the leading member of Philip III's Council of State or, if after March 31, 1621, and before Zúñiga's death in October 1622, the principal minister of the young Philip IV. In the opinion of Zúñiga as in that of his nephew and successor, the count of Olivares, the truce had not worked. The United Provinces had prospered at the expense of Spain's overseas trade; Spain had grown weaker. A return to war, in the opinion of many, would restore the discipline and the vigor the nation had shown in the sixteenth century. Between 1620 and 1622 war was imminent or had begun. At such a time

---

gitimate son, Don Hernando de Toledo; and *Don Juan de Austria en Flandes,* a dramatization of episodes in the title character's governorship of the Netherlands. See S. Griswold Morley and Courtney Bruerton, *The Chronology of Lope de Vega's "Comedias"* (New York: Modern Language Association, 1940), pp. 252 and 276–77.

Unless otherwise stated, attributions of plays to Lope and dates given for them are based on Morley and Bruerton.

[22] Ibid., pp. 195, 172.

[23] Ibid., p. 229.

Lope's portrayal of heroic feats in a campaign of 1595 could be interpreted as a call to arms.

Los españoles en Flandes and *El asalto de Mastrique* reveal from first to last Lope's intention to dramatize, within limits of fidelity approximating those of English history plays of the era, notable events in the Revolt of the Netherlands. Both of them include fictional characters and episodes, but these are subordinate, needed components of plays intended to please audiences. Lope's protagonists, Don Juan of Austria and Alexander Farnese, prince of Parma, are convincing dramatic characters who respond to historical situations and in a measure—Parma more than Don Juan—determine the course of events.

As his source for the plays, Lope turned to the chronicle of a Spanish officer who was a witness to many of the events he describes: Captain Alonso Vázquez's *Los sucesos de Flandes y Francia del tiempo de Alejandro Farnese.* Lope read it in manuscript; it was not published until late in the nineteenth century.[24] The chronicle is accurate and detailed, including, in addition to accounts of major events, anecdotes about Parma's campaigns.[25] Lope followed it with some care, with the result that his plays are historically accurate insofar as accuracy is consistent with fiercely partisan interpretation of events and with omission of reference to important events and such important persons as Queen Elizabeth and the prince of Orange.

Los españoles and *El asalto* are not among Lope's best plays. Yet they reveal a quality absent in most of the best ones, a willingness to question Spanish policy: in these plays, the policy of continuing the war in the Netherlands. When Lope wrote them, intermittent war in the Netherlands had lasted some thirty years; and it was to continue for an additional fifty years, establishing Spain's reputation for oppression and bigotry,

[24] S. A. Vosters, "Lope y Calderón, Vázquez y Hugo, Maastricht y Breda," *Revista de Literatura*, 24 (1963), 128–29. The chronicle was first published in CODOIN, 72–74 (1879–80).

[25] Francisco Barado y Font emphasizes the accuracy and fullness of Vázquez's narrative: *Literatura militar española* (Barcelona: Tipografía La Academia, 1890), p. 247.

damaging her military reputation. Always he writes as a patriot; but here his patriotism does not prevent him from depicting Spanish soldiers as predators, living on the land, who have earned the hatred of the natives, nor from depicting in *El asalto* the brutal horror of siege warfare. A reading of *Los españoles* and *El asalto* suggests qualification in the description of Lope's work as uniformly laudatory of the Spain of his own era.

We may consider Fernando Lázaro Carreter's criticism of him. His youth, Lázaro notes, coincided with the final period of Spain's imperial greatness; his age, with the period in which decadence had set in, though the territories of the empire remained. "Lope passed all those years," Lázaro writes,

> intimately bound to Spain, celebrating its military, political, and religious glories, almost never attempting to come to grips critically with the reality of the nation.[26]

This is a comprehensive criticism to which no comprehensive rebuttal can be made. But, as Lázaro implies, exceptions exist. I would regard these two Flanders plays as exceptions: as plays that implicitly criticize Spain's determination to carry on the war in the Low Countries.

Pobreza no es vileza, on the other hand, is no exception; written about twenty years later, it is exuberantly bellicose. It differs also in that the historical action is encompassed by a fictional plot. Although Lope portrays a military campaign, following carefully in factual detail another chronicle written by a Spanish officer,[27] he devotes the larger part of the play to nonhistorical episodes. He fuses novelistic materials and dramatized history without distortion of the latter, employing scenes devoted to Spanish victories in 1595 to reinforce a plot turning on a problem of personal honor.

[26] Lázaro Carreter, *Lope de Vega: Introducción a su vida y obra* (Salamanca: Ediciones Anaya, 1966), p. 7.

[27] Captain Diego de Villalobos y Benavides, *Comentarios de las cosas sucedidas en los Países Baxos de Flandes, desde el año de 1594 hasta el de 1598* (Madrid: Luis Sanchez, 1612). I refer to the edition prepared by Alejandro Llorente (Madrid: Alfonso Durán, 1876).

In its historical dimension, *Pobreza no es vileza* has resemblances to *Los españoles* and *El asalto*. But there is one notable
difference. In *Pobreza* the enemy are not rebellious
Netherlanders, but troops in the army of King Henry IV, who
in 1593 had been converted to Catholicism and in 1594 had
been crowned in Chartres cathedral. (In September 1595, long
before Lope wrote the play, Clement VIII gave Henry absolu-
tion.) He remained an ally of the English and of the rebellious
provinces in the Netherlands, and some Protestants served in
his army. But Lope could not plausibly portray the Spanish
campaign of 1595 as a crusade against heresy as he had portrayed the campaigns represented in the earlier plays. He includes few references to the enemy, naming only one of the
leaders, the commander of the garrison at Châtelet. He writes
nothing about French strategy or about King Henry IV, who
early in 1595 had declared war on Spain.

★

An understanding of Lope's silence about sovereigns, notably
King Henry IV and Queen Elizabeth, requires attention to the
restraints imposed on him both by governmental censorship,
which forbade reference to sensitive political subjects, and by
the principle of decorum in characterization. To turn from the
comedia to contemporary Spanish nondramatic poetry is to be
reminded of the strength of these restraints. Lope does not include Queen Elizabeth (Isabel, Isabela) as a character in any of
his surviving plays;[28] references to her in dialogue may exist,
but they are in any event rare.

Apart from his reverential and ordinarily brief introduction
of Spanish kings—or emblematic representations of them as
symbols of Spain's imperial destiny—Lope includes only a few
recent Christian sovereigns among his characters.[29] Of them, I

---

[28] See S. Griswold Morley and Richard W. Tyler, *Los nombres de personajes
en las comedias de Lope de Vega: estudio de onomatología: University of California
Publications in Modern Philology* 55 (Berkeley and Los Angeles: University of
California Press, 1961), Parts 1 and 2.

[29] Among them are Francis I of France in *Carlos V en Francia* and Don Sebastian of Portugal in *La tragedia del rey Don Sebastián*.

know of only one who is portrayed as a villain, Boris Godunov, the emperor of Russia (1598–1605) in *El gran duque de
Moscovia y emperador perseguido*. In Lope's mind this might not
have been an exception, for Godunov belonged to the Eastern
Orthodox church and, furthermore, usurped the throne that
rightfully (in the play, if not in history) belonged to Demetrius
(the pseudo-Demetrius of history), a Roman Catholic whose
claim was supported by the Roman Catholic king of Poland.

His remarks in *El arte nuevo de hacer comedias en este tiempo*
(published in 1609) on decorum in characterization reveal assumptions that explain why he would have found it difficult to
introduce as a character a sovereign whom—on the showing of
his non-dramatic poems—he hated as heartily as he hated
Queen Elizabeth. He comments on stage dialogue (ll. 269–73):

> *Si hablare el Rey, imite cuanto pueda*
> *La gravedad real; si el viejo hablare*
> *Procure una modestia sentenciosa;*
> *Descriva los amantes con afectos*
> *Que muevan con estremo a quien escucha.*[30]

> If the king speaks, approximate royal dignity as closely as possible;
> if an old man speaks, try to convey a modest sententiousness; let
> lovers speak with such feeling that they stir the emotions of those
> who hear them.

(English critics, including John Dryden and Thomas Rymer,
would later write in much the same vein.)[31] Because he could
not represent her with the qualities appropriate to her rank,
Lope did not represent Queen Elizabeth at all.

Lope writes in *El arte nuevo* that Philip II had been dis-
pleased, for reasons Lope did not know, in seeing a king portrayed in a play. However, Lope does not interpret Philip's dis-
pleasure as preventing dramatists from including kings among

---

[30] In Lope de Vega, *El arte nuevo* . . . , ed. Prades, p. 296. The passage is
quoted from the edition of 1613.

[31] "All crown'd heads by *Poetical right* are *Heroes*." Thomas Rymer, *The
Tragedies of the Last Age* (1678 [1677]). Dryden expresses a similar opinion in
The Grounds of Criticism in Tragedy (1679).

their characters (ll. 157–64).[32] His plays portray Spanish and foreign kings, but not modern English ones. In at least two of his plays, *La nueva victoria de Don Gonzalo de Córdoba* (1622) and *El Brasil restituido* (1625), he includes hostile reference to James I's son-in-law, the elector Palatine, Frederick V, whom the English considered the rightful king of Bohemia.[33] But Lope would have regarded him as an heretical German prince who had unsuccessfully attempted to usurp the throne of Bohemia.

To judge from the remarks of a Protestant propagandist writing in the Netherlands in 1624, some Spanish dramatists, untroubled by the principle of decorum, wrote critically not only about Elizabeth but also about Henry VIII, James I, and other English sovereigns.[34] Here it should be added that Tirso de Molina—the most audacious politically of the three principal dramatists—includes in his *No hay peor sordo* (III.vii) hostile conversational allusion to Henry VIII and to his "illegitimate" daughter, Elizabeth, as having corrupted England.[35] However biased Calderón may be in his interpretation of the English Reformation in *La cisma de Inglaterra*, his portrayal of Henry VIII is consistent with dramatic decorum as Lope describes it in *El arte nuevo*.

The reasons for Lope's silence about Elizabeth—and Henry IV as well—are apparent. Those for his silence about William I, prince of Orange, are more obscure. The prince's rank, "stadhouder" or governor, provides no explanation. He was neither a sovereign nor of royal birth. In the years Lope writes about in *Los españoles* and *El asalto*, Prince William I was the formidable and uncompromising leader of the Revolt against Spain: the single individual in the Netherlands not included in King Philip II's general pardon of October 30, 1576. The king referred to Orange as the originator and perpetuator of all Spain's troubles in the Netherlands.[36] Perhaps the circum-

---

[32] *El arte nuevo*, ed. Prades, p. 291.

[33] Ed. Acad., 13, *Le nueva victoria*, p. 127a; *El Brasil*, p. 85b.

[34] Thomas Scot, *Vox Regis*, p. 10.

[35] Ed. Blanca de los Ríos, 3: 1056a.

[36] *Correspondance de Philippe II sur les affaires des Pays Bas*, ed. L. P. Gachard, 4 (Brussels: Librairie Ancienne et Moderne, 1861), 455.

stances of his assassination in 1584, four years after Philip II
had declared him an outlaw and had placed a large price on his
head, made it impolitic for Lope to say much about him.
Prince William had responded to the king's denunciation of
him in his *Apology* (published in 1581), the most influential of
all the documents occasioned by the Revolt in darkening Philip's name.

★

Though Lope was reticent in portraying monarchs, he was less
wary in portraying their descendants, even one descendant
who was a great general—Alexander Farnese, prince of
Parma. *Los españoles en Flandes* provides a good introduction to
Parma, a man far more important in the history of the Netherlands than Don Juan of Austria, his uncle. He was the son of
the sovereign duke of Parma and Margaret of Austria, an illegitimate daughter of Charles V, who had herself been governess of the Netherlands prior to the arrival of the duke of Alba.
Parma, born in 1545, was probably two years older than Don
Juan; as youths they were frequently together, and in the great
naval victory over the Turks at Lepanto, they fought together,
Parma under Don Juan's command. Regarded by military ex-
perts as the most able general of his time, Parma won repeated
victories in the Netherlands, and he reinforced his military
achievements with skillful diplomacy. He did not suppress the
Revolt, but he came closer to doing so than any other general
employed by the kings of Spain. His successes made practicable King Philip's plans for the Great Armada.

Although the events of July 1588 prevented Parma from
leading an invading army into England, he had fought Englishmen in the Netherlands for many years. As early as the battle of Gembloux, January 31, 1578, Parma faced English volunteers and Scots mercenaries.[37] (The month before, an
English agent reported the arrival of 3,000 Scots to Lord Bur-
leigh.)[38] Lope does not include reference to them, but he in-

[37] Charles H. Wilson, *Elizabeth and the Revolt of the Netherlands*, p. 59.
[38] Léon van der Essen, *Alexandre Farnèse, prince de Parme, gouverneur général
des Pays-Bas (1545–1592)*, 1 (Brussels: Librairie Nationale d'Art et d'Histoire,
1933), 202.

cludes prominent reference to John Casimir, son of the elector Palatine, Frederick III, and a leader of German mercenaries, who later in 1578 received a subsidy from Queen Elizabeth.[39] Don Juan mentions the danger from Germany as he welcomes the return of Spanish troops. No longer, he says, will he fear the leader of the Netherlands army or Casimir, with his large force of Germans. As events would reveal, he had no reason to fear Casimir, who proved to be ineffectual.[40]

Los españoles en Flandes is an apt title for the play, one that places emphasis on the Spanish people, here soldiers in the Netherlands. It suggests a quality, in this play as in many others by Lope, that separates his drama from that of nearly all his contemporaries and seventeenth-century successors in Europe: his attention, without condescension, to men in the lowest rank of society.[41] In this military play, the lowest level is that of the common soldiers, not often portrayed by other dramatists with a respect comparable to that Lope shows for them. This respect appears consistently in his plays, providing a contrast with Shakespeare, whose soldiers are figures of fun, bumpkins such as Falstaff's recruits in *2 Henry IV* (III.ii).[42]

Lope takes care to give common soldiers individuality, to make distinctions among them. In both *Los españoles* and *El asalto*, a soldier has a major role: Chavarría and Alonso García, respectively, each of them winning the confidence of the

[39] Charles H. Wilson, *Elizabeth and the Revolt of the Netherlands*, p. 64.
[40] Ibid.
[41] See Américo Castro, *De la edad conflictiva, I: el drama de la honra en España y en su literatura*, 2nd edn. (Madrid: Taurus, 1963), passim; and Lázaro Carreter, *Lope de Vega: Introducción*, pp. 203–05.
[42] See Paul A. Jorgensen, *Shakespeare's Military World* (Berkeley and Los Angeles: University of California Press, 1956), pp. 120, 133.

Leo Salingar contrasts Shakespeare's and Lope's attitudes toward the lowest class of society: "He [Shakespeare] shows none of the interest in the condition of the peasants as a subject for drama that appears in the writings of Ruzzante or Lope de Vega; he is a national playwright, but he looks towards London. And even in his urban scenes, he shows little or nothing of the working life of the craftsman or apprentice or the ordinary shopkeeper in staple trades, by comparison with a contemporary like Dekker. . . ." *Shakespeare and the Traditions of Comedy*, p. 255.

prince of Parma. Yet in personal qualities they are totally different—Chavarría is gregarious, boastful, eager for battle; García is contemplative, troubled by the brutality of war, dubious that military glory is worth its costs in human life. Chavarría meets Parma, who is travelling to the Netherlands incognito, in a town in Lombardy. Not knowing the prince's identity, the soldier mistakes him for a petty thief and accuses him of stealing a missing cape. The prince accepts the mistake in good humor, recognizes in Chavarría the qualities of a soldier, and takes him into his service. When Parma joins Don Juan in the Netherlands, Chavarría rides at his side.

Alonso García has a more central role, not in the action of *El asalto* (for until late in the third act he remains a choral character, commenting on what passes before him), but rather as a guide to the meaning of the savage fighting portrayed in the play. Starting as a disbeliever, he responds gallantly when Parma entrusts a dangerous assignment to him; and when battle is joined within the city walls, he shares the passions aroused. Parma must deny his request to continue fighting after victory is won.

★

Los españoles en Flandes opens with a sense of urgency. While visiting his mother at her residence near Naples, Parma receives orders from King Philip to assume command of the Spanish troops in Milan and to lead them to the Netherlands, where Don Juan, the governor, is in danger. When Parma learns from the messenger that the troops have already left Milan and are on the march, he sets out on horseback with one attendant. In depicting the journey, Lope follows his source, Vázquez's narrative of Parma's campaigns in the Netherlands and France.[43]

(Attention to the historical circumstances of Don Juan's governorship will explain the reasons for Parma's hurried journey. Don Juan, an illegitimate son of Charles V, had gone

---

[43] Vázquez, *Los sucesos de Flandes y Francia del tiempo de Alejandro Farnese*, CODOIN 72:68–70. See S. A. Vosters, "Lope y Calderón, Vázquez y Hugo, Maastricht y Breda," pp. 128–29.

to the Netherlands as royal governor in 1576, arriving on November 3, the day before mutinous soldiers in the Spanish army sacked Antwerp, killing over 8,000 persons. The atrocity brought the provinces together for the first time since the Revolt began. On November 8, delegates from all the provinces signed a treaty of union, the Pacification of Ghent, negotiated with the prime purpose of expelling the Spaniards. Don Juan accepted the pacification in a separate treaty of February 12, 1577, the Perpetual Edict, in which the Netherlanders gained self-government and the withdrawal of Spanish troops in exchange for their pledge to recognize his position as governor. For sixteen months he presided uneasily over a resentful populace, until, in response to warnings that he would be assassinated, he withdrew to the citadel of Namur. When King Philip learned of Don Juan's danger, he ordered troops to return, with Parma as their leader.)

The first act and the beginning of the second portray opposing attitudes toward the troops' return. Don Juan in conversation with the duke of Ariscote (Aerschot) and the marquis of Abre (Havré) refers to the troops as essential to the peace of the Netherlands: as soon as they were gone, insurrection followed. Aerschot denies that there was just cause for recalling them. He is restrained in Don Juan's presence, but when he finds himself alone with Havré (his brother), he vents his anger:

> Ya vuelven los españoles,
> Los que haciendo tantos robos,
> Son de nuestra sangre lobos,
> De nuestra plata crisoles.   (Ed. Acad. 12:360a)

Now the Spaniards return, those who robbing much are smelters of our silver plate, wolves who suck our blood.

Aerschot appears in the play as a despicable character. Yet his villainy does not undercut these lines.

The count of Bossu, like the duke of Aerschot an historical figure, accuses the duke of responsibility for the recall of the soldiers. Only a single Spaniard remained, he says, referring to

Don Juan; you and your followers treated him unjustly and encouraged the common people to do so. Whatever the historical Bossu thought of the duke, the historical Aerschot had a measure of responsibility for the return of the troops. He was the principal proponent of the treaty known as the Perpetual Edict, derisively called at the time "the peace of the duke of Aerschot,"[44] which, in its failure to require a meeting of the States-General to negotiate a religious settlement, caused renewed hostilities between the Calvinist maritime provinces and the Catholic southern provinces.[45] Yet Zeeland and Holland would have demanded religious toleration, at least within their own borders, which to King Philip was an unacceptable concession.

The count of Berlaymont, historically one of the Walloons who took Don Juan's side, appears prominently in the play as the victor in the first battle of the campaign, at the town of Ruremonde.[46] Bossu, commander of the States' army, mentions the battle, attributing the Spanish victory to the improvement in morale occasioned by Parma's arrival. Later, Don Juan and Parma congratulate Berlaymont, who praises Parma, adding—in a seeming reference to the Battle of Lepanto—that the prince was trained in the school of Don Juan. From Parma, he predicts, peace will come to the Netherlands. Piqued by jealousy, it would appear, Don Juan responds to the extravagant praise of his nephew by changing the subject: he describes to Berlaymont King Philip's empire.

Lope's concern with decorum prevented direct criticism of Don Juan: many characters, including Parma, praise him. But there are hints of an uncertain relationship between the two leaders.[47] Don Juan addresses Parma formally, at times defer-

---

[44] Pieter Geyl, *The Revolt of the Netherlands (1555–1609)* (London: Williams & Norgate, 1945), p. 154

[45] Wernham, *Before the Armada*, pp. 329–30; Charles H. Wilson, *Elizabeth and the Revolt of the Netherlands*, p. 43.

[46] See Essen, *Farnèse*, 1:205.

[47] Alonso Vázquez writes that, before the prince's arrival, Don Juan had heard a report that his mother, the duchess of Parma, was to be appointed

entially; and just before the Battle of Gembloux, he offers him the royal standard of command. After Parma refuses it and leaves to join the cavalry, Don Juan remarks that he resembles Alexander the Great—a conventional comparison used in praise of military leaders, which gains force here from Parma's Christian name. Parma appears to better advantage than Don Juan—a more inspiring leader, a better tactician, a more audacious soldier. Lope wrote with knowledge of his later career.

Parma was married; Don Juan was not. Lope turns to dramatic advantage Don Juan's reputation for attractiveness to women.[48] Madama Rosela, a kinswoman of the duke of Aerschot, is infatuated with Don Juan; her brother, a Netherlands patriot, hates him as a symbol of their national servitude to the extent that he undertakes the suicidal task of attempting to kill him. When Rosela learns that Don Juan's life is in danger, she disguises herself, makes her way to him as he plans the impending Battle of Gembloux, and warns him. Before he can send her away, her brother fires at him, misses, and is killed by soldiers—but not before he can shout his defiance:

> *¡Agora es tiempo, valor,*
> *Que des libertad á Flandes!*

Courage! Now is the time that you give liberty to the Netherlands.

A soldier finds and reads aloud a message written on a paper clutched in the dead man's hand:

> *"Adolfo soy, que por librar la patria*
> *Troqué la vida á tanta fama y gloria,*
> *Y dí la muerte al español del Austria."*   (Ed. Acad. 12:386b, 387a)

"I am Adolpho, who, in order to liberate my country, exchanged life for fame and glory. I killed the Spaniard of Austria."

---

governess again and that Parma himself was to be her captain-general: Vázquez, CODOIN, 72:70.

[48] In *Pobreza no es vileza*, a character tells an anecdote that has as its point Don Juan's attractiveness to highborn ladies: a French lady, on seeing his gallant demeanor, became so enamored of him that she wore beneath her dress a red sash in honor of Spain (Ed. Acad. 12:513a).

Lope does not portray rebels sympathetically. But in this episode he acknowledges that some of them oppose Spain on principle.

In anticipation of the battle, Don Juan withdraws for solitary prayer, holding the royal standard as he looks at an image of Christ. He prays for divine support in his war against the "rebelde flamenco pertinaz." A character personifying Don Juan's imagination appears, standing on a platform[49] at a height above the stage, and addresses him. Reminding him that he fights for religion, his Imagination encourages him, first by describing Philip's empire in Europe, Asia, Africa, and America, and then by showing him a symbolical representation of it. A curtain is drawn, uncovering a portrait of the king, in which three matrons stand around him holding a globe of the world above his head.

The devotional interlude ends with the sound of a drum and of the Spanish war cry, "¡Cierra España!" Startled by the war cry, Don Juan asks on whose order the squadrons have attacked. The count of Berlaymont answers, describing the battle, undertaken on Parma's initiative, that has already been won. (Lope follows Alonso Vázquez closely in Berlaymont's battle narrative.)[50] Although the infantry had not yet arrived, Parma had seen the enemy vulnerable and had ordered the cavalry to charge. They had hesitated a moment because the order had not come from Don Juan. Parma vigorously asserted his own authority and led an overwhelmingly successful attack.[51]

[49] On a *bofetón*: "This was a device which either rotated or sprang open to enable characters to appear and disappear as if by magic": Shergold, *History of the Spanish Stage*, pp. 222–23.

[50] Vázquez, *Los sucesos*, CODOIN, 72:89–94.

[51] In 1590 Sir Roger Williams described the circumstances that led to the Spanish victory: "The shamefull Ouerthrow at *Iubeleo* [Gembloux], where lesse than 600. Horsmen of *Don Iohn de Austria*, ouerthrew 15000. against reason, onelie for want of Chiefes to keepe order. The occasion of this charge came through a Captaine of Horsmen, which discouered their disorder of March, and procured the rest to followe, desiring leaue of *Octauia Gonzaga* his Generall, to charge." Williams, *A Briefe discourse of Warre*, in *The Works of Sir Roger Williams*, ed. John X. Evans (Oxford: Clarendon Press, 1972), p. 10.

The infantry arrived and, although tired from a long march, completed the rout of the States' army.

In a later conversation, Parma reports to Don Juan that 12,000 of the enemy were killed and 4,000 captured. Don Juan attributes the victory to God—and, after the Deity, to Parma. Lope closes the play with this triumph that marked the return of Spanish troops.

No character in *Los españoles en Flandes* alludes to a possible invasion of England, though Vázquez in Lope's source does so. Referring to an effort by Queen Elizabeth in January 1578 to avert resumption of war, Vázquez describes Don Juan's courteous reception of her ambassador (Sir Thomas Leighton) and his refusal to grant her request for an armistice.[52] The queen believed, Vázquez writes, that if King Philip were not burdened by the Revolt of the Netherlands, he would have troops available for waging wars in England,

> which he had wished to do for a long time in order to extirpate the heresies of that kingdom and liberate the large number of English Catholics who lived under severe oppression from a queen who was their determined enemy.[53]

But even such victories as Gembloux did not end the Revolt.

Lope justly portrays the battle as a major victory for Spain. Although the count of Bossu's army was numerically superior, many of its officers were absent, and it lacked sufficient strength in cavalry to stop Parma's sudden charge. The States had vainly hoped for cavalry from Queen Elizabeth,[54] but despite her overtures of friendship and messages of encouragement, support apart from volunteers and subsidies would not

---

Evans notes that Parma was in command (p. 165). For a modern account of the battle, see Essen, *Farnèse*, 1:211–17.

[52] At the time she sent Leighton to the Netherlands, Queen Elizabeth sent Sir Thomas Wilks to Spain to request that Don Juan be recalled: John Black, *The Reign of Elizabeth* (Oxford: Clarendon Press, 1936), p. 295; Wernham, *Before the Armada*, p. 331.

[53] Vázquez, *Los sucesos*, CODOIN, 72:71–72.

[54] See Charles H. Wilson, *Elizabeth and the Revolt of the Netherlands*, pp. 59–61.

be forthcoming until 1585.[55] Fortunately for Prince William
and those of his countrymen who shared his hostility toward
Spain, Don Juan did not receive enough money from King
Philip to enable him to maintain the momentum generated at
Gembloux. The Netherlanders gained time to strengthen the
defenses of Brussels and other strong places in the South. On
Don Juan's death in October 1578, the prince of Parma became
governor, and a new era began.

★

Los españoles en Flandes closes with the victory at Gembloux on
January 31, 1578. *El asalto de Mastrique por el Príncipe de Parma*,
a dramatic chronicle of the first of Parma's major sieges, opens
on March 7, 1579, the day before the Spanish attack on the
city. More carefully written than *Los españoles*, it is a more important play, a remarkably detailed portrayal of siege warfare.
Lope follows Vázquez's narrative closely, and although he includes fictional characters, he gives them unimportant roles.[56]
This is a play of darker tone than *Los españoles*, one in which
Lope's ambivalence about Spain's war in the Netherlands appears more emphatically.

Parma's stated motive in besieging Maastricht is as crassly
prudential as Henry IV's recommendation of foreign wars to
divert the "giddy minds" of rebellious subjects (*2 Henry IV*,
IV.v.212–15). Parma attacks the city, he explains to his council
of war, to prevent mutiny:[57]

[55] Black, *Reign of Elizabeth*, p. 296.

[56] On Lope's use of his source, see S. A. Vosters, "Lope y Calderón, Vázquez y Hugo, Maastricht y Breda," pp. 127–36.

[57] Parma's fear of mutiny was well founded. In the Netherlands in "the last
quarter of the sixteenth century," there were "over forty . . . concerted Span-
ish mutinies": Charles H. Wilson, *The Transformation of Europe, 1558–1648*
(Berkeley and Los Angeles: University of California Press, 1976), p. 154.
Geoffrey Parker prints a detailed list of the mutinies from 1570 until 1607: *The
Army of Flanders and the Spanish Road, 1567–1659* (Cambridge: Cambridge
University Press, 1972), pp. 290–92. See also Parker, "Mutiny and Discontent
in the Spanish Army of Flanders, 1572–1607," in his *Spain and the Netherlands*,
pp. 106–21.
Parma's success at Maastricht as well as in later sieges is the more remarka-

Señores, ya habéis visto y advertido
En la poca asistencia, aunque con causa,
Que el Rey, nuestro señor, hace á este ejército;

. . . .

Mayormente, los fuertes españoles,
Que en país tan remoto de su patria,
No tienen otro amparo que el del cielo,
Tengo temor que amotinarse quieren,[58]
Porque la sed y hambre los aflige
Y ha mucho tiempo que la paga esperan,
Si no es que los empleo en algún sitio
De tierra, que pudiese la esperanza
Del saco entretenellos algún tiempo.   (Ed. Acad. 12:440b)

Señores, you have already seen and taken notice of the meager support the king, our master—for compelling reasons—can give this
army. . . . Principally, I am concerned that the valiant Spaniards—
in a country so distant from their own and having no shelter except
the sky—will mutiny if they are not employed in a siege that can
keep them occupied and give them hope [of profit from] the sack
[of a city]. They suffer from hunger and thirst, and for a long time
they have not been paid.

The capture of Maastricht will enable the troops to pay themselves with plunder—a general's cruel solution to a difficult
problem. The historical general had more comprehensive reasons for the siege.

Yet Lope portrays Parma admiringly. Even in the first scene,
as soldiers talk about the inadequacy of their food and the ar-
rears in their pay, it becomes apparent that in the short time he
has been in the Netherlands, he has won a reputation as an extraordinarily able general. He has become known to his enemies, as well as to his own troops, as a consistently victorious
leader. Before the siege begins, an aide to the governor of
Maastricht describes him as another Alexander the Great.

---

ble in view of his distance from Spain and the limited financial support King
Philip could give him.

[58] In Calderón's *El sitio de Bredá*, about a Spanish siege in 1624–25, the general, Spínola, speaks about mutiny in a similar vein in his own preliminary
council of war. Ed. Valbuena Briones, 1:75a

Lope depicts Parma's versatility, his ability to meet the exigencies of situations, often in unorthodox ways. In the course of the siege, he borrows money from his Spanish troops and with it buys food and munitions in the nearby region of Liège. The men will be able to repay themselves, he explains, by sacking Maastricht. His officers and men are reluctant to undertake the labor of digging trenches and constructing equipment needed for scaling the city walls. He overcomes their reluctance by taking a shovel in hand and commencing to dig a trench.[59] His design of a platform to be placed adjacent to the walls compels the admiration of an expert engineer. He is resolute, refusing to consider proposals that he raise the siege. He alone makes command decisions. Lope's praise of his protagonist can in this instance be the more convincing because the historical figure possessed the qualities attributed to him. Lope's admiration of Parma, however, does not prevent him from portraying the brutality of the siege: the mutilation of bodies and the deaths that the campaign causes.

The Spaniards meet unexpectedly strong resistance from Maastricht. Parma intentionally began the siege on a market day (as became his custom in his later sieges—beginning them, if not on a market day, then on a festival), assuming that many peasants from nearby villages would then be in the city and that the additional people would more rapidly exhaust the available food.[60] In this instance, the stratagem works to his disadvantage: the city has a large store of supplies. Just before the siege begins, Maastricht's governor explains to an aide that, knowing the peasants are stubborn fighters when cornered, he has prevented them from leaving. During the siege they are kept busy day and night working on the city's fortifications. The historical Parma found himself confronted with

[59] This detail was probably suggested to Lope by a passage in Cervantes' *Comedia del cerco de Numancia*, in *Obras completas: Comedias y entremeses*, ed. Rodolfo Schevill and Adolfo Bonilla, 5 (Madrid: Gráficas Reunidas, 1920), 117. The Roman leader Scipio, like Parma, takes a shovel in hand to overcome the reluctance of his men to work. (I am indebted to Professor Willard F. King for the reference.)

[60] Essen, *Farnèse*, 2:152.

a multinational garrison of 1,200, made up of English, Scots, and French soldiers, supported by a larger group of 4,000 men-in-arms consisting of the peasants and the residents of the city.[61] Because the peasants were within the walls, Parma was deprived of his usual supply of forced labor for digging trenches and building fortifications.[62]

The Netherlanders repulse the first penetration within the city, inflicting heavy losses. The Spaniards succeed in a second attempt, though at the expense of many men. Lope does not include a final estimate of the losses in Parma's army, which was made up of Walloons and Germans as well as Spaniards. They are believed to have been about 2,500.[63] Lope overstates the number of those killed in Maastricht, but he does so in a passage that obscures the historical reality of a massacre. At dawn of the day of victory (June 29, 1579), the soldiers leaped from the walls into the city, Captain Castro reports to Parma, and within half an hour killed more than 14,000 persons. They were killed, Castro says, in vengeance—honorably exacted— for the Spaniards who had lost their lives. Parma offers no objection to the assertion that the Spaniards acted honorably. Although he orders that acts of violence be stopped, he permits all of Spanish nationality to enter the city and join in the sack, recalling that earlier Spaniards had given him their gold. (His Walloon and German troops had refused his request.)

Although Lope's source, Vázquez, does not refer to the number of persons killed in Maastricht, he says enough for it to be apparent that Parma's troops committed an atrocity: the excited and angered soldiers, he writes, killed indiscriminately all persons they encountered, including women and children.[64]

★

Lope portrays forthrightly the brutality of the siege. The play provides, more clearly than *Los españoles*, a "double vision" of

---

[61] Ibid.

[62] Ibid., 2:152–56.

[63] Ibid., 2:188.

[64] Vázquez, *Los sucesos*, CODOIN, 72:214–15. Essen estimates the number killed to have been about 10,000: *Farnèse*, 2:188.

war, of victory bought at an absurdly high price. Alonso García, a soldier from Toledo, opens the play with a soliloquy about the exposure to the cold of winter and heat of summer, the broken arms and legs, and the deaths by the hundreds that are the price of military glory. He asks, in a conversation that follows, if any good purpose is served by Parma's campaign. A companion scolds him and praises Parma. But García continues to interject expressions of doubt. The most remarkable of his comments on the war appears late in the final act in a soliloquy that includes an epic catalogue of heroes fighting under Parma's command and a reference to the world-wide empire of King Philip. García's tone is not confident or expansive; it is, on the contrary, elegiac: would Maastricht, even if captured, be worth the loss of so many gallant men?

> Pero, ¿ qué os digo, si, en fin,
> Tras tanto valor y fuerzas,
> De ochocientos españoles
> Las vidas, Mastrique cuesta,
> Sin veintidós capitanes
> Que honrar el mundo pudieran?   (Ed. Acad. 12:469b)

But what can I say to you if, in the end, after so many courageous acts and feats of arms, the capture of Maastricht costs the lives of eight hundred Spaniards, without taking into account those of twenty-two captains who could have done honor to the world?

Yet García undergoes a change of heart when Parma himself speaks to him, calling on him as a man of Toledo to perform an important and dangerous act. (The change in García from cynical doubter to brave soldier is similar to the transformation of a character in Lope's later *El Brasil restituido* [1625], after his general has reprimanded him for cowardice.) Precisely at dawn of the day Parma has chosen for the final battle, García signals the attack by leaping from an enclosed area in the walls into Maastricht, yelling the Spanish battle cry.[65]

More surprising than García's cynical commentary on the war is an expression of doubt by Parma, the exemplar of heroic fortitude and devotion to duty. For a moment, at least, he

---

[65] Lope departs from Vázquez here: *Los sucesos*, CODOIN, 72:214.

questions the justice of the war. At the time he speaks, he begins to feel the chills and fever that mark the onset of a grave illness: his self-questioning, in contrast to his customary assurance, can be explained psychologically as the result of a sudden diminution in vigor that accompanies his illness. His words nevertheless reveal a sensitivity to the human consequences of the siege:

> Guerra ¿quién te inventó? Si soy injusta,
> Mi origen fué de un ángel la malicia;
> Si soy justa, inventóme la justicia,
> Porque con la razón la guerra es justa.
> . . . .
> ¿Qué haré, guerra, qué haré? Sequir la guerra,
> Y abrase el fuego los flamencos hielos,
> Hasta que se reduzca al Rey su tierra.   (Ed. Acad. 12:471a)

War, who invented you? If I am unjust, my origin was the malice of an angel; if I am just, justice invented me, because war for a legitimate reason is just. . . . What shall I do, war, what shall I do? Continue the war and unleash fire on the Flemish frosts until the king's land has been restored to him.

Repressing his doubts, he gives a soldier's answer to his scruples: the war is just and he will carry on.

For a time, however, Parma is unable to carry on. Seized by a sudden fever, he relinquishes his sword and baton of command; as he becomes delirious, he allows himself to be taken to his bed. Lope follows Vázquez's account of the illness, which came a short time before the decisive battle.[66] When Parma's attendants undress him, they discover an inflamed swelling on his shoulder. When it is lanced, his delirium leaves him; and he reassumes command in time to plan the final battle.

At this point, Lope follows a pattern present in *Los españoles en Flandes*. Parma prays for divine assistance in his war against heretics. But he cannot lead the fighting within Maastricht because of his illness. In this Lope follows his source, although he addresses only indirectly a subject implicit in Vázquez's

---

[66] Ibid., 72:212–21.

narrative: that Parma's presence in the city might have prevented the indiscriminate slaughter of which his army was
guilty.

Although *El asalto de Mastrique* may be interpreted as a play
that is critical of Spain's war in the Netherlands, it includes
nothing that would justify our considering it as critical of
Spanish imperialism. Although the sombre, unflinching portrayal of siege warfare in *El asalto* reminds us of Cervantes'
portrayal of it in *La Numancia*, the classic siege play of the
Spanish Golden Age, Lope stops short of the more fundamental kind of questioning of Spanish imperial policy implicit in
the earlier play. In *El asalto* Lope would seem to conclude, with
the Parma of his play, that Spain's war in the Netherlands is
horrible but may be necessary; in *La Numancia* Cervantes concludes—not overtly, to be sure—that Spain's foreign wars on
both sides of the Atlantic are horrible and unnecessary.[67]

★

Unlike Don Juan, Parma did not underestimate the difficulty
of a successful invasion of England; and again unlike him, he
thought the war in the Netherlands should be won before an
invasion was launched. After he captured Antwerp in August
1585, he seemed close to total success in the Netherlands,
which could come only with the conquest of Zeeland and Holland. But the fall of Antwerp and the assassination the previous year of Prince William of Orange led Queen Elizabeth
after long hesitation to send an English army in support of the
Netherlanders; and English soldiers and money enabled the
Dutch to slow Parma's advance. After the execution of Queen
Mary Stuart in February 1587, Parma turned his attention
from the reconquest to preparations for launching the barges

---

[67] Willard F. King, describing the close relationship between *La Numancia*
and Ercilla's epic, *La Araucana* (one of Cervantes' principal sources), writes
that both works portray heroic "resistance to aggression by an imperial power
represented as brave, intelligent, and honorable" ("Cervantes' *Numancia* and
Imperial Spain," *MLN* 94 [1979]: 200–21; quotation, p. 215. See also Carroll
Johnson, "*La Numancia* and the Structure of Cervantine Ambiguity," *Ideologies
and Literature* 3 [1980]: 87, 93 n. 28).

intended to transport his soldiers to England under cover of a Spanish fleet.[68]

Understandably the *comedia* includes little about the Invincible Armada. But Spanish nondramatic poetry, by Luis de Góngora as well as by Lope, provides distinguished comment on it. In their poems Lope and Góngora express hostility to England and to Queen Elizabeth uninhibited by stage censorship or dramatic decorum. Both men, as well as Antonio Coello (in his play *El Conde de Sex*), associate Elizabeth with the defeat of the Armada.

Góngora's "De la armada que fué a Inglaterra" reveals the religious conviction that animated the abortive attack. In the Latinate syntax for which he is famous, Góngora approaches his subject by indirection. His lament for the Armada becomes a lament for England. Had the fleet been successful, Spain could have rescued the heretic nation from the infamy to which her queen had reduced her. His denunciation of Elizabeth gains force from its juxtaposition with lines recalling the heroic past of England,

> *de Arturos, de Eduardos i de Enricos,*
> *Ricos de fortaleza, i de fee ricos;*
> *Ahora condenada a infamia eterna*[69]
>> *Por la que te govierna*
>> *Con la mano ocupada*
> *Dèl huso en vez de sceptro i de la espada;*
> *Muger de muchos, i de muchos nuera,*
>> *O Reina torpe, Reina no, mas loba*
>>> *Libidinosa i fiera,*
> *Fiamma dal ciel su le tue trezze piova!*[70]

of Arthurs, of Edwards, and of Henrys, rich in courage and in faith, now condemned to eternal infamy.

. . . .

Wife of many, and daughter-in-law of many; oh lewd queen; no,

---

[68] Mattingly, *The Defeat of the Spanish Armada*, p. 61.

[69] The following three lines must remain (in words Edward Gibbon used in a similar situation) "veiled in the obscurity of a learned language."

[70] D. Luis de Góngora, *Obras poéticas*, ed. R. Foulché-Delbosc, I (New York: The Hispanic Society of America, 1921), 109.

not a queen but a lascivious and fierce she-wolf: let a flame from
heaven rain upon your head!

Góngora employs a line in Italian, from Petrarch, to express
his intensity of feeling.[71]

These lines convey regret for what Góngora regards as the
tragedy of England—and, as a corollary not stated in the
poem, of the Protestant part of northern Europe. Don Juan of
Austria's belief that Spain's problems in the Netherlands had
their origin in England and could most effectively be opposed
there was shared during his life and for decades after his death
by many of his countrymen. England as the natural leader of
the Protestant states could be and often was regarded as the defender of the Reformation and the fomenter of heresy on the
Continent. The unfulfilled mission of the Armada was more
comprehensive than the restoration of England and Scotland
to the Catholic faith.

Góngora and Lope were Spaniards of the same generation,
and their personal differences notwithstanding, their conceptions of the Armada's mission were largely the same. Lope's
well-known sonnet, "Famosa armada de estandartes llena,"
about the Armada as it appeared in Lisbon harbor before sailing, includes an affirmation that the Catholic faith alone sends
it from the shores of Spain to oppose the falsehood of a siren
(Queen Elizabeth).[72] His bitter lines on Elizabeth among his
group of short poems conceived as "Epitafios fúnebres" include an apparent reference to the English use of fireships
against the Armada: "Jezebel," he calls the queen, "cruel incen-
diary of the sea."[73]

In Book I of *La corona trágica*, his long poem on Mary, queen
of Scots, Lope denounces Elizabeth as Mary's executioner. In
a vitriolic stanza on Elizabeth, he expresses regret that Philip II
(when he was in England as the husband of Queen Mary Tu-

[71] The line in Italian is the first line of sonnet 104 in Petrarch's *Rime*, Part
One: Robert Jammes, *Etudes sur l'oeuvre poétique de Don Luis de Góngora y Ar-
gote* (Bordeaux: Institut d'Etudes Ibériques et Ibéro-Américanes de l'Univer-
sité de Bordeaux, 1967), p. 253 n. 14.

[72] Lope de Vega, *Rimas humanas*, Part One, in *Colección de las obras sueltas*, 4
(Madrid: Imprenta de Don Antonio de Sancha, 1776), 212.

[73] *Rimas humanas*, Part Two, in ibid., 4:395.

dor) had not killed her.[74] He devotes several stanzas of Book III to the Armada, referring to his own service in it. While he was still too young to grow a beard, he writes (with some exaggeration), he entered the king's service so that he could take part in the Catholic expedition. He describes the storms out of the north the fleet encountered, referring to thunder that resembled gunfire and lightning that illuminated the topsails. The weather, he implies (with some justice), defeated the Spanish fleet. Elizabeth triumphed, and Mary's tears were not avenged.[75]

To turn from the harlot Elizabeth of Spanish nondramatic poetry to the dignified queen of Antonio Coello's play, *El Conde de Sex* (1633), is to be reminded of the shaping force of literary theory in historical drama. In this play, based on the Elizabeth and Essex story, the dramatist, guided by theory, represents the queen as an exemplary sovereign: she suppresses her love for Essex even as she condemns him to death for treason. In Coello's time most Spaniards believed Elizabeth to have been promiscuous, the mistress of Essex and other men. Yet she was a queen, and the principle of decorum, derived from Aristotle's assertion that in drama the truth of poetry should take precedence over the truth of history, required that the character be endowed with qualities appropriate to her supreme rank.[76]

Coello associates Queen Elizabeth with the Armada. (His is the only reference I have encountered in the *comedia* to the subject.) The earl of Essex implies, unhistorically, that he had been admiral of the English fleet,

>   *cuando Filipo*
> *Segundo, español monarca,*

[74] *La corona trágica*, Book I, in ibid., 4:5.

[75] *La corona trágica*, Book III, in ibid., 4:61–62.

[76] Edward M. Wilson and Duncan Moir, *The Golden Age: Drama, 1492–1700*, in *A Literary History of Spain*, gen. ed. R. O. Jones, 3 (New York: Barnes and Noble, 1971), 135–36. Moir quotes Bances Candamo's comments of 1689 or 1690 on the play. See also Francisco Antonio de Bances Candamo, *Theatro de los theatros de los passados y presentes siglos*, ed. Moir (London: Tamesis Books, 1970), pp. lxxxvi–lxxxviii, 34–35, 70 n. 18, 130 n. 15.

contra Ingalaterra hizo
la armada mayor que nunca
con pesadumbre de pino
la espalda oprimió salobre
de aquese monstruo de vidrio;
y que a mí la Reina entonces
me envió con sus navíos
a procurar resistir
tan poderoso enemigo.[77]

when Philip the Second, the Spanish monarch, sent the largest armada that ever lay heavy—with the weight of [ships made of] pines—upon that monster of glass [the sea]; the queen sent me with her ships to try to withstand such a powerful enemy.

Lord Howard of Effingham, not Essex, was the admiral of the fleet that defeated the Invincible Armada. However, there is the truth of poetry in Coello's representation of Essex as a naval hero: in June 1596, when Philip II was preparing an armada to be sent in support of Irish rebels, Essex led a fleet in a destructive attack on Cádiz. (Philip launched his armada, bound for Ireland, in October, but an autumn storm caused heavy losses and forced it back to Spain.)

Lope's association in *La corona trágica* of the execution of Mary Stuart with Philip II's launching the Armada in 1588 is historically sound: the death of the Catholic heir to the English throne set in motion the sequence of events that reached their climax in the narrow seas that separate England from the Netherlands and France.

★

The defeat of the Armada seems in retrospect a more decisive event in the long war between England and Spain than it seemed in 1588 or the dozen years that followed. Englishmen expected King Philip to try again, as he did, unsuccessfully, in 1597 as well as in 1596. Despite losses, Spanish naval strength

---

[77] Coello, *El Conde de Sex*, ed. Donald E. Schmiedel (Madrid: Editorial Playor, 1973), p. 93. The play is the earliest dramatization of the Elizabeth and Essex story.

became greater in the 1590s than it had ever been before.[78] In that decade Spain's revenue from the silver mines of America reached its peak,[79] providing wealth for the construction of ships and for foreign adventures directed against France as well as against England and the Netherlands. With Philip's many commitments, money remained a problem, and unpaid troops in Spanish service continued to mutiny; but only death would put an end to the king's aggression.

Parma had identified in advance a major weakness in the Spanish plan for the Great Armada: the lack of a deep-water port near England to serve as a base for the galleons. In July 1588 some of them foundered on the sandbanks of Flanders. In anticipation of subsequent expeditions, King Philip attempted to provide a base on the coast of France for use against England directly or by way of Ireland—a strategy Queen Elizabeth was compelled to oppose. Although the war in the Netherlands and English participation in it continued, after 1588 the focus of the queen's attention turned to France.

Henry IV, the legitimate heir to the French throne, succeeded Henry III in August 1589. But before he became acknowledged king of a united France, Henry IV faced years of war against a coalition of French Catholic, Spanish, and Papal troops. He found allies in Prince Maurice of Nassau and in Queen Elizabeth.

In the months of 1589 following his accession, the queen sent an army to France under Lord Willoughby, as well as a loan of £20,000 to King Henry. In the five following years she sent more money and more troops under several commanders including the earl of Essex, Sir John Norris, and Sir Roger Williams. The English effort was defensive, calculated to prevent Spain from capturing Channel ports, and was concentrated in the coastal areas, a strategy that was effective though costly in lives.[80] In heavy fighting, the English prevented the

---

[78] Black, *Reign of Elizabeth*, p. 353.

[79] Charles H. Wilson, *Transformation of Europe*, p. 170.

[80] J. B. Black notes that in the five years from the autumn of 1589 until the autumn of 1594, about 20,000 Englishmen were sent to France and about half of them failed to return: *Reign of Elizabeth*, p. 362.

Spanish army from gaining control of Brittany, a province important in the event of a Spanish strike against Ireland. King Henry's conversion to Catholicism in 1593 alarmed the English, but it did not end the alliance, nor did it end Spain's opposition to him, though it weakened the position of the French members of the Catholic League, which was subsidized by King Philip.

The accession of Henry IV and Spain's intervention in France provided the United Provinces of the Netherlands with an opportunity they exploited in full measure. On orders from his king, Parma spent a large part of the last three years of his life, 1589 to 1592, in France; and although he achieved the objectives assigned to him, his absence left the command of Spanish forces in the Netherlands to men of lesser ability. In 1590 Prince Maurice, the son of William I, launched a counteroffensive, and in the campaigns of five successive years, through 1594, he won back many towns Parma had captured. In 1595 and 1596 he encountered reverses, but thereafter his advance continued.

In these years the Spanish Army of Flanders had to oppose Prince Maurice's troops as well as those of King Henry, the latter frequently reenforced by the Dutch, as in the autumn of 1595, when the States-General sent twenty-two companies for the defense of Cambrai. These troops arrived too late to save the town, though they were useful to King Henry later.[81] The Spanish captured Cambrai in a campaign that Lope portrays in *Pobreza no es vileza.*

★

Although Lope subordinates history to fiction in *Pobreza*, he nevertheless conveys the political temper of the southern Netherlands in the late sixteenth century, and he chronicles a successful military campaign. He refers to the fictional as well as the historical component of the play in his dedicatory epistle to the duke of Maqueda:

[81] Jan den Tex, *Oldenbarnevelt*, 2 vols., 1 (Cambridge: Cambridge University Press, 1973), 203–04.

This play is about war. Although its title is *Pobreza no es vileza* for a character who is a brave soldier, it celebrates feats of arms and victories in the Netherlands of the valorous Don Enrique de Toledo, Count of Fuentes.   (Ed. Acad. 12:479)

The victories are those the count of Fuentes won against the French in or near the province of Picardy in 1595; the heroic soldier (the "valiente" whose experiences occasion the play's title) is a fictional character, Don Juan de Mendoza, a nobleman who with his sister has fled Spain, both of them in disguise and with little money, in the aftermath of a duel he fought near Toledo to protect her. In his role as protagonist, Mendoza enlivens and gives focus to Lope's dramatic rendering of Fuentes' campaign. In the final act a minor character names the battles in which Mendoza has fought:

> *Dicen que todo el verano*
> *Valientemente ha servido*
> > *En Chatelete y en Han,*
> *Clari y Cambray, y en la gloria*
> *Que dió á España la victoria*
> *Del socorro de Durlán.*   (Ed. Acad. 12:505a)

They say that he has served courageously all summer at Châtelet, Han, Clari, and Cambrai, as well as in the relief of Durlán, a victory that brought glory to Spain.

All these were successful battles that seemed to contemporaries and near contemporaries the more impressive in that they followed five successive years of reverses for the Spanish and were to be followed by other unsuccessful years.[82]

Menéndez y Pelayo and at least one other well-informed critic, Damien Saunol, believed *Pobreza no es vileza* to be the best of the plays Lope wrote about the war in the Netherlands.[83] It is indeed more entertaining than the others, though *El asalto de Mastrique*, in its examination of the human price

---

[82] Damien Saunol, "Autour des Sources de *Pobreza no es vileza*," *BH* 48 (1946): 239; Jan den Tex, *Oldenbarnevelt*, 1: 201.

[83] See Menéndez y Pelayo, Ed. Acad. 12:cxlv–clii; Saunol, "Autour des Sources," p. 238.

paid for military victory, is more searchingly honest. Lope devotes few passages to details of siege warfare of the kind that give *El asalto* a documentary interest. Yet he is punctiliously accurate when he writes about Fuentes' campaign, even at times echoing the phrasing of his source, the commentaries written by a captain who served in the Spanish army.[84] Lope moves rapidly through his military history, pausing only for the portrayal of the siege of Châtelet, in which Mendoza first distinguishes himself.

In his opening scene, Lope conveys the time of the dramatic action, the troubled state of the southern Netherlands, the wretched condition to which Spanish soldiers have been reduced by the nonpayment of their wages, and the lack of principle of a fictional Walloon nobleman, Count Fabio. Rosela, Fabio's sister, who shares her brother's political attitudes and his moral insensitivity, has recently returned from Brussels to the family's country seat. A page and a maidservant express concern for her safety in the midst of war, the page adding that neutrality is no longer possible for her brother. To Rosela's answer that he is now loyal to Spain, the maidservant replies sarcastically that to be so in their region no longer requires courage.

The servants' fears are quickly justified: four Spanish soldiers, driven by hunger, come to rob Rosela of her jewels. But Mendoza, who has heard Rosela's cries, comes to confront them. The soldiers know and respect him; and although they dispute his right, as a soldier without rank, to give them orders, his determination prevails. His appearance and bearing prevail with Rosela as well, who perceives that, notwithstanding his tattered clothing, he is no ordinary soldier. When his sister Laura and his servant join them, Rosela invites them to be her guests. Mendoza must go to Brussels, he explains, but he accepts her invitation on behalf of his sister and his servant.

Mendoza's conversations in Brussels turn to military af-

---

[84] Captain Diego de Villalobos y Benavides, *Comentarios*. I follow the edition prepared by Alejandro Llorente (Madrid: 1876). On Lope's use of his source, see Saunol, "Autour des Sources," pp. 238–46.

fairs.[85] The count of Fuentes, he learns from a fellow soldier, is
ready to leave Brussels with an army of 8,000 men to besiege
Châtelet. The number will suffice, Mendoza comments: "Con
tan gran capitán tan poca gente." Here as elsewhere he praises
Fuentes extravagantly.

Fuentes himself soon enters, telling his aide that he will meet
all those who wish to talk to him. When Mendoza approaches,
the count greets him warmly despite the poverty apparent in
his clothing. Mendoza gives him a letter of introduction from
a person of high rank who reveals Mendoza's true identity and
the reason for his abrupt departure from Spain. Fuentes treats
him respectfully, asking him to remain even after Count Fabio
joins them; and he privately gives Mendoza money with
which to buy appropriate clothes. Mendoza, more zealous
than ever to distinguish himself in the forthcoming campaign,
then conducts Laura and his servant to Rosela, who assures
Mendoza that she will protect his sister: "You may be confident, señor, that you leave her in trust to me on my honor as a
noblewoman" (Ed. Acad. 12: 494a), and in parting she affec-
tionately gives him a scarf to wear into battle.

Fuentes' campaign provides occasion for Lope to praise
Spanish heroes collectively and two of them, Fuentes and the
duke of Pastrana,[86] individually. He elaborates a brief descrip-
tion in his source of the armor Pastrana wore when he left
Brussels at the head of his troops to join Fuentes at Châtelet.
Mendoza speaks to Fuentes:

> ¡Oh, si viera, señor, Vuestra Excelencia,
> Con unas armas que de fuegos llaman,
>
> . . . .
>
> Que por valiente y gentilhombre aclaman,
> Dijera, al ver su rostro, que había sido
> Adonis en diamante convertido!   (Ed. Acad. 12:497b)[87]

[85] In these passages Lope follows the *Comentarios* of Villalobos y Benavides.

[86] Lope wrote a sonnet on the occasion of Pastrana's early death: "Quién
llora aqui? Tres somos, quita el manto." Sonnet 100, *Rimas humanas*, Part One,
in *Obras sueltas*, 4:239.

[87] See Villalobos y Benavides, *Comentarios*, pp. 32–34. There is an apparent
reference to Pastrana's armor in George Chapman's *The Conspiracy . . . of*

Oh, if you could see, your excellency, his armor shining like fire
. . . that proclaims him a courageous gentleman; you would say,
on seeing his face, that Adonis had been transformed into diamond!

In his military passages, Lope writes in superlatives, drawing
on classical literature as well as Spanish history in his praise of
the soldiers and their leaders.

He pauses for an account of fortifications and tactics only in
the scenes devoted to the siege of Châtelet. A soldier reports to
Fuentes that the enemy garrison has been firing burning arrows from the walls of the citadel into nearby houses, where
grain is stored. The high walls and deep fortifications and
moat surrounding the citadel will protect it from artillery and
underground tunnels for planting mines.

On the day Fuentes chooses for his attack, Mendoza reports
that the Spanish artillery has made little impact on the fortifications. Determined to proceed, Fuentes gives marching orders to his captains. Mendoza recognizes that the day will be
climactic for himself. As he hears his comrades sound the battle cry, he receives the shattering news that his sister has been
raped by Fabio. Caught in a dilemma of claims on his honor,
Mendoza perceives that he can avenge his sister at once only by
leaving the battlefield. He makes the necessary decision to fulfill his soldier's duty first, a decision that has a quality of desperation in it, intensifying the savagery with which he fights.

Lope returns to his novelistic plot in his final act. Mendoza
has won the honor he desired, but he wishes his identity to be
concealed until he can confront Fabio. Laura, believing herself
to be without resources, unable even to return to Spain, has remained at Fabio's estate. Mendoza returns and demands that
Fabio face him with his sword. Fabio refuses, saying that he
will not fight a social inferior. Mendoza describes his own and
Laura's—properly, Doña Ana's—illustrious ancestry. Fabio's
answer, late in the final act, signals a change in him. He will
not give Mendoza satisfaction in a duel but in another manner,
"y no seas / tan español en la honra." He wishes to marry Doña

---

Charles Duke of Byron (1608) in *Chapman: The Tragedies*, ed. Thomas Marc
Parrot (New York: E. P. Dutton, 1910), p. 166.

Ana, and he will do so when Mendoza's true identity and name, Don Juan de Mendoza, are known in Brussels. Fabio adds another condition: that Mendoza accept a Netherlands wife, one of high rank and with a large dowry—his sister Rosela, though he does not say so.

When Mendoza learns the identity of his prospective bride, he denounces her for failing to protect his sister. But when she responds in a spirited gesture, his affection overcomes his desire for revenge. The count of Fuentes, Mendoza's kinsman, enters and presides over the resolution. To him Rosela offers an explanation for her failure to protect Laura that would have had more force in the seventeenth century than it has in the egalitarian twentieth century: because of his poverty she had failed to recognize Mendoza as a nobleman with honor to defend. Fuentes brings the play to a close by determining that Mendoza shall marry Rosela and Fabio, Ana.

The play is morally out of balance, partly because of the intrusion of Lope's distrust of and hostility toward the southern Netherlands' nobility. Fabio, a boastful liar, offers his services to Fuentes, who proposes that he join the cavalry commanded by the duke of Pastrana. But he takes no part in military action, choosing to spend the summer on his country estate. Both Fabio and his sister are flawed characters, and their marriages to the Spanish brother and sister are best regarded as a necessity of Lope's crowded plot.[88]

The crowded plot—and the compression in the portrayal of Fuentes' campaign that is its consequence—preclude the double vision of war that gives importance to *El asalto*. Classical allusion and catalogues of heroes take the place of acerbic commentary on the brutality of war. More neatly organized than *Los españoles* and more diverting than either that play or *El asalto*, *Pobreza* is a successful entertainment including a tribute to a Spanish general.

---

[88] On the theme of offended honor in the play, see Donald R. Larson, *The Honor Plays of Lope de Vega* (Cambridge, Mass.: Harvard University Press, 1977), p. 170.

Chapter Three

QUEEN ELIZABETH I'S WAR

AGAINST SPAIN

KING MIDAS:

Have not I made the sea to groan under the number of my ships, and have they not perished, that there was not two left to make a number?

. . . .

Have not I enticed the subjects of my neighbor princes to destroy their natural kings . . . ?

JOHN LYLY, *Midas* (1590)

IN A TRIBUTE to Queen Elizabeth written five years after her death, Francis Bacon described the danger from Spain she had confronted. Until about 1581, he writes, she was lenient with, in a limited measure even tolerant of, English Catholics.

> For up to that year there was no penalty of a grievous kind imposed by previous laws upon popish subjects. But just then the ambitious and vast design of Spain for the subjugation of the kingdom came gradually to light. Of this a principal part was the raising up within the bowels of the realm of a disaffected and revolutionary party which should join with the invading enemy; and the hope of effecting this lay in our religious dissensions.[1]

Elizabeth was confronted, that is, by the threat of a Spanish invasion supported by a rebellion of English Catholics.

During her reign English dramatists could not write openly about the danger Bacon describes, and even in James I's time the subject was sensitive, requiring circumspection. Yet they could approach it indirectly by writing about recent times in a foreign country, as Marlowe and Chapman did in *The Massacre at Paris* and *The Conspiracy and Tragedy of Charles, Duke of By-*

---

[1] Bacon, "In Felicem memoriam Elizabethae," trans. James Spedding, in Spedding et al., *The Works of Francis Bacon*, 11 (Boston: Brown and Taggard, 1860), 455.

ron respectively, or about remote times in England, as Shakespeare did in *King John*.

★

Shakespeare wrote most of his histories during the 1590s, a
decade during which war between Catholic and Protestant was
only the width of the Channel away from England, and, in
King John, he wrote about the conflict and its consequences for
his country.[2] The remoteness in time of John's reign, 1199 to
1216, as well as the historical record of the reign, gave Shakespeare freedom to write about sensitive doctrinal and political
problems: about the relationship between the English sovereign and the pope; the defense of England from foreign invasion supported by internal rebellion; and—at a time when
there was no undisputed heir to Queen Elizabeth's throne—
the nature of hereditary succession.

The presence among Shakespeare's characters of King
John's niece Blanche of Castile can remind us that the Spanish
and Catholic offensive against Protestant England included a
dynastic claim to the throne. In an attempt to take advantage
of the ambiguities clouding succession to Queen Elizabeth, the
Habsburgs and their supporters among the English Catholics
put forward as claimant the infanta Isabel, Philip II's older
daughter. The Spanish claim had been argued in England for a
long time, at least since 1571, when there had been talk of an
invasion led by the duke of Alba.[3] "R. Doleman" (probably a
pseudonym of Robert Parsons) summarized the arguments for
the infanta in a book published in Antwerp in 1594, *A Conference about the Next Succession to the Crowne of Ingland*. The author gained adventitious attention for his work by prefixing to
it a dedicatory epistle to the earl of Essex, one that embarrassed

---

[2] In this play alone, J. Dover Wilson writes, "Shakespeare deals directly
with the main issue of his age, viz. the religious question and the conflict between the English monarchy and the Papacy" (*King John*, ed. Wilson [Cam-
bridge: Cambridge University Press, 1936], p. viii).

[3] See Wernham, *Before the Armada*, pp. 312–13; and Marie Axton, *The
Queen's Two Bodies: Drama and the Elizabethan Succession* (London: Royal Historical Society, 1977), pp. 91–92.

Essex, though he soon cleared himself of complicity in writing it.[4] In any event, surviving comments on and answers to Doleman's book assure us that it gained a wide audience, including persons in high place. Lord Burghley read it, making notes in which he described it as "seditious." The author, says Burghley, "argues against the King of Scots, and in favour of an Infanta of Spain, or the King of Spain and his son."[5]

In *A Conference about the Next Succession*, Doleman considers theoretical issues first. Then he examines claims made for persons regarded as possible heirs to Elizabeth, adducing disqualifications for those who are not Spanish. In stating his case, he traces parallel dynastic lines back to William the Conqueror, concluding that his living representative is the infanta Isabel.

Among the historical figures he finds important for supporting Isabel's claim are two who are represented in the dramatis personae of *King John*: Constance of Brittany and Blanche of Castile, the daughter of Alfonso VIII of Castile and granddaughter and, allegedly, heir of Henry II of England. Blanche married Louis VIII of France, who, according to Doleman, became also king of England when King John was deposed for murdering his nephew Arthur. From Louis VIII and Blanche all subsequent kings of France were descended—as was the infanta Isabel, the granddaughter of Henry II of France. Although excluded from succession to the French crown by Salic Law,[6] the infanta was, Doleman asserts, the inheritor of the French right to the English crown inasmuch as King John had been deposed before the birth of his heir, Henry III.[7] Furthermore, Isabel's ancestor Blanche had an additional claim through her mother, King John's elder sister and nearest relative when he lost his crown.[8]

Doleman finds parallel support for the infanta's claim

[4] Lily B. Campbell, *Shakespeare's "Histories": Mirrors of Elizabethan Policy* (San Marino: The Huntington Library, 1947), pp. 176–80.

[5] *C.S.P., Domestic, 1595–97*, p. 157. Quoted from Campbell, *Shakespeare's "Histories,"* p. 180. See ibid., pp. 179–82.

[6] See *A Conference*, Part One, p. 31; Part Two, p. 153.

[7] *A Conference*, Part Two, pp. 25, 153.

[8] Ibid., Part Two, p. 153.

through her descent from Constance of Brittany. Constance was the heiress of her father, fourth duke of Brittany, a direct descendant of the Conqueror. Although her son Arthur died without issue, Constance—in the words of *A Conference*—"marryed agayne with a prince of her owne house . . . and by him she had issue that hath indured until this day, the last whereof hitherto is the lady Isabella infanta of Spaine" and her younger sister.[9]

Shakespeare shows no more patience than we would expect with a dynastic claim that favors the medieval over the recent past and that is based on a selective use of history and pseudo-history. We need not assume that he had read *A Conference*, a summary statement of long-used arguments, to believe he had some familiarity with the nature of the Spanish claim. The Constance of *King John*, far from surviving her grief over the death of Arthur to remarry and beget other children, dies "in a frenzy" (IV.ii.122). The Blanche of the play does indeed marry the dauphin (who later became King Louis VIII). But the marriage has grave consequences for King John, who arranged it, and for England: the dauphin leads a French invasion under cover of Blanche's dynastic claim, which also provides John's subjects with a pretext for an unsuccessful rebellion.[10] John dies a king, the dauphin returns to France, and Prince Henry succeeds his father as Henry III.

★

Shakespeare illustrates problems of succession in a monarchy, but he does so with reference to the beginning of John's reign, not its end. Whatever the nature of the historical figure's claim to succeed his brother King Richard, John of the play is portrayed as legally, at least, a usurper. Yet he is king, and he is confronted by a powerful and aggressive foreign power, France. The dauphin is eager to exploit the dissension among Englishmen arising from John's treatment of his nephew Arthur, the son of John's older brother Geoffrey, who died be-

[9] Ibid., Part Two, p. 18.
[10] See Axton, *The Queen's Two Bodies*, p. 110.

fore he could inherit the throne. Arthur is a child, too young to rule.[11] In the opening scene, John's mother, Eleanor of Aquitaine, reminds John of his disputed accession. When he boasts of his "strong possession" and his "right," Eleanor answers:

Your strong possession much more than your right,
Or else it must go wrong with you and me. (I.i.40–41)

They speak privately after the French ambassador, on behalf of his master, has asserted the claim of Arthur.

Yet it becomes apparent that hereditary right to the throne is qualified by circumstances. The king of France and the dauphin, while supporting Arthur's claim, look covetously at the extensive French domains then held by England. They ignore Arthur when John agrees to end a war with France by a marital alliance: Blanche will marry the dauphin. John offers his niece with the promise that "Her dowry shall weigh equal with a queen" (II.i.486). In fact, he offers something more than a queen's dowry—most of the French provinces held by the English crown. Later, when the papal legate Pandulph, angered by John's defiance of the pope, wishes the dauphin to lead an invading army into England, he tells the dauphin that he will be able to claim the throne. Pandulph predicts that John will kill Arthur and in doing so will alienate his subjects; the dauphin can then assert the right of Blanche, granddaughter of Henry II. Salisbury and Pembroke, to judge from their overt statements, are alienated from John not by his alleged usurpation but by their suspicion that he has murdered Arthur.[12] The bastard son of King Richard, Faulconbridge, the most percep-

[11] See Hugh M. Richmond, *Shakespeare's Political Plays* (New York: Random House, 1967), pp. 99–102.

[12] These two lords abandon John and join the dauphin less abruptly and for baser motives than at first appears: close attention to the time scheme of the play reveals that even when they affirm their loyalty to John in IV.ii, they have already been in communication with the dauphin and have received assurance of favorable treatment from him (James L. Calderwood, "Commodity and Honour in *King John*," *University of Toronto Quarterly* 29 [1960]; repr. in *Shakespeare: The Histories*, ed. Eugene M. Waith [Englewood Cliffs. N.J.: Prentice-Hall, 1965], pp.89–91).

tive and patriotic of the characters, recognizes the legitimacy of Arthur's claim (IV.iii.140–43).[13] But he supports John before as well as after the death of Arthur. In the moral climate of the play, the conception of legal right in isolation from qualifying circumstances has limited meaning.[14]

The peace between England and France made with the marital alliance is broken when, at the command of Cardinal Pandulph, King Philip of France renounces the alliance and again makes war. John, more successful in this campaign than earlier, captures Arthur, whom he places in the custody of Hubert de Burgh. Up to this time, John has appeared as a not overscrupulous opportunist, in his moral qualities resembling the ambitious dauphin. Now, however, in the climactic scene of the play, he instructs Hubert to take the boy to England and kill him.

In a pathetic scene, Hubert attempts to carry out, not John's initial instructions, but subsequent written instructions scarcely less cruel: not to kill Arthur but to blind him. Compassion overcomes him; he will not harm the boy, he tells him, but will convey false reports to the king. This scene more than any other signals John's depravity and makes plausible his nobles' desertion to join the invading army of the dauphin. Recognizing John's vulnerability, they choose what they regard as the stronger side even before their suspicions concerning Arthur have been confirmed.

Their calculations fail to take the bastard son of Richard Coeur-de-Lion into account. Faulconbridge can turn from the shattering discovery of the lifeless body of Arthur, the legitimate king, to a vigorous confrontation of the French army and the English rebels. Unlike Salisbury and Pembroke, he can perceive that John, his failings notwithstanding, remains king,

---

[13] Axton, *The Queen's Two Bodies*, pp. 109–10.

[14] Peter Saccio writes about John's disputed claim: "Most Tudor historians do not question the legitimacy of John's crown. In Holinshed there is no serious doubt about his right: Richard I wills all his dominions to John . . ." (*Shakespeare's English Kings: History, Chronicle, and Drama* [New York: Oxford University Press, 1977], pp. 202–03).

entitled to the loyalty of Englishmen.[15] No longer an insouciant adventurer, Faulconbridge becomes the military leader of England, Richard *redivivus*, providing a focus for patriotic resistance to foreign invasion. Among the leaders, only he disproves his own earlier assertion that men are uniformly self-serving (II.i.561–98).[16]

Shakespeare closes the play with the Bastard's triumphant and defiant lines that sound as though he refers to England as an island fortress. Neither he nor any other character mentions the nation's loss of portions of her French domains. Earlier in the final act Salisbury refers to England as a nation held in "Neptune's arms" (v.ii.34). In John's time, England had not yet lost all of France, but it serves Shakespeare's patriotic purpose to identify John's realm with Elizabeth's.[17] As in other aspects of the play, Shakespeare develops a paradox: that in the loss of Continental possessions England grows stronger.

In 1946 E.M.W. Tillyard described *King John* as "but mildly Protestant in tone."[18] Presumably, he used the qualifiers "but mildly" to distinguish the portrayal of religious issues in it from those in such vehemently Protestant renderings of the history of the reign as Shakespeare's source play, the anonymous *Troublesome Reign of King John* (printed in 1591). Although Shakespeare followed the plot of *The Troublesome Reign* with moderate fidelity, he rewrote it, darkening the character of the king; and in doing so he softened qualities that

---

[15] See Richmond, *Shakespeare's Political Plays*, pp. 116–17.

[16] Adrien Bonjour finds the structural pattern in the play in the contrasting fortunes of John and the Bastard: "John's career represents a falling curve, the Bastard's career a rising curve; and both curves, perfectly contrasted, are linked into a single pattern" ("The Road to Swinstead Abbey: A Study of the Sense and Structure of *King John*," *ELH* 18 [1951]: 270).

[17] Shakespeare does not address the moral problem latent in John's huge gift to France of Crown lands, as his niece's dowry, in order to protect his throne. Holinshed reveals that many of his French territories were in revolt against him. See Holinshed, The Third Volume of Chronicles (edition of 1587), in *Narrative and Dramatic Sources of Shakespeare*, ed. Bullough, 4:25–35.

[18] Tillyard, *Shakespeare's History Plays* (New York: Macmillan, 1946), p. 215.

give the earlier play a more emphatic Protestant ring.[19] A reading of Shakespeare's play with a knowledge of the history of the 1590s can leave little doubt about its Protestant bias. Yet Shakespeare, though he includes patriotic lines, refuses as firmly to simplify problems of church government as he does those of royal succession.

His subject presented him with another paradox: a wicked king, John, like the good Queen Elizabeth, had asserted England's independence of the pope, who in retaliation had excommunicated him, just as Pius V had excommunicated Elizabeth. A wicked man, in brief, had defiantly taken a position that at the time the play was first performed was regarded as just and courageous. Shakespeare accepted the paradox, refusing to resolve it as John Bale among others had done by altering the record of John's reign,[20] and in doing so he retained the subtlety of good history.

The antagonism between the king and the pope first becomes evident early in the third act, just after the marriage of the dauphin and John's niece has sealed an alliance between England and France. Shakespeare's timing of Cardinal Pandulph's entrance accentuates the intrusiveness of the papal legate. He joins the wedding party, including the two kings and the duke of Austria, after the ceremony. Ignoring the events that have brought the kings together, Pandulph querulously asks John why he had refused to allow the man chosen by the pope to become archbishop of Canterbury. The subject has not been mentioned previously. John replies indignantly:

What earthly name to interrogatories
Can taste the free breath of a sacred king?   (III.i.73–74)

---

[19] E.A.J. Honigmann has demonstrated that Shakespeare made use of Holinshed as well as *The Troublesome Reign*: *King John*, ed. Honigmann, New Arden (London: Methuen, 1954), pp. xii–xiii.

[20] In *King Johan* (ca. 1560), a morality play, Bale portrays "John as a martyr-king, forced against his will to submit to papal tyranny": Bale, *King Johan*, ed. Barry B. Adams (San Marino: The Huntington Library, 1969), p. 25. Bale includes lines that suggest priests had falsified the history of John's reign.

Tell the pope, he continues,

>   that no Italian priest
> Shall tithe or toll in our dominions.   (III.i.79–80)

Pandulph's answer recalls Pius V's Bull of 1570 directed against Queen Elizabeth:[21]

> Thou shalt stand curs'd and excommunicate:
> And bless'd shall he be that doth revolt
> From his allegiance to an heretic;
> And meritorious shall that hand be call'd,
> Canonized[22] and worshipp'd as a saint,
> That takes away by any secret course
> Thy hateful life.   (III.i.98–105)

Pius V's Bull had the practical consequence of encouraging English conspirators such as the duke of Norfolk and foreign ones such as Don Juan of Austria and the duke of Guise. The attempts on the queen's life would have reminded Shakespeare's audience that Pandulph's act was not an empty gesture.

Pandulph calls on the king of France, as "champion of our church," to reinforce the excommunication by making war on John. Philip's reluctance to renounce the newly sworn peace and his eloquent description of the human experience of war force Pandulph to a reasoned exposition of his demand.

Philip's prior oath to defend the church, he argues, renders the subsequent oath to keep peace with John invalid, now that the church has declared John to be an enemy. Pandulph speaks at length, developing his argument in sententious paradoxes. To some readers of the play, Pandulph's lines have seemed "inconsequent or ridiculously subtle."[23] Samuel Johnson disagreed, defending Pandulph's rhetoric as well as his logic. The

---

[21] *King John*, ed. J. Dover Wilson, p. 138.

[22] The pope offered canonization as a reward for the murder of Queen Elizabeth: *King John*, ed. Honigmann, pp. xlvi, 65 n. 103.

[23] *Johnson on Shakespeare*, in *Works*, ed. Sherbo, 7 (1968), 419.

logic is indeed impeccable. Of the rhetoric, one can at least observe that it is employed to persuade one king to resume war with another. Pandulph concludes his argument with a threat: Philip himself will be excommunicated if he fails to obey the legate of the pope. Unlike John, Philip is intimidated and agrees to do as he is told.

After John has led his troops back to England, Pandulph's willingness to shed blood appears again when he persuades the dauphin to pursue the king with an invading army. Yet, when the dauphin, supported by John's rebellious nobles as well as his French troops, seems to be near victory, Pandulph orders him to withdraw. "King John hath reconcil'd / Himself to Rome," he explains (v.ii.69–70). This time the dauphin protests the church's intrusion in matters of state: "Am I Rome's slave?" (v.ii.97).

John yields his crown to the church out of military expediency: his lines spoken just after Pandulph returns his crown to him, "as holding of the Pope," reveal that he wishes the cardinal to act as a peacemaker at a time when his English and French enemies threaten him.[24] Faulconbridge soon after, speaking as he says for the king, repudiates John's submission. He speaks to the dauphin in the presence of Pandulph:

> for at hand—
> Not trusting to this halting legate here,
> Whom he hath us'd rather for sport than need—
> Is warlike John.   (v.ii.173–76)

We conclude a reading of the play with the impression that Pandulph is indeed an "Italian priest" meddling in English affairs.[25]

Samuel Johnson, in his comments on King John's defiant

---

[24] Calderwood, "Commodity and Honour in *King John*," in *Shakespeare: The Histories*, ed. Waith, pp. 95–96.

[25] David Bevington writes that "anticlericalism is staple in Shakespeare's plays." He notes, however, that Shakespeare does not follow *The Troublesome Reign* to the extent of portraying an international Catholic league: Bevington, *Tudor Drama and Politics*, pp. 197, 201.

answer to Pandulph, calls attention to the topical allusions in the play:

> This must have been at the time when it was written, in our struggles with popery, a very captivating scene.
>
> So many passages remain in which Shakespeare evidently takes his advantage of the facts then recent, and of the passions then in motion, that I cannot but suspect that time has obscured much of his art, and that many allusions yet remain undiscovered, which perhaps may be gradually retrieved by succeeding commentators.[26]

In the two hundred years since Johnson wrote, the commentators have proved his prediction accurate.

In its topical allusions, *King John* is unambiguously Protestant. I have referred to the similarity of Pandulph's excommunication of King John and Pope Pius V's Bull of 1570. King Philip of France, "champion of our church," as Pandulph calls him, would have put men in mind of Philip of Spain.[27] In the 1590s reference to the threat of invasion of England was in its nature anti-Catholic. E.A.J. Honigmann refers to the "Protestant (Armada) bravado" in the play,[28] bravado well illustrated by the Bastard's lines at the end of the fifth act. When read with attention to the circumstances of the era, they appear as a declaration of England's invulnerability to invasion so long as Englishmen remain loyal to their sovereign.

But in the 1590s Englishmen knew that they must soon have a new sovereign, and in the absence of a direct heir to the queen or of a successor designated by Elizabeth herself or by Parliament, they knew that contention for the crown could lead to war. James VI of Scotland was next in line of succession, but even so there were complications: his foreign birth; Henry VIII's will (providing that the line of Henry's younger sister should be preferred over that of his older sister, from whom James was descended); James's mother's treasonous conspir-

---

[26] *Johnson on Shakespeare* in *Works*, ed. Sherbo, 7:417.

[27] See Richmond, *Shakespeare's Political Plays*, pp. 111. Geoffrey Bullough notes that there may be an indirect reference in II.i.56–75 to Essex's raid on Cádiz in 1596: *Narrative and Dramatic Sources of Shakespeare*, ed. Bullough, 4:3.

[28] *King John*, ed. Honigmann, p. lxxxiii, n. 1.

acy against Elizabeth. All this and more led to uncertainties that account for the attention given to Doleman's *A Conference about the Next Succession to the Crowne of Ingland.*

★

Marlowe's criticism of the Catholic church is at once more vehement than Shakespeare's and more comprehensive. In several plays—*The Jew of Malta, Dr. Faustus,* and *Edward II*—he includes passages ranging from ridicule of Catholic institutions to expressions of hatred of the church. In *The Massacre at Paris* he portrays Catholicism as an aggressive, international league led by the pope and the king of Spain. The St. Bartholomew's Day Massacre, dramatized in the early scenes of the play, provided a historical subject that in its nature emphasized the international aspect of Catholic aggression.

The Revolt of the Netherlands, and more immediately the duke of Alba's siege of Mons in the summer of 1572, set in motion the train of events that led to the Massacre. Four years earlier, in 1568, the prince of Orange had negotiated an agreement of mutual assistance with the two leaders of the Huguenots, Gaspard de Coligny, admiral of France, and the prince of Condé. The latter was killed in battle in 1569.[29] The marriage, August 18, 1572, of the nineteen-year-old king of Navarre to Marguerite of Valois, the sister of Charles IX, brought Coligny and other Huguenot leaders from all regions of France to Paris. To judge from a letter he wrote to his wife the day of the wedding, Coligny expected to lead an army into the Netherlands with the permission of the king on Monday, August 25, or within a few days thereafter.[30] However, on the morning of Friday, August 22, an assassin, apparently employed by the duke of Guise, wounded Coligny, though not dangerously. The king visited him the same afternoon and promised an investigation.

What happened in the interval between the king's conver-

[29] Geyl, *Revolt of the Netherlands,* p. 111.
[30] Nicola M. Sutherland, *The Massacre of St. Bartholomew and the European Conflict* (London: Macmillan, 1973), pp. 308–09.

sation with Coligny on Friday afternoon and the beginning of the slaughter late Saturday night is variously reported and cannot be determined in detail.[31] Although the opportunity presented to the Catholics by the presence in Paris of nearly all the Huguenot leaders had been noted—by Philip II, among others[32]—the Massacre seems not to have been planned far in advance, but rather to have been hastily decided on by the queen mother, who earlier had authorized the duke of Guise to kill his enemy, Coligny. The Massacre, on this assumption, was undertaken to prevent Coligny and his fellow Huguenots from demanding vengeance for the bungled attempt on Coligny's life. It would furthermore prevent the imminent departure of Coligny and his army into the Netherlands, where an attack on Alba's army could lead France to war with Spain. "War or peace with Spain," N. M. Sutherland writes, "was . . . the core and focus of the crisis. . . ."[33] Queen Catherine saw that France, weakened by the wars of religion, could not sustain a war with Spain.[34]

The Huguenots took the side of the prince of Orange; the Catholic extremists, led by the duke of Guise, took that of Philip II. When the assassin failed in the first attempt to kill Coligny, Guise and his followers were at hand to lead the general slaughter.[35] Beginning about midnight Saturday and continuing for several days, Guise and those who followed him or followed his example killed over three thousand persons in Paris and more in the provinces, including nearly all the Huguenot leaders except Navarre and Condé, both of whom were very young.

For a short time the Massacre improved the position of the Spaniards in the Netherlands by preventing the Huguenots from sending an army to support the rebels. But its long-term consequences are problematical. It strengthened the resolve of

---

[31] On the contemporary accounts of the Massacre, see ibid., pp. 312–37.

[32] Ibid., p. 295.

[33] Ibid., p. 334.

[34] Sir John E. Neale, *The Age of Catherine de Medici* (New York: Barnes & Noble, 1959), pp. 75–79.

[35] Ibid., p. 78.

Protestants in the Netherlands, in France, and elsewhere, including England. Marlowe provides in *The Massacre at Paris*, written eighteen or more years after the event, a literary reminder of the shocked response of Elizabethans to the atrocity.[36]

The Massacre at Paris has survived in a corrupt, memorial text, perhaps about half of its original length, a text sufficiently remote from Marlowe's manuscript to make critical judgment hazardous.[37] The lurid nature of some passages may be the consequence of interpolations into or alterations of Marlowe's play. But the rendering in rapidly paced episodes of seventeen years of French history is seemingly little affected by the defective text: Marlowe must be responsible for much of the vehement anti-Catholicism. We seem to have the bare bones of his play without the reflective dimension: without, that is, the passages in which characters talk about motives and the meaning of events.[38]

The play reflects literary sources Marlowe employed in writing it, pamphlets of Protestant controversialists that kept French and English readers informed of the course of events leading to the accession of Henry IV. A specific source has been identified for the early scenes that culminate in the Massacre: François Hotman's *A True and plaine report of the Furious outrages of Fraunce*.[39] No single source for the later scenes is known and one may not exist; Marlowe presumably drew from one or more of the large number of pamphlets on recent French history that were published in England, many of them

[36] On its impact in England, see A. G. Dickens, "The Elizabethans and St. Bartholomew," in *The Massacre of St. Bartholomew: Reappraisals and Documents*, ed. Alfred Soman (The Hague: Martinus Nijhoff, 1974), pp. 52–70.

[37] A surviving fragment of what may be presumed to be close to what he wrote suggests the magnitude of our loss. See Frank P. Wilson, *Marlowe and the Early Shakespeare* (Oxford: Clarendon Press, 1953), pp. 89–90.

[38] J. B. Steane, *Marlowe: A Critical Study* (Cambridge: Cambridge University Press, 1964), pp. 237–38.

[39] Paul H. Kocher, "François Hotman and Marlowe's *The Massacre at Paris*," *PMLA* 56 (1941): 349–68.

written in French and translated into English.[40] The details of the propagandists' accusations appear in the play, though Marlowe refuses to linger over Protestant grievances.

Marlowe's play, F. P. Wilson noted, has "a kind of plot which Shakespeare did not touch."[41] Nor did Lope "touch" that "kind of plot," even though he wrote plays about recent events. Marlowe ignores principles of decorum that Lope carefully observes. Three of Marlowe's characters are kings of France: Charles IX, Henry III, and Henry IV, the last the reigning king at the time the play was first performed.[42] Henry IV alone has qualities appropriate to his rank. (He was still a Protestant when Marlowe wrote, and an ally of Queen Elizabeth.) Charles is irresolute, easily manipulated by his mother and the duke of Guise. Persuaded by his mother, he reluctantly approves plans for the Massacre; but he is appalled by the slaughter and becomes remorseful before he is poisoned and dies. Henry III, who appears as the duke of Anjou in the early scenes, disguises himself and takes a sadistic part in the murders. The larger part of the play portrays the fifteen years of his reign, troubled years made more difficult by the failure of his leadership. Only in Henry IV does France gain a sovereign strong enough to restore order.

Although French history provides his subject, Marlowe

---

[40] Paul H. Kocher, "Contemporary Pamphlet Backgrounds for Marlowe's *The Massacre at Paris*," *Modern Language Quarterly* 8 (1947): 151–73, 309–18. See also A. G. Dickens, "The Elizabethans and St. Bartholomew," in *Massacre of St. Bartholomew*, ed. Soman, pp. 52–70.

[41] Wilson, *Marlowe and the Early Shakespeare*, p. 90.

[42] *The Massacre at Paris* was remembered in France some ten years after its first performance. In July 1602, when Ralph Winwood, English ambassador to France, protested to the French Council of State the planned performance of a play about Queen Elizabeth, the chancellor issued an order restraining the company of actors. However, according to Winwood, some persons present recalled "that the *Massacre* of St. *Bartholomews* hath ben publickly acted, and this King represented upon the Stage." "*Mr.* Winwood *to Mr. Secretary* Cecyll, *Paris, 7th July* 1602. O.S.," in *Memorials of Affairs of State in the Reigns of Q. Elizabeth and K. James I. Collected (Chiefly) from the Original Papers of . . . Sir Ralph Winwood*, ed. Edmund Sawyer, 1 (London: W. B. for T. Ward, 1725), 425.

keeps Spain and the pope in view as the source of the affliction that has overcome France.

> *Spaine* is the counsell chamber of the pope,
> *Spaine* is the place where he makes peace and warre,
> (Scene xiv; Ed. Bowers, 1:387)[43]

Navarre exclaims early in Henry III's reign. Navarre, as well as the duke of Guise himself, speaks repeatedly of Spain as Guise's patron and the paymaster of his private army. The duke will seize the crown of France, he says in soliloquy, or destroy the nation in seditious wars:

> For this, from *Spaine* the stately Catholickes
> Sends Indian golde to coyne me French ecues:
> For this have I a largesse from the Pope,
> A pension and a dispensation too.   (Scene ii; Ed. Bowers, 1:366)

He first aligns himself with Henry III against Navarre—Catholics against a Protestant; but finding subordination to the king intolerable, he makes war on him. Seemingly close to victory, in possession of Paris and supported by the army of the league, he oversteps himself. He enters a trap the king has prepared for him at Blois, where he is fatally stabbed. Calling on the pope for vengeance, he attributes his death to his alliance with Philip II and the prince of Parma.

The names of Philip and of Parma, spoken by Guise as he lies dying, call up a recollection of the Spanish Armada, defeated in July 1588, five months before he was killed. Upon seeing his dead body, Henry III enumerates his crimes, mentioning the Armada among them:

> Did he not cause the King of *Spaines* huge fleete,
> To threaten *England* and to menace me?
> (Scene xix; Ed. Bowers, 1:398)

Matters were not so simple as the king implies, but Guise had indeed played an important role in the preliminaries to the

---

[43] Here as elsewhere I refer to *The Complete Works of Christopher Marlowe,* ed. Fredson Bowers, 1 (Cambridge: Cambridge University Press, 1973).

launching of the Armada. Parma by his victories had removed the threat of interference in the Netherlands; the league led by Guise had neutralized France.[44]

The duke of Guise, little less ambitious than Tamburlaine and as free of moral restraint as the Jew of Malta, resembles Barabas and Tamberlaine, though with the important difference that Navarre (Henry IV), not he, dominates the political plot: the movement from near anarchy apparent in the Massacre scenes to the final promise (and at the time of the play's first performance, probably in 1592 or 1593, it could be only a promise) of a return to stability implied in the accession of a strong and capable king.[45] The play ends, not with the assassination of Guise, but with that of Henry III, who as he lies dying addresses a warning to the English.

Navarre as Henry IV speaks the final, vindictive lines, predicting not peace but vigorous war against international Catholicism. If his role throughout the play be examined, he can be seen to share qualities with Guise: ambition, opportunism, and vengefulness.[46] Yet Henry IV was a Protestant hero in England at the time Marlowe wrote, and the dramatic character commands the sympathy, even the admiration, of spectators and readers.

★

Chapman, like Marlowe, turned to recent French history. In two plays with a single title, *The Conspiracy and Tragedy of Charles, Duke of Byron*, he writes about events that occurred in France during the closing years of Elizabeth's life, after her military assistance to Henry IV had ceased to be necessary. By 1595, when the queen withdrew most of the English troops from France, Henry had largely suppressed the French Catholic League. In that year he formally declared war on the

[44] See De Lamar Jensen, "Franco-Spanish Diplomacy and the Armada," in Charles H. Carter, ed., *From the Renaissance to the Counter-Reformation* (New York: Random House, 1965), pp. 213–29.

[45] See Steane, *Marlowe*, pp. 243–45.

[46] See Judith Weil, *Christopher Marlowe: Merlin's Prophet* (Cambridge: Cambridge University Press, 1977), pp. 89–92.

league's patron, Philip II. But France and Spain had actually
been at war a long time, and by 1598 Henry and Philip II found
it to their mutual advantage to accept a negotiated peace, embodied in the Treaty of Vervins, ratified in May not long before Philip II died in September 1598.

Chapman places an early scene of the *Conspiracy* in Brussels
at the time of the ratification of the Treaty of Vervins, some
nine years after Henry's accession. The historical King Henry
had, indeed, as Marlowe's character predicts in the final lines
of the play, fought Spanish armies and French armies, the latter subsidized and reenforced by the king of Spain. Lope's *Pobreza no es vileza* portrays a campaign of 1595 in which the
Army of Flanders fought Henry's troops on France's northern
border.

Unlike Marlowe, Chapman largely ignores religious issues.
His Henry IV faces conspiracies, but ones that have their
origins in the interplay of personal ambitions and dynastic ri-
valries, not in the hostility of Catholics and Protestants. The
historical king had become a Catholic and made his peace with
the pope years before the time span represented in the Byron
plays. Chapman does not refer to a religious dimension in
either the domestic or foreign opposition King Henry encounters.[47]

The peace that followed the Treaty of Vervins was less than
comprehensive. Before consenting to it, Henry promised an
embassy of the States-General financial support to be provided
over a four-year period as well as support by troops, engineers,
and commanders, should they be required.[48] France needed
peace, but Henry, like Elizabeth, could not allow Spain to con-

---

[47] Referring to Chapman's avoidance of the "common anti-Spanish, anti-
Papal animus of his contemporaries," Thomas Marc Parrott wrote in 1910 that
"the apology for the Duke of Guise and the eulogy of Philip II which he puts
into the mouths of Clermont [in *The Revenge of Bussy D'Ambois*] and Byron
[in *The . . . Tragedy of . . . Byron*] respectively show, at the very least, that he
possessed the faculty, rare enough at all times, naturally and notably rare in his
age, of seeing both sides of a great world-struggle" (Parrott, ed., Chapman,
Tragedies, p. 687).

[48] Jan den Tex, *Oldenbarnevelt*, 1:271. Den Tex writes that the Treaty of Vervins "led to a sort of cold war between France and Spain": ibid., 1:203.

quer all the Netherlands. Philip III and his *privado* ("favorite"), the duke of Lerma, not wishing a direct confrontation with the French king, resorted to subversion. For the dozen years before Ravaillac's assassination of Henry IV altered the balance of power, life in France was uneasy—these were years made dangerous by the plots and counterplots of men and women playing for high stakes.

In *The Conspiracy and Tragedy of . . . Byron* (written 1607–1608)[49] Chapman reveals an understanding of the altered nature of international politics after 1598. For almost forty years France had been too deeply troubled by internal dissensions to take an important role in European affairs. The neutralization of France by her civil wars had prevented a French challenge to Philip II's hegemony in Italy. But Philip's death and the emergence of Henry IV as the able leader of a unified country meant that the princes of Italy could look to either France or Spain for patronage. The duke of Savoy, whom Chapman portrays in *The Conspiracy . . . of . . . Byron*, was one of the first to attempt to exploit the altered relationships.

The strategic position of Savoy in the Alpine barrier between France and Italy gave it an importance disproportionate to its size and resources. To Spain, it provided a link in the "Spanish road," the military corridor along which men, supplies, equipment, and treasure moved from Milan to the Netherlands;[50] to France, Savoy could provide access to Italy, as it did in the time of Francis I and Charles V. The two countries had sought marital alliances with Savoy: Charles Emmanuel I, the duke in 1600, was the grandson of Francis I and the son-in-law of Philip II.

★

Although Chapman writes about French history, following his source within the limits of fidelity customary in drama, he directs the plays to English concerns. The French King Henry

⁴⁹ Albert H. Tricomi, "The Dates of the Plays of George Chapman," *ELR* 12 (1982): 265.

⁵⁰ See Geoffrey Parker, *Army of Flanders*, pp. 66–71.

IV of the plays confronts the problem familiar to Queen Elizabeth of preparing to defend a kingdom from foreign invasion supported by rebellion.[51] Chapman could give his subject a more immediate relevance to English affairs because of the parallel between the career of his protagonist, Charles of Gontaut, duke of Byron, and that of Robert Devereux, second earl of Essex, both of them executed for treason, the latter in February 1601, the former in July 1602. The parallel was striking if not exact: Byron had conspired with the count of Fuentes, the Spanish governor of Milan, in anticipation of a Spanish invasion of France; Essex had been suspected of favoring a Spanish successor to Queen Elizabeth. I have referred to the epistle addressed to him prefixed to *A Conference about the Next Succession to the Crown of England*. It caused Essex embarrassment, but no more than that.

A dedication addressed to him in 1599 before he sailed to Ireland to take up his command there caused him more trouble. The author, Sir John Hayward, had a sensitive subject, *The First Part of the Life and Reign of King Henry IV*. In his epistle Hayward described Essex's present eminence and predicted even greater eminence for him. The book and the dedication were brought forward as evidence of Essex's intentions when he was arrested upon his unauthorized return from Ireland in September 1599. He had violated the queen's orders in granting a truce to the leader of the Irish rebellion, the earl of Tyrone—an offense that could be construed as aid to Spain, for Tyrone was in league with Philip III. After a trial and house arrest, Essex was released by the queen in August 1600, but he failed to regain her confidence. In frustration—and in financial straits—he led his short-lived conspiracy and rebellion in London early in February 1601 and was executed on February 25.[52]

In the first decade of the century, the association of Byron with Essex was inevitable.[53] When the historical Henry IV told

[51] See Jean Jacquot, *George Chapman (1559–1634): sa vie, sa poésie, son théatre, sa pensée* (Paris: Société d'Edition *Les Belles Lettres*, 1951), p. 145.

[52] Campbell, *Shakespeare's "Histories,"* pp. 187–88.

[53] Millar MacLure calls attention to a French work published in 1607 about them: *Histoire de la vie et mort du Comte d'Essex avec un discours grave et eloquent*

the English ambassador about Byron's conspiracy the day after Byron was arrested, the ambassador replied

> that as her Majestie could not but condole with him, *for the late feeling which she hath had of the like Misfortune*, that his owne Creature, whom he had charged with so many Honors, should practize against the Repose of his Realme, so could she not but rejoyce . . . with him, that . . . so dangerous a Complott hath been discovered.[54]

In the *Tragedy*, Byron twice associates himself with Essex (IV.i. 133–35; v.iii. 139–42). Most members of Chapman's first audience had some knowledge of Byron, who had been in England in September 1601 on a diplomatic mission. They could perceive the resemblances between Byron and Essex.

The historical Byron, like Essex, had something of the Marlovian overreacher in him. Both were soldiers who had won lavish rewards as well as personal favor from their sovereigns. In peacetime they could find neither channels for their energy nor scope for their ambition.[55] They had reached the highest eminence short of sovereignty. Byron was a duke; Essex was an earl in an England that had no dukes. What, then, did they want?

We can reply, at least for the Byron of Chapman's play. He wanted sovereignty—and the offer of that was the bait that lured him to betray his master.[56] La Fin,[57] whose betrayal of Byron parallels the latter's betrayal of King Henry, describes the reward offered to him:

---

de la Royne d'Angleterre, au Duc de Biron sur ce sujet (MacLure, *George Chapman: A Critical Study* [Toronto: University of Toronto Press, 1966], p. 133).

[54] "Winwood to Cecyll, Paris, 17th June 1602. o.s.," in *Memorials of Affairs of State*, ed. Sawyer, 1:417.

[55] On the discontent of Essex and other English soldiers of high rank, see Jorgensen, *Shakespeare's Military World*, pp. 221–22; *Chapman's The Conspiracy and Tragedy of Charles, Duke of Byron*, ed. George Ray, 2 vols., 1 (New York: Garland, 1979), 103–06. Quotations from the plays are based on this edition.

[56] Janin speaks of his ambition: "Yea, at so unbeliev'd a pitch he aim'd That he hath said his heart would still complain Till he aspir'd the style of Sovereign" (*Tragedy*, i.i.26–28).

[57] Jacques of La Fin, Sieur of Beauvais-la-Nocle.

> It is for these parts [Byron's abilities] that the Spanish King
> Hath sworn to win them to his side
> At any price or peril, that great Savoy
> Offers his princely daughter and a dowry
> Amounting to five hundred thousand crowns
> With full transport of all the sovereign rights
> Belonging to the state of Burgundy.   (*Tragedy*, 1.ii.60–66)

Except for the money, the details La Fin mentions correspond to those Edward Grimeston, Chapman's source, describes as comprising the object of Byron's ambition: "In his Heart he aspired to be Duke of *Burgundy*, Son in Lawe to the Duke of *Savoy*, and Nephew to the King of *Spaine*."[58]

Chapman's Byron aspires to a lesser eminence than Marlowe's duke of Guise, who sought to become, with Philip II's support, king of France.[59] Byron aims at the sovereignty of a dukedom, to be won with the support of the duke of Savoy and the count of Fuentes. He aimed lower than Guise, but to him the objective represented a greater and more unrealistic ambition. He was nevertheless dangerous. His conspiracy was the more dangerous because peace in France was precarious, recently established after forty years of intermittent civil war. Henry IV was a more able man than the three Valois kings who, with their mother, Queen Catherine, had ruled France before him. Yet he "enjoy'd but an unequal nook" (*Tragedy*, 1.i.101) of France when, with Queen Elizabeth's aid, he under-

---

[58] Grimeston, *A General Inventorie of the History of France* (London: George Eld, 1607), p. 992. In a separate passage, Grimeston suggests that the duke of Savoy made an empty promise to entrap Byron (p. 961): "The Duke of *Savoy* gave him more hope, then assurance of [marriage to his daughter]."

George Ray includes a useful appendix made up of relevant quotations from Grimeston's *General Inventorie* in each of his two volumes, devoted respectively to the *Conspiracy* and the *Tragedy*. However, my own references to and quotations from Grimeston are independent of Ray's.

[59] A passage in the *Tragedy* (III.i.53–56) has at times been misinterpreted as meaning that Byron wished to be king of France. Peter Ure, for example, writes: "Byron's conspiracy is, unequivocally, a league with foreign princes to overthrow Henry and deliver the crown of France into Byron's own hands (*Tragedy*, III, i, 53–56). . . ." Ure, "The Main Outline of Chapman's Byron," *Studies in Philology* 47 (1950): 583.

took the campaigns that brought the Catholic League to submission and Philip II to the Treaty of Vervins. In his conversation with Queen Elizabeth—reported, not dramatized—the Byron of the play attributes King Henry's inability to come to England to the political unrest in France,

> . . . the green roots of war
> Not yet so close cut up but he may dash
> Against their relics to his utter ruin,
> Without more near eyes fix'd upon his feet
> Than those that look out of his country's soil.
>
> (*Conspiracy*, IV.i.63–67)

The Byron plays are histories,[60] and attention to them with reference to Chapman's source—Grimeston's *General Inventorie of the History of France*—and other early records, as well as to modern scholarship, can clarify obscure passages. Chapman is frequently elliptical in exposition, omitting needed transitions; but he does not include passages that cannot be explained. Most of his references to affairs of state are historically accurate; they can be documented.

The two plays present two distinct phases in Byron's conspiring: the first, with the duke of Savoy, who uses his relationship with Byron as a cover for an attempt to exchange his alliance with Philip III for an alliance with Henry IV; the second, with the Spanish governor of northern Italy, the count of Fuentes (the general praised by Lope in *Pobreza no es vileza*).

---

[60] Chapman left open the question whether *The Conspiracy and Tragedy of . . . Byron* should be regarded as a single play in two parts or as separate plays. He wrote a single title, a single dedication, and a single prologue. Yet he took care to provide the *Conspiracy* with a conclusion and the *Tragedy* with introductory exposition: they can be performed separately. In short, we are free to consider them as one double play, or as companion pieces: independent plays with similarities of theme and plot.

Because the differences between the *Conspiracy* and the *Tragedy* seem to me more impressive than the resemblances, I choose to regard them as separate plays. The plays differ from one another in expository manner: the *Conspiracy*, loosely plotted, episodic, lacking a clear and sustained focus, at times not intelligible except in retrospect, when additional information is conveyed in subsequent passages; the *Tragedy*, without obscurity, structured for clarity of focus on the tragic agony of the protagonist.

The time limits of the *Conspiracy* are fixed by the arrival in the
opening scene of the duke of Savoy at the French court (on December 27, 1599) and his departure (March 1, 1600)[61] at the
end of the play. However, several events represented, reported, or mentioned fall outside those limits. About twenty-
two months elapse between the close of the *Conspiracy* and the
opening of the *Tragedy*. Chapman focuses the later play on
events of the five to six months prior to Byron's death on July
29, 1602.[62] The play opens with the king, reluctantly convinced of Byron's guilt, planning to lure him to court; it closes
with Byron's execution.

★

Passages appearing in the opening and closing scenes of the
Conspiracy illustrate the obscurity that results from Chapman's
delayed exposition. The duke of Savoy accompanied by several of his courtiers arrives at the court of King Henry. He
speaks of his purpose in coming to France. "All you can say
against my coming here," he tells his followers,

> Is that which I confess may for the time
> Breed strange affections in my brother Spain,
> But when I shall have time to make my cannons
> The long-tongu'd heralds of my hidden drifts,
> Our reconcilement will be made with triumphs.   (1.i.18–23)

The reason for his alienation from his brother-in-law, Philip
III, becomes apparent in remarks that follow: his resentment
that his wife's dowry was inconsiderable in comparison with
that given with her sister, "the Infanta, wedded by the Archduke," who has "the French County and Low Provinces" (ll.
40–41)—that is, Franche-Comté and the Spanish Netherlands.[63] The duke has come to entreat Henry to relinquish his

---

[61] Winwood, *Memorials*, 1:136, 153.

[62] Ibid., 1:417. In mid-June of 1602, King Henry told the English ambassador at his court, Ralph Winwood, that for the previous four months he had
had "perfect Knowledge of . . . [Byron's] Confederacy."

[63] In an effort to achieve a settlement in the Netherlands before he died,
Philip II ceded sovereignty of the region to his daughter Isabel and arranged a

claim to a territory in the Alps of strategic importance to both France and Spain, the Marquisate of Saluces,[64] long a possession of France but since 1588 occupied by Savoy. One of the duke's followers urges caution in the negotiations with King Henry, lest the duke

> endanger Spain's whole loss
> For hope of some poor fragment here in France.   (ll. 48–49)

The Duke replies that he has a hidden objective in France,

> And for my loss of Spain, it is agreed
> That I should slight it.   (ll. 50–51)

But the "hidden objective" he divulges to his courtiers, to induce Byron to betray Henry IV, would not alienate Spain. Clarification does not come until the final scene of the play, when King Henry speaks as the duke of Savoy prepares to depart:

> where you have propos'd
> (In your advices) my design for Milan,
> I will have no war with the King of Spain
> Unless his hopes prove weary of our peace.   (v.ii.198–201)

Here, Chapman introduces a new subject—a proposal by the duke of Savoy to ally himself to France in opposition to the Habsburgs—of which there is no anticipation apart from the references in the opening scene to the duke's hostility to Spain. The duke offers assistance to King Henry for an attack on Milan, expecting in return to be permitted to keep Saluces.[65]

---

marriage for her to her Austrian cousin, the archduke Albert, who had followed Fuentes as governor.

[64] See Geoffrey Parker, *Army of Flanders*, pp. 68–69; and Ciriaco Pérez Bustamente, *Felipe III: Historia*, 24 (1979), 274.

[65] The duke wanted to retain Saluces, Grimeston writes, because of its importance in the defense of Savoy against the Swiss. In his effort to induce Henry to allow him to have it, he proposed that France attack the German empire as well as Milan, "giving him very plausible meanes, if they had beene as easie in the execution as in the discourse: shewing that for all the fruite of the conquest, he desired nothing but to hold . . . *Salusse*." Chapman ignores Grimeston's reference to Germany. (Grimeston, *General Inventorie*, pp. 900–

(Spanish leaders learned from informants at the French
court much of what passed between the duke and the king.
Knowing that the duke was untrustworthy, they sent the
count of Fuentes to keep a watchful eye on what passed in
northern Italy. The letter of instructions given to Fuentes cor-
roborates Grimeston's account of the duke's negotiations with
King Henry.)[66]

Even if not fully understood by a spectator or reader, the
passages on the negotiations serve a dramaturgical purpose.
They convey the pomposity and deviousness of the duke of
Savoy, qualities of the historical figure as well as of the dramatic character—personal characteristics accentuated in the
last scene by the contrast established between the duke and
King Henry. Unlike the king, Byron fails to perceive the duke
of Savoy as a flawed leader.

In the play, as in its source, the duke uses a stratagem to alienate the king and Byron: he praises the latter extravagantly
to the king, giving Byron credit for battles the king has won.
Henry listens patiently and replies with moderation: "We must
not give to one to take away from many" (ii.ii.214). His rejoin-
der provides Chapman with an occasion to recall England's
part in Henry's wars against the Catholic League. The king
praises "The general, My Lor' Norris, sent from England,"
and

> Colonel Williams,
> A worthy captain, and more like the Duke [Byron]
> Because he was less temperate than the general.   (ii.ii.216, 224–26)

Praise for Sir John Norris and Sir Roger Williams, but none
for the earl of Essex. Talking to Byron later, Savoy implies

---

01. Grimeston here translates the French of Pierre Matthieu, *Histoire de France
. . . durant sept annees de paix*, 1 [Paris: Jacques Bessin (1606)], 510–11.)

[66] Fuentes' letter of instructions, signed by King Philip, May 19, 1600, addressed the problems he would confront with respect to Savoy. He was told to
give especial attention to the duke's negotiations with King Henry about Saluces (Archivo General de Simancas: Secretaria de Estado. Leg. 1.288: Instruc-
ciones al Conde de Fuentes, Gobernador y Capitán General del Estado de
Milán.—El Rey. Madrid, May 19, 1600. Cited by Julio Fuentes, *El Conde de
Fuentes y su tiempo: estudios de historia militar, siglos XVI á XVII*, 1 [Madrid: Imprenta del Patronato de Huérfanos de Administración Militar, 1908], 167–80).

that the king has slighted his accomplishments. At this Byron, in contrast with the king, replies in a torrent of rebuttal. He thanks the duke of Savoy for "the many secret bounties" he has received and assures him "that all my most deserts are at your service" (III.ii.33, 36). We learn no details. Savoy advises Byron to conceal his dissatisfaction; before they can say more, they are interrupted.

Although Byron cannot be circumspect, the king continues to show him favor:

> And now for England you shall go, my Lord,
> Our Lord Ambassador to that matchless Queen.   (III.ii.274–75)

Henry praises Elizabeth, making no reference to the strained relations with England that followed his treaty of peace with Spain. (This historical Henry's praise of Elizabeth in a letter to the duke of Sully written not long after her death reveals his esteem for her.)

The reported account of Byron's embassy to England that comprises the fourth act and most of the events that are represented in the fifth are introduced anachronistically: Byron went to England in September 1601; episodes of the fifth act occurred historically after France's short war with Savoy in the latter part of 1600. The crucial episode in which Byron momentarily wishes to kill the king—when Henry refuses his request to be allowed to name the commander of the citadel of Bourg—could have taken place only after the war, in the course of which troops led by Byron himself captured Bourg. During the peace negotiations with Savoy in January 1601, Byron made a partial confession to the king, who was already suspicious of him, and received a pardon. Although Byron acknowledges guilt in the final act of the *Conspiracy*, his guilt—so far as we learn—derives from an intention to commit treasonable acts rather than from actually committing them.

★

In the *Conspiracy*, anachronism abounds; in the *Tragedy*, in important events, it does not exist. The difference may be associated with the more compact, less digressive structure of the

latter play. With few sidelong glances, Chapman directs attention to the treason of Byron, Auvergne, and their confeder-
ates, to its potential consequences for France, and, with in-
creasing intensity as the play moves to its catastrophe, to the
inward drama of Byron's mind.

In the opening scene King Henry and his councillors conclude that Byron has relapsed into conspiracy. A courtier refers
to the danger he presents:

> And from what ground, my Lord, rise all the levies
> Now made in Italy? From whence should spring
> The warlike humor of the Count Fuentes,
> The restless stirrings of the Duke of Savoy,
> . . . .
> But from some hope of inward aid from hence?   (1.i.29–32, 38)

King Henry agrees: Spain's affairs are not in a condition to permit an attack on France "without treason bred in our own
breasts." Confronted by the danger of renewed war, the king
makes plans for the arrest and trial of Byron, procuring in-
criminating documents from La Fin.[67] Neither the king nor
any other character mentions Auvergne, who is later arrested
as a co-conspirator.

Henry's instructions about the use to be made of the documents in Byron's trial may be relevant to a scene that Chapman was forced to cancel after the French ambassador to England complained about the play to the lord treasurer, the earl
of Salisbury (Robert Cecil). Henry speaks to the lord chancellor:

>   of many pieces,
> More than is here, of his conspiracies
> . . . .
> You only shall reserve these seven and twenty,
> Which are not those that most conclude against him
> But mention only him, since I am loath
> To have the rest of the conspirators known.   (1.iii.69–70, 72–75)

---

[67] On the historical role of La Fin in betraying the conspiracy, see Berthold
Zeller, "La Conspiration du Maréchal de Biron," in the [French] Académie des
sciences morales et politiques, *Compte-Rendu* 111 (1879), 141–45.

The king to this point has not mentioned Auvergne, though he may be presumed to know of Auvergne's guilt.[68] Yet later the king orders Auvergne as well as Byron arrested.

The cancelled scene apparently came at the beginning of Act II, just after the scene in which Henry determines that some of the evidence should be withheld.[69] Our information about the nature of it is limited to what the French ambassador reported to his government on April 8, 1608:

> About mid-Lent [March 6] the actors who, at my instigation, had been forbidden to perform the play about the late Marshall Biron, noting that the Court was not in London, performed it. Not only that: they included in the play the Queen and Madame de Verneuil, the former speaking harshly to the latter and giving her a slap on the face. When I was informed of this several days ago, I went at once to see the Earl of Salisbury and complained to him that the company had not only violated the prohibition placed on them, but had also added to the play material which was more important and which had nothing to do with Marshall Biron. All of it was false. He [Lord Salisbury] became very angry and sent at once to have the actors arrested.[70]

Madame de Verneuil—or Henriette d'Entragues, marquise de Verneuil—King Henry's mistress, was the half-sister of the count of Auvergne. The count was the illegitimate son of King

[68] According to Sully, King Henry decided at the same time to arrest Byron and Auvergne but not others such as the duke of Bouillon who were under suspicion but of whose guilt he did not have documentary proof. See Maximilien de Béthune, Duc de Sully, *Mémoires de sage et royales oeconomies d'estat*, ed. Joseph F. Michaud, I (Paris: Imprimerie de Firmin Didot Frères, 1837), 395.

[69] The absence of an act division in the first quarto suggests that some tampering with the text occurred at this point. See Chapman, *Tragedies*, ed. Parrott, p. 612, n.I.iii.102; *Chapman's Byron*, ed. Ray, 2:382–86.

[70] Translated from John B. Gabel, "The Original Version of Chapman's *Tragedy of Byron*," *JEGP* 63 (1964): 434.

Virginia C. Gildersleeve suggests "that it was the scandal attendant upon these dramas [The *Conspiracy* and the *Tragedy*] which caused the edict against 'the representing of any modern Christian kings' ": *Government Regulation of Elizabethan Drama*, pp. 105–07.

Charles IX, and apart from his own children, he was the last of the royal House of Valois.

Before King Henry married Marie de Medici in 1600, he had given Henriette d'Entragues a written promise of marriage if she should bear him a son within a specified period of time.[71] She, her father, and her brother Auvergne believed that this promise made the king's marriage to Marie unlawful. All three of them were arrested late in 1604, more than two years after Byron's execution (but before Chapman wrote the plays), on charges of treasonable conspiracy with Spain. In the summer of that year, the king had forced the Entragues to return the promise of marriage to him by threatening to execute Henriette's father if they failed to do so.[72]

With these facts in mind, let us return to the French ambassador's letter of protest. He describes the offensive scene as one dealing with subjects more important than those portrayed in the rest of the play. The interpolated material, he writes, had nothing to do with Byron and it was a fabrication, without a basis in truth. The surviving play, in which the scene is omitted, does not include an explanation of why Auvergne comes to be arrested despite the king's earlier decision to the contrary. It would seem to follow from the ambassador's account of the cancelled scene and from the absence of a needed transition in this carefully constructed play that the missing scene included reference to Henriette d'Entrague's claims and to her half-brother's support of them.[73]

[71] Jean-Pierre Babelon, *Henri IV* (Paris: Librairie Arthème Fayard, 1982), p. 848.

[72] Pierre de l'Estoile, *Journal pour le règne de Henri IV*, ed. André Martin, 2 ([Paris]: Librairie Gallimard, 1958), 152.

[73] I will venture a more specific conjecture: that in the missing scene Madame de Verneuil claimed to be the king's legitimate wife, that the queen roundly contradicted her, and that one or the other of them referred to Auvergne as conspiring with Spain in an effort to have his sister's claims recognized. A scene of this kind would conform to the details mentioned by the ambassador and it could explain Auvergne's arrest. Furthermore, it would not represent a turning away from the central preoccupations of the play. Chap-

King Henry closes all that remains of Act II (a court masque) with an ironic remark:

> Come, let us in and thank them and prepare
> To entertain our trusty friend Byron.   (II.i.135–36)

Act III opens with Byron, not yet aware of the danger threatening him, talking exuberantly to Auvergne. He refers to the glorious prospect in store for him:

> And whatsoever good shall come of me,
> Pursu'd by all the Catholic Princes' aids
> With whom I join, and whose whole states propos'd
> To win my valor, promise me a throne,
> All shall be, equal with myself, thine own.   (III.i.53–57)

Byron's fantasy is soon punctured by the successive arrival of two noblemen who bring him the king's summons to court. He refuses to go, even when the second tells him he cannot escape. He reverses himself only when he receives false reassurances from La Fin that the king suspects nothing.[74]

Chapman remains faithful to his source in the latter part of the play, though increasingly, as Byron comes to understand that he cannot escape death, dramatic poetry that is all Chapman's own becomes the focus of attention. However, Chapman takes a lead from Grimeston for a striking passage of dialogue appearing midway in the scene that closes with the arrest of Byron and Auvergne. Byron, who moments before has learned from Auvergne that they are "undone," plays at cards with the queen, Epernon, and Montigny. Grimeston writes that Byron dined at Montigny's lodging, where "he fel to comend the deceased King of *Spaine*, his Piety, Justice and

---

man is unlikely to have written a scene devoted to a scolding match, as the ambassador's account of it might superficially suggest.

[74] In historical fact, La Fin's misrepresentation was only one of several reasons for Byron's decision to obey the king. Among others, Sully (then the marquis of Rosny) had taken military precautions that would have made it impossible for Byron to defend himself in Burgundy (Sully, *Mémoires*, 1:396–97).

Liberality."[75] Chapman's Byron turns to the subject by way of a reference to a playing card, the King of Hearts:

> Whose name yields well the memory of that king,
> Who was indeed the worthy king of hearts,
> And had both of his subjects' hearts and strangers'
> Much more than all the kings of Christendom.   (IV.ii.118–21)

When the chancellor objects that King Philip won his followers with gold, Byron counters:

> He won them chiefly
> With his so general piety and justice.   (ll. 122–23)

To the bare statement he adds fourteen lines of plausible, well-argued supporting details, comparing Philip's role in widening the boundaries of civilization and curbing savage cruelties to that of Alexander the Great, with the difference that Philip (ll. 136–37)

> Expell'd profane idolatry, and from earth
> Rais'd temples to the Highest.

Again the chancellor questions Philip's motives, and again Byron replies with cogent, detailed argument.

Montigny closes the exchange, in lines taken with few changes from the *General Inventorie*.[76] "The greatest commendation we can give" to King Philip, he says—and his lines imply an association of the Spanish and French kings, on the one hand, and, on the other, Don Carlos and Byron—is that he had his eldest son justly put to death "Because he sought to trouble his estates" (ll. 158–62).

Byron's and Montigny's remarks are dramatically apt: the latter's provide a warning of the arrest and death so soon to come; the former's express defiance as Byron feels the king's power closing on him. At the time he praises Philip II, Byron is a discredited character, from whom we are accustomed to

[75] Grimeston, *General Inventorie*, p. 968.
[76] Ibid.

hear irresponsible pronouncements. Yet he puts aside his customary hyperbole in favor of reasoned argument;[77] his defects of character notwithstanding, some of his lines have the ring of truth.

The indictment of Byron in the trial scene (v.ii), based on Grimeston,[78] provides a recapitulation of much that is represented or referred to in the *Conspiracy* and *Tragedy*. Byron denies all but one of the charges made against him with systematic and detailed argument, mistakenly believing that he has convinced the court. He pleads guilty to the final charge, that he conspired with Savoy and Fuentes "Touching the ruin of King and realm" (v.ii.66), urging in mitigation of the crime his desperation on seeing another person given command of the citadel at Bourg, which he had captured.

The historical detail serves as scaffolding for Chapman's poetry in this final act, in which the verdict of the court compels Byron to confront death. Dramaturgical reasons lead Chapman to focus on Byron's progressive abandonment of self-delusion as he comes to acknowledge the imminence of death. Political reasons led King Henry to narrow the focus of public attention to the one man.[79] He did not wish to reveal the extent of the conspiracy, which threatened him with renewed civil war supported—at least in the world of the play—by a Spanish

[77] A passage with similar voltage, defending Henry, third duke of Guise, and the St. Bartholomew's Day Massacre, appears in *The Revenge of Bussy D'Ambois* (11.i.204–34). In this instance, the defense is spoken by Clermont, the protagonist, in many respects an admirable character. Yet his defense of what seems indefensible to the Protestant mind may be regarded as an aspect of Chapman's characterization of him as intellectually inflexible: see Julius W. Lever, *The Tragedy of State* (London: Methuen, 1971), pp. 51–52.

Alvin Kernan refers to Chapman as the "most openly philosophical and political of the playwrights of his age." Kernan et al., *The Revels History of Drama in English . . . 1576–1613*, 3 (London: Methuen, 1975), 387.

[78] Grimeston, *General Inventorie*, p. 975.

[79] Sully (*Mémoires*, 1:400) comments on the king's decision to punish Byron alone: "The King, after the death of Marshall Biron decided—in consultation with you [Sully]—to suppress the remainder of the evidence and to pardon all those who might have or had in fact participated [in the conspiracy] in any way whatever."

invasion. Early in the fifth act, Chapman's King Henry refers to a Spanish army, levied by the count of Fuentes, that has crossed the Alps (v.i.14–23).[80] Thereafter Chapman ignores the subject, as he turns to Byron's trial and execution. (During the month in which Byron was executed, Fuentes, on orders from Madrid, dispersed the army he had assembled.)[81]

★

Chapman's Henry IV reveals many of the qualities attributed to Queen Elizabeth in the earlier play (*Conspiracy*, III.ii.277–84). The dramatic character, like the historical King Henry, is generous in rewarding Byron, slow to take offense, quick to forgive, and yet decisive, possessing a ruler's toughness of mind. The Henry IV of history had other less admirable qualities, some of them apparent in his relationship with Henriette d'Entragues. Having spent much of his life in war, he was pugnacious as well as tough-minded. While he lived, he provided a check to Spain's ambitions. His death at the hands of an assassin, May 14, 1610, left France vulnerable, with his widow as regent. Louis XIII, his son and heir, was nine years old. Until the emergence of Cardinal Richelieu as the king's chief minister in 1624, France was again neutralized as a European power.

Writing on June 5, 1610, Luis Cabrera de Córdoba described the sense of relief Henry IV's death brought to Spain: "The news about the King of France is regarded as something marvelous, sent from heaven, coming at a time when weapons were being provided in many places in expectation of an attack

---

[80] In assembling a large army in Northern Italy and in joining the duke of Savoy in conspiring with Byron, the historical count of Fuentes was apparently acting on his own initiative, without authorization from King Philip III or the duke of Lerma. J. H. Elliott refers to him as one of "the great Italian proconsuls," who "conducted over the years a militant and aggressive policy entirely at variance with that of Madrid": *Imperial Spain*, p. 320. See also Edouard Rott, *Henri IV: Les Suisses et la Haute Italie, la lutte pour les Alpes (1598–1610)* (Paris: E. Plon, 1882), pp. 110–14.

[81] Rott, *Henri IV*, p. 114.

somewhere by the army he had assembled." "May it please God," Cabrera adds, "that it will be the cause of much peace in Christendom."[82]

★

King Henry died by violence at the age of fifty-six. Queen Elizabeth had died quietly seven years earlier at sixty-nine. Unlike Henry's, her death caused no political crisis. The king of Scotland succeeded the queen peacefully, without overt opposition. James had not been confident that success would come easily: like many of his contemporaries, he anticipated Catholic—especially Spanish—opposition.

Catholics in England and on the Continent had long talked about a Spanish successor to Elizabeth: their arguments are well represented in Doleman's *Conference about the Next Succession to the Crowne of Ingland.* Why, when the time for action came, were they so passive?[83]

Their natural leader, Philip III, was in a measure responsible for their inactivity. Throughout his reign, before and after the death of Elizabeth, English Catholics looked to him for protection.[84] Before the queen died, they looked to him also for leadership in organizing support for a Catholic rival to James. Excessively cautious and secretive, Philip was slow to commit himself to any candidate, and slow to alter his position when events required that he do so. He did not inform his advisors

---

[82] Luis Cabrera de Córdoba, *Relaciones de las cosas sucedidas en la corte de España, desde 1599 hasta 1614* (Madrid: Imprenta de J. Martín Alegría, 1857), p. 407.

[83] Albert J. Loomie, S.J., provides a comprehensive answer to this question: "Philip III and the Stuart Succession in England, 1600–1603," *Revue Belge de Philologie et d'Histoire* 43 (1965): 492–514. See also Helen Georgia Stafford's chapter, "Foreign Affairs, 1598–1603," in her *James VI of Scotland and the Throne of England* (New York: D. Appleton-Century, 1940), pp. 225–49.

[84] For the period after March 1603, see the collection of documents pertaining to English Catholics edited by Albert J. Loomie, S.J., *Spain and the Jacobean Catholics, Vol. 1, 1603–12,* 64 (Catholic Record Society: 1973); *Vol. II, 1613–24,* 67 (Catholic Record Society: 1978).

of his choice, his sister Isabel, until early in 1601.[85] He then met insurmountable obstacles to her candidacy—above all from Isabel herself, who refused to have anything to do with the English succession. She distrusted her brother, believing that he put her forward as a means to gain her sovereignty of the Netherlands. Henry IV opposed Isabel or any other Habsburg, fearing encirclement by Habsburg dominions. The pope, like the French king, resisted an enhancement of Spain's power. He urged Henry and Philip to join in supporting some Catholic claimant who was aligned with neither of them. When it was too late to matter, in March 1603, Philip accepted Henry's proposal that the candidate should be a native Englishman.[86]

In any event, the strength of the king of Scotland's position was such that it made doubtful the ultimate success of any Catholic. What had earlier seemed impediments ceased to matter in 1603. James was next in succession to Elizabeth by the law of primogeniture; he had had her unspoken support; for two years prior to her death, he had been in secret correspondence with her secretary, Robert Cecil;[87] he could summon military support if needed. It is not surprising that he claimed his English crown so easily.

[85] Loomie, "Philip III and the Stuart Succession," p. 502.

[86] Ibid., pp. 512–13.

[87] For an account of the accession of King James with emphasis on the diplomacy of Robert Cecil, see Joel Hurstfield, "The Succession Struggle," in *Elizabethan Government and Society*, ed. Bindoff, pp. 369–96.

Chapter Four

KING JAMES I'S PEACE AND

THE PALATINATE

Hee too late is conscious,
That his ambition to incroach upon
His neighbours territories, with the danger of
His liberty, nay his life, hath brought in question
His owne inheritance . . .

> *(The ambassador of the duke of Urbino, referring to the duke)*
> PHILIP MASSINGER, *The Maid of Honour* (*c.* 1621–1622)

WITHIN A dozen years before and after 1600, European leaders witnessed a series of events that seemed to point to peace: the Treaty of Vervins in 1598 ended the war between Spain and France; the Treaty of London in 1604 ended the war between Spain and England; Philip III and James I, who in 1598 and 1603 respectively succeeded to the Spanish and English crowns, were each less inclined to war than their predecessors; Spain and the United Provinces agreed to a ceasefire in 1607 and, two years later, to a twelve-year truce; the assassination of Henry IV in 1610 stopped his threat of aggression. Europe enjoyed an interval of peace—a *Pax Hispanica*, H. R. Trevor-Roper calls it.[1] But it proved to be a brief one: a revolt in Bohemia in 1618 set in train another series of events that resulted in the Thirty Years' War, accurately described as the first world war. Again Catholic and Protestant armies clashed, and again Spanish and English dramatists addressed the issues in contention.

★

The peace between Spain and England negotiated in 1604 lasted for twenty years, with important consequences for Eng-

---

[1] Trevor-Roper, "Spain and Europe 1598–1621" in *The New Cambridge Modern History*, ed. J. P. Cooper, 4 (Cambridge: Cambridge University Press, 1970), 269.

lish literature. Although the long Elizabethan war had not prevented Englishmen, including the queen herself, from reading
Spanish,[2] it prevented them from seeing the *comedia* in the theatres of Spain during the formative years of Lope de Vega's career, beginning in the late 1580s. The English had access to
Spanish books, including plays, many of which were printed
in the Netherlands;[3] and some presumably saw Spanish plays
in Amsterdam, either in the original language or in translation.[4] But King James reopened the way to Spain itself. Diplomatic relations were resumed, English merchants gained access to Spanish ports, and Englishmen—some of them with
literary interests who became translators—traveled or resided
in Spain, at times on governmental missions, at other times to
see the country and learn Spanish. Referring to her husband's
youthful travels, Lady Fanshawe writes that in the early 1630s,
after a year's residence in Paris, "he [Sir Richard Fanshawe]
travelled to Madrid in Spain, there to learn that language. At
the same time for that purpose went the late Earle of Carnar-

  [2] Gustav Ungerer, *Anglo-Spanish Relations in Tudor Literature* (Berne:
Francke Verlag, 1956), pp. 43–44; Dale B. J. Randall, *The Golden Tapestry: A
Critical Survey of Non-chivalric Spanish Fiction in English Translation, 1543–1657*
(Durham, N.C.: Duke University Press, 1963), pp. 231–33.
  [3] Henry Thomas writes that "Spanish books began to be printed in the
Netherlands not long after Charles V inherited this portion of the Austrian do-
minions; . . . nearly all the books were printed in Antwerp, which, as a pro-
ducer of Spanish books in this century, ranks with the Castilian cities of the
second class."
  There is good reason to believe "that the Netherlands were the chief source
of supply of Spanish books for the English market" in the sixteenth century:
Thomas, "The Output of Spanish Books in the Sixteenth Century," *The Library*, 4th Ser., 1 (1920–21): 85–86. See also Thomas, *Short-Title Catalogues of
Spanish, Spanish-American and Portuguese Books Printed before 1601 in the British
Museum* (London: British Museum, 1966), and Jonas A. Van Praag, *La Comedia espagnole aux Pays-Bas au XVIIᵉ et au XVIIIᵉ siècle* (Amsterdam: H. J.
Paris, 1922).
  [4] J. Te Winkel, "De Invloed der Spaansche Letterkunde op de Nederlandsche in de Seventiende Eeuw," *Tijdschrift voor Nederlandsche Taal- en Letterkunde* 1 (1881): 59–114; Jacob A. Worp, *Geschiedenis van het Drama en van het
Tooneel in Nederland*, 1 (Groningen: J. B. Wolters, 1904), 389–99. In 2 (1908):
127–29, Worp provides a list of Netherland plays that are translations or adaptations of Spanish ones. See also Henry W. Sullivan, *Calderón in the German
Lands and the Low Countries*, pp. 45–47.

van, and my Lord of Bedford, and Lord John B[erkeley], and
severall other gentlemen."[5] Spain had become a place to be visited on a grand tour, and it was the Spain of the Golden Age in
drama.[6]

In 1610, Ben Jonson gave jocular expression to the English
admiration of all things Spanish in King James's reign. Face
speaks:

> Aske from your courtier, to your innes of court-man,
> To your mere millaner, they will tell you all,
> Your *Spanish* iennet is the best horse. Your *Spanish*
> Stoupe is the best garbe. Your *Spanish* beard
> Is the best cut. Your *Spanish* ruffes are the best
> Weare. Your *Spanish Pauin* the best daunce.
> Your *Spanish* titillation in a gloue
> The best perfume. And, for your *Spanish* pike,
> And *Spanish* blade, let your poore Captaine speake.
>   (*The Alchemist*, IV.iv)[7]

The ironical burden of Jonson's lines conveys the ambiguity of
attitude toward Spain characteristic of James's reign and the
peaceful part of Charles's. Many Englishmen admired the nation's wealth and military power, but many feared her cunning
and ambition. Influential noblemen in the courts of both James
and Charles favored close alliance with Spain. With important
qualifications, both kings followed foreign policies that were
pro-Spanish.[8] But their Parliaments, especially the House of
Commons, remained stubbornly hostile to Spain. The memory of 1588 lingered; the fear of aggressive Spanish Catholicism was reenforced by rivalry in overseas trade.

[5] *The Memoirs of Anne, Lady Halkett and Ann, Lady Fanshawe*, ed. John Loftis
(Oxford: Clarendon Press, 1979), p. 113.

[6] John Walter Stoye, *English Travellers Abroad, 1604–1667: Their Influence in
English Society and Politics* (London: Jonathan Cape, 1952), pp. 325–90.

[7] Jonson, *The Alchemist*, ed. C. H. Herford, Percy and Evelyn Simpson, 5
(Oxford: Clarendon Press, 1937), 372.

For an account of the circumstances that led to admiration for Spain
throughout Europe in the middle years of Philip III's reign, see Trevor-Roper,
"Spain and Europe," in *New Cambridge Modern History*, 4:260–82.

[8] See C. V. Wedgwood, *Poetry and Politics under the Stuarts* (Cambridge:
Cambridge University Press, 1960), p. 154.

James's policy remained Protestant during the lifetime of Robert Cecil, earl of Salisbury, who as lord treasurer was the king's chief minister. One of Salisbury's last acts, in fact, was to negotiate a marriage between the king's daughter, Elizabeth, and Frederick V, elector of the Palatinate and a leader of the German Protestant Union.[9] Through this marriage—in February 1613—James entered an alliance with the German Protestant states that was to have long-lasting consequences for England and for western Europe.

Frederick, a Calvinist and one of the seven princes of Germany entitled to a vote in imperial elections, was the hereditary ruler of the Palatinate, the collective name of two separate German regions about two hundred miles apart: to the west, the Lower or Rhenish Palatinate, bisected by the Rhine; to the east, the Upper Palatinate, north of the Danube, bisected by the Nab River. Although both regions were compact and of about the same size, the Lower Palatinate, in one of the loveliest and most fertile parts of Germany, was rich, the Upper Palatinate poor. The location of Frederick's territories held a potential for conflict with the Habsburgs: the lands to the west lay across Spain's military corridor to the Netherlands; those to the east bordered on Bohemia, where a Habsburg king ruled a Protestant state.[10]

King James, anxious to balance the Protestant alliance that came with his daughter's marriage, wished his son and heir to marry a Catholic. Only a French or Spanish marital alliance could advance his objectives in foreign policy. Since he disliked the regent of France, Marie de Medici, and since in any event he thought more was to be gained, in munificence of dowry as well as in international politics, from Spain than from France, he opted for Spain.[11]

---

[9] Although there had been occasional talk of a Catholic marriage for Princess Elizabeth, King James had never seriously considered one. See Maurice Lee, Jr., *James I and Henri IV: An Essay in English Foreign Policy, 1603–1610* (Urbana: University of Illinois Press, 1970), p. 178.

[10] Robert Zaller, *The Parliament of 1621: A Study in Constitutional Conflict* (Berkeley: University of California Press, 1971), p. 8.

[11] Lee, *James I and Henri IV*, pp. 178–79.

In the event, the Spanish match never occurred, either for Prince Henry, who died in 1612, or for his younger brother, Prince Charles. Nevertheless, talk of it, plans for it, and, after Charles's futile journey to Madrid in 1623, hostilities resulting from its failure were divisive in English political life. James failed to understand the depth of his people's aversion to the prospect of a Spanish bride for his heir; they, in turn, did not understand his reasons for desiring a Spanish alliance. He believed that an alliance with Spain would remove a threat to the peace of his kingdom. Furthermore, he needed the dowry a Spanish match would bring.

★

Diplomatic missions to Spain, some for negotiations pertaining to the projected marriage, some for other purposes, provided occasions for Englishmen to see Spanish plays and dramatic entertainments.

The earl of Nottingham, who in 1588 as Lord Howard of Effingham had commanded the English fleet that defeated the Armada, went to Spain in 1605 with a large number of attendants to witness Philip III's ratification of the peace treaty in Valladolid, then the capital city.[12] Contemporary accounts of Nottingham's embassy help to explain why many Englishmen thought that Spain was very rich. Soon after Nottingham's squadron arrived at Corunna, the entertainments began.[13] Robert Treswell describes some of them. In the marketplace at Corunna, a square space "of twenty yeards or more" was railed in "with Scaffolds, built of purpose" around it "wherein the English were very sufficiently appointed and placed. . . . His Lordship and other the Noblemen were placed in severall windowes, in a very faire roome in the Kings State-

---

[12] For a detailed account of Nottingham's mission, see Robert W. Kenny, "Peace with Spain, 1605," *History Today* 20 (1970): 198–208.

[13] Discussing the structure of seating arrangements in the Renaissance English theatre, Leslie Hotson has quoted from and commented on some of the accounts of Spanish dramatic entertainment to which I refer. He mentions other accounts as well: *Shakespeare's Wooden O* (London: Rupert Hart-Davis, 1960), pp. 70–77, 89–90, 105–15, 216–17, 221–22, 224, 233–35.

house. . . . Ladies and better sort of the towne" were similarly accommodated. All this sounds much like the improvised theatres and the seating arrangements in them in Spanish towns that did not have permanent theatres. The entertainment, in its emphasis on spectacle, sounds as though it was intended for an audience that could not understand Spanish.[14]

The festivities at Corunna proved to be the beginning of varied entertainment, including bullfights and jousts, provided for the English.[15] They also attended religious ceremonies, as on the occasion in Valladolid when the king's son, the future King Philip IV, was christened.[16] On Corpus Christi day, they saw performances of *autos sacramentales*.[17] And on June 7, the duke of Lerma entertained them with a performance of Lope de Vega's *El caballero de Illescas* in the courtyard of his palace.[18]

The king and the duke of Lerma were both present for an elaborate evening party, June 16, in a large and handsome hall of the royal palace. A Spanish account of the entertainment on that occasion survives;[19] so do two in English, one by Robert Treswell and one by the author of an anonymous pamphlet. I quote from the latter. After all were seated,

> there were men sung upon both sides, presently there was a Curtaine drawne, and there entred five and twentie Violins and Cornets, playing very sweetly. . . . Then began the Musicke, and in

[14] Treswell, *A Relation of Such Things as were observed to happen in the Journey of . . . Charles Earle of Nottingham . . .* (London: 1605), pp. 21–23 (STC #24268).

[15] *The Royal Entertainement of . . . The Earle of Nottingham* (London: 1605), pp. 13–15 (STC #13857). For a modern account of the entertainment, see Luis Astrana Marín, *La vida turbulenta de Quevedo*, 2d edn. (Madrid: Editorial "Gran Capitán," 1945), pp. 114–18.

[16] *Royal Entertainement*, pp. 9–10.

[17] Astrana Marín, *Quevedo*, p. 115.

[18] Astrana Marín, *Quevedo*, p. 115; Shergold, *The Spanish Stage*, p. 246. I have seen no reference to the performance in the English pamphlets describing Nottingham's embassy. Probably most of the Englishmen were unable to understand Lope's dialogue. This is apparently the earliest known occasion when Englishmen saw the performance of a *comedia* in Spain.

[19] By Pinheiro da Veiga: quoted by Astrana Marín, *Quevedo*, pp. 116–17.

maner of a Cloude [the curtain] did open, which shined and glit-
tered like Starres over head. . . . There came downe the King and
Queene, and the Duke of Lermo, with an other Ladie, let downe all
foure as if they came out of a Cloud. It was a verie glorious shew to
see them come down.

The King and Queen daunced hand in hand, and the Duke of
Lermo, and the other Ladie, untill they came to the Throne.[20]

The spectacle and ceremony, with the king and queen taking
leading roles, remind us of the court masques Ben Jonson and
Inigo Jones prepared for Charles I.

In 1617 Englishmen went again to the duke of Lerma's palace, but on this occasion they were received coolly, and they
narrowly missed seeing a play that includes thinly disguised,
jesting allusions to Prince Charles's long-range courtship of
the infanta. This was a sensitive subject to address even in innuendo, and we may be confident the dramatist, Luis Vélez de
Guevara, knew before he wrote his play, El caballero del sol,[21]
that the king and the duke of Lerma opposed the English marriage. Philip III was unwilling for Charles to marry his daughter unless he should become a Catholic, an unlikely occur-
rence, as the king understood. But Philip allowed negotiations
to proceed lest he drive King James into closer alliance with
Spain's enemies. Furthermore, Philip apparently saw in the
negotiations a means to improve conditions for English Catholics.

King James had sent Sir John Digby to Spain as a special am-

---

[20] *Royal Entertainement*, pp. 16–17.

[21] Some well-informed scholars assumed until a few years ago that *El caballero del sol* had been lost. See Shergold, *Spanish Stage*, p. 255, and Gareth A.
Davies, "Luis Vélez de Guevara and Court Life," in C. George Peale, ed., *An-
tigüedad y actualidad de Luis Vélez de Guevara: estudios críticos* (Amsterdam and
Philadelphia: John Benjamins Publishing Co., 1983), p. 35, n. 9. The play survives in copies of a *suelta* (Seville: Francisco de Leefdael, n.d.), one of which is
held by the British Library (B.L., 11728 f.86).

On the political dimension of the play, see A. Valbuena Briones, "Una incursión en las comedias novelescas de Luis Vélez de Guevara y su relación con
Calderón," in Peale, ed., *Vélez*, pp. 45–46. In note 29, pp. 49–51, Valbuena
Briones quotes passages that reveal the nature of Vélez's allusions to the marriage negotiations.

bassador for consultations about terms for a marriage. Knowing that King Philip would be at Lerma, the *privado*'s palace, Digby went with his attendants to the nearby city of Burgos to wait until the Spanish king would receive him. His stay in the region coincided with an elaborate fiesta lasting several days that the duke of Lerma had prepared in honor of the royal visit.[22]

Our information about the activities of Digby and those accompanying him comes largely from a diary kept by Sir Robert Phelips, one of the ambassador's attendants.[23] Phelips' phrasing is at times obscure, and his dates can be misleading in that he refers to both the Old and the New Style calendars. However, his narrative may be supplemented by reports written by the Tuscan ambassador for the information of his government.[24] On Sunday, October 8, 1617 (N.S.), the ambassador wrote that Digby would arrive the following Tuesday at a village near Lerma. The next Sunday, he wrote again, describing the performance on the previous Tuesday evening of *El caballero del sol* before an audience that included the king. He referred to the staging of the play on a quay extending into a river opposite another quay on the other side, where spectators sat. The Tuscan ambassador added that the English ambassador and his retinue arrived the same evening at the nearby village, where their lodging and meals were provided by the Spanish king.[25]

This report establishes a firm date for the arrival of the English—Tuesday, October 10 (N.S.). Phelips also specifies Tuesday: he too was using the New Style calendar. According to Phelips, Digby learned on Sunday (October 8) that coaches would be sent to take him and his attendants to the village near Lerma, where "a house and all other necessaryes" would be ready by Tuesday afternoon, and that the king would receive

---

[22] On the fiesta, see Shergold, *Spanish Stage*, pp. 255–58.

[23] The diary was printed by the Historical Manuscripts Commission, *Appendix to the First Report* (1870), pp. 59–60.

[24] I am indebted to Professor Shirley B. Whitaker for generously making available to me information from the Tuscan archives.

[25] Archivo di Stato di Firenze, Mediceo, *filza* 4945.

him on Thursday. All went as planned until the ambassador's party reached the village at the time specified, only to learn that no orders had been given for their reception. Messages passed to and from the palace, Digby complaining of the indignity shown him, the duke of Lerma's secretary insisting that appropriate orders had been given. With night coming on, an unfurnished house was found for Digby's accommodation.[26] Meanwhile, only a mile away at Lerma, *El caballero del sol* was being performed.

The coincidence of these events suggests the possibility that the English were purposely kept away by a stratagem. At least two of them, Digby himself[27] and Francis Cottington, knew the Spanish language and the circumstances of the negotiations well enough to have understood the dramatist's veiled political jests. Without more complete information, we cannot know precisely what happened.

Attention to Vélez's play will reveal why it would have been offensive to English diplomats. The Tuscan ambassador summarized its improbable, chivalric plot in his report written October 15:

Four princes of high rank court the beautiful Diana, *signora* of Naples [a city often used in Golden Age drama to signify a Spanish one]. Not attracted to any of them, she falls in love with an English prince, who has fled from his native country because of the death of his wife, intending always to travel. He has come by chance to

---

[26] H.M.C., *Appendix to the First Report*, p. 59.

[27] On August 3/13, 1617, Gondomar wrote from London to the duke of Lerma about Digby's forthcoming visit. He urged Lerma to be cautious in his dealings with the experienced English diplomat: "Sir John Digby is subtle and attentive, and thus it is necessary that in general he be welcomed and shown all good will. I think that it is of the utmost importance that great care be taken in details of relations with him because, since he has been in Spain so many years, he will leave no way untried to learn what he can, and his primary duty is to get at once to the heart of the business. I regard it as a certainty that if he understands that nothing can be accomplished, he will depart at once." (In Antonio Ballesteros y Beretta, ed., *Correspondencia oficial de Don Diego Sarmiento de Acuña, Conde de Gondomar*, DIE, 89–90.)

the Neapolitan coast, where he meets Diana. After some adventures he marries her.[28]

All this reminds us, and Vélez intended that the play do so, of the books of knightly adventure that turned Don Quixote's head: *El caballero* includes two characters, *graciosos*, cut to the pattern of Cervantes' knight and his squire, called in the play Don Roque and Merlín. Vélez becomes more specific in portraying Don Roque and the title character, an English prince named Febo, who in certain respects resemble, respectively, the count of Gondomar, then the Spanish ambassador in England, and Prince Charles. Gondomar was known to be the principal Spanish proponent of the marital alliance.[29] Febo tells of his ancestry and of the circumstances that led him to fall in love with Sol, his first wife:

> *De ricos, y nobles padres*
> *heredero naci, y noble,*
> *en Londres, para desdichas,*
> *que es de Ingalaterra Corte.*
> *Truxo entre varios retratos*
> *un Embaxador a Londres,*
> *para que fuesse el primero*
> *veneno de mis amores,*
> *uno milagroso, y raro*
> *del Sol, hija de los Condes*
> *de Galizia, donde el Cielo*
> *cifrò en un Sol muchos Soles.*[30]

I was born, the heir of a rich and noble family, in London, which unfortunately is the capital of England. An ambassador brought to London, among various portraits, a miraculous and precious one of Sol—so that it should be the first poison of my loves—the daughter of the count of Galicia, a region where heaven made many suns into one sun.

Febo tells of falling so intensely in love with the portrait that he became ill.

[28] A.S.F., Mediceo, *filza* 4945.
[29] See Valbuena Briones, "Una incursión," in Peale, ed., *Vélez*, p. 46.
[30] Vélez, *El caballero del sol* (B.L., 11728 f.86), p. 4.

tratar mis padres disponen
el casamiento con ella,
despachando Embaxadores.
Eran en nobleza iguales,
que si eran los suyos Condes
de Galizia, eran los mios
de Ingalatera señores.[31]

My parents undertook negotiations for my marriage with her, sending ambassadors. Our families were of equal rank in nobility, for if her ancestors were counts of Galicia, mine were sovereign lords of England.

The king of England was equal in rank to the count of Galicia!

The references to Galicia and the word play on *sol* ("sun") are aspects of the political innuendo: the count of Gondomar was a native of that province; in his letters he frequently complained about the English climate, and he was known to wish to return to the Spanish sun. Furthermore, the behavior of the character Don Roque could be interpreted by persons critical of Gondomar as a burlesque of Gondomar's own behavior.[32]

The Tuscan ambassador's account of the entertainment omits reference to the double identity of Febo's first wife, Sol: she was the daughter of the count of Galicia, we are told, but she was also the sun in the heavens. Her "death" was not that of a mortal but rather a return to her heavenly sphere. Her celestial identity is the more prominent in the play. Febo, whose name resembles that of Phoebus Apollo, had learned from an ambassador about the existence of Sol: that is, he learned that there was a sun, which, according to Gondomar, was rarely seen in the northerly latitudes of England. Febo fell in love with Sol's picture, and he later married her. But she was the sun, and, if Gondomar's exaggerated reports about the English weather were to be believed, she could spend but little time in London.

On his travels Febo arrives at Naples and meets Diana (whose name is that of a moon goddess). Late in the play, Sol

---

[31] Ibid.
[32] Valbuena Briones, "Una incursión," p. 46.

appears to Febo, telling him to look for Diana and to protect her; she, Sol, must return to heaven.[33] At the play's end, Febo arrives in England with Diana and her former suitors, whom he introduces to his father, Lisandro, king of England. Don Roque, who has also come with Febo, loquaciously introduces himself to the king.[34]

There is no mistaking the topical allusions to Prince Charles's courtship, to the English weather, and to Gondomar's dislike of it. The performance at approximately the time of Digby's planned arrival suggests an indifference toward King James, who was known to have a conception of kingship incompatible with theatrical jests about his heir. Whether or not the duke of Lerma was responsible for keeping the English away from the performance, he must have perceived that they would have been offended by the play.

Sir Robert Phelips, who could have known only what he had been told about *El caballero del sol*, described the play very briefly in his diary. On Friday (October 13 [N.S.]), not long before the Englishmen left their lodgings near Lerma, he says, a messenger came from the count of Saldaña, the duke's younger son, "to thank him [Digby] for the honour he dyde him in beholding the sports" ("sports" apparently meaning spectacles or dramatic entertainments). Phelips continues:

> . . . and if I mistake not, the Conde of Lenos [Lemos], a son in law of the same dukes [Lerma] (who had at that tyme sett forth a Comedye in which there was presented an English prince comming awoing to a Spanish princes[s], which in spight of all competition he obtayned), did lykewyse send his lordship a compliment that he should be glad to have him and his company present, when itt was presented before the King.[35]

These remarks are misleading: the king had already seen a performance of *El caballero del sol*; the invitation to Digby to at-

---

[33] Vélez, *El caballero del sol*, p. 30.

[34] Ibid., p. 32.

[35] H.M.C., *Appendix to the First Report*, p. 59.

I quoted Phelip's account of Vélez's play in an earlier draft of this chapter, not knowing that the play could be identified. Professor Shirley B. Whitaker called my attention to *El caballero del sol*.

tend a play when it was presented before the king probably referred to a second, anonymous one, *La casa confusa*, performed in a church at nightfall with the king present.[36] Phelips's imprecisions are to be accounted for by his imperfect comprehension of conversations carried on in Spanish.

★

The diplomatic maneuvers for a Spanish bride for Prince Charles were soon to be played out against the cruel reality of the Thirty Years' War. Charles's brother-in-law, the elector Frederick V, became a central figure in the first phase of the war, which began with a disputed succession to the crown of Bohemia. Traditionally the king of Bohemia had also been the Holy Roman Emperor and head of the House of Habsburg, with Prague as his capital. But the Diet of Prague claimed a right to elect a king, and in a political situation clouded by the departure from Bohemia of the aged and childless emperor Matthias (who died soon after), the Protestant nobility refused to accept his designated successor, the Catholic Ferdinand of Styria.[37] In his place they elected Frederick, who unwisely accepted.[38] At about the same time as his election, Ferdinand became emperor.

By his acceptance of the Bohemian crown, Frederick aroused the Catholic states of Germany against him, and he failed to attract significant support from the Protestant states,

---

[36] See Shergold, *Spanish Stage*, pp. 256–57.

[37] In *La ventura con el nombre*, Tirso seemingly refers to the first phase, in Bohemia, of the Thirty Years' War. See Ruth Lee Kennedy, "Tirso's 'La ventura con el nombre': Its Source and Date of Composition," *Bulletin of the Comediantes* 21 (1969): 35–45.

The play has a Bohemian locale, in Prague, in residences of the sovereigns, and in a village. Nominally about a dynasty that came to an end early in the fourteenth century, the play includes details that suggest Tirso wrote with the events of 1620 in mind. An invading Saxon army threatens to capture Prague, which is beset by uncertainty concerning succession. The lawful successor assumes command of the Bohemian forces and defeats the Saxons.

[38] The complexities of the conditions under which Frederick was elected king defy brief statement. For a lucid exposition of them, see Georges Pagès, trans. David Maland and John Hooper, *The Thirty Years War, 1618–1648* (New York: Harper & Row, 1970), pp. 41–67.

whose rulers were not necessarily pleased to see one of their own advanced to a dignity above them. Frederick's father-in-law, King James, had opposed his acceptance of the Bohemian invitation, disliking the precedent of subjects deposing their sovereign, and in any event understanding that English naval power would be of little use in a land-locked country.[39] Frederick lacked the personal qualities of leadership as well as the military strength needed to maintain his position, and after a single year in Prague he was driven into exile, in November 1620, by troops in the service of the emperor Ferdinand.

Even earlier, in August 1620, Frederick's fortunes were disastrously worsened when, on orders from the archduke Albert, Ambrosio Spínola led an army of 25,000 from the Netherlands into the Lower Palatinate, where within six months he gained control of about half of it. Albert (the husband of the infanta Isabel) held lands within the empire and was, in theory at least, subject to the emperor: the invasion of the Lower Palatinate was made on behalf of the emperor as an act of retribution for Frederick's insubordination in usurping Ferdinand's Bohemian crown.[40]

In his adversity, Frederick refused to recognize military and political realities, thus complicating the efforts of King James and others who tried to aid him through diplomacy.[41] Nor did the emperor relent in his hostility, despite efforts by the king of Spain to limit reprisals.[42] On January 22, 1621, Ferdinand pronounced the ban of the empire on Frederick, rendering him an outlaw, and in the summer of 1621 the army of the Catholic League, commanded and paid by the duke of Bavaria, occupied the Upper Palatinate. Ferdinand had promised to repay

[39] See Conrad Russell, *The Crisis of Parliaments: English History, 1509–1660* (London: Oxford University Press, 1971), pp. 290–92.

[40] Charles Howard Carter, *The Secret Diplomacy of the Habsburgs, 1598–1625* (New York: Columbia University Press, 1964), p. 176. See also Anna Egler, *Die Spanier in der linksrheinischen Pfalz, 1620–1632: Invasion, Verwaltung, Rekatholisierung* (Mainz: Selbstverlag der Gesellschaft für mittelrheinische Kirchengeschichte, 1971), pp. 25–26.

[41] Anton Gindely, *History of the Thirty Years' War*, trans. Andrew Ten Brook, 2 vols. (New York: G. P. Putnam's Sons, 1884), 1:312–16.

[42] Ibid., 1:314.

the duke for his military support in Bohemia by conveying to him Frederick's electoral dignity and at least a portion of his territories. Ultimately, the duke gained not only the electoral vote but both the Upper and Lower Palatinate, though for his lifetime only.[43]

The invasion of the Palatinate, "the ancient patrimony of the King's children" (in Francis Bacon's phrase), aroused deep emotions in England. It violated a just inheritance; it also extended the domain of Catholicism. Although James had opposed Frederick's Bohemian adventure, he and Charles after him felt an obligation to help Frederick regain his electorate. But their ability to do so was limited. In 1620, James gave permission for a regiment of volunteers commanded by Sir Horace Vere to go to the Palatinate to reinforce the troops of the Protestant Union and the Dutch Republic who were fighting on behalf of Frederick. Although the force included able men and was led by an experienced and able officer, it was too small to accomplish much.[44]

Not long after news of Spínola's invasion of the Lower Palatinate reached England, James made a sustained effort to aid Frederick. He complained bitterly to the Spanish ambassador, Gondomar, and in the early autumn of 1620, he declared publicly that if the Palatinate were not restored by spring he would go to war.[45] He would need money to wage war on the Continent, and to give force to his threat he summoned Parliament. The Parliament of 1621 shared the widespread indignation at the invasion, and before the first session was adjourned, the House of Commons promised to assist the king "with

[43] On the transactions between the emperor and the duke of Bavaria, see C. V. Wedgwood, *The Thirty Years War* (1938; repr. New York: Methuen, 1981), pp. 141–65.

[44] Markam, "*The Fighting Veres*," pp. 394–420. A member of Vere's regiment, Arthur Wilson, provided an account in his autobiography of the expedition sent to aid Frederick: Wilson, *Observations of God's Providence, in the Tract of my Life*, printed as an appendix to an edition of Wilson's play, *The Inconstant Lady* (Oxford: Samuel Collingwood, 1814).

See also Egler, *Die Spanier in der linksrheinischen Pfalz*, pp. 48, 51, 60, 61, 65–67.

[45] Robert Zaller, *The Parliament of 1621*, p. 17.

their lives and fortunes" should war become necessary.[46] In the second session the Commons were of similar mind. But the king knew he could not expect Parliament to supply him, over a protracted period of time, with a sufficiently large army for him successfully to influence a European war. Diplomacy seemed to offer the only viable means of restoring Frederick's territories.

At the end of November 1621, James learned through intercepted letters from the emperor directed to the king of Spain that the emperor intended to convey Frederick's electorate to the duke of Bavaria. James learned at the same time that the Spanish had not deceived him; they opposed the transfer of the electorate. He believed that only through the Spanish as intermediaries could he hope to influence a decision by the emperor. Having no more need of the Parliament, he dissolved it. And through his ambassador in Madrid, he expressed his good will to the king of Spain and his desire to cooperate with him.[47]

That James did not do more to assist Frederick has often been attributed to the diplomatic skill of the resident Spanish ambassador, whose mission at the time was to keep England neutral. Don Diego Sarmiento de Acuña, from 1617 count of Gondomar, held his position from 1613 until 1622, except for an interval between 1618 to 1620. He was an astute and well-educated man, devoted to the service of the king of Spain and the Catholic faith. Sir John Digby, English ambassador to Madrid at the time of Gondomar's appointment, described his abilities and his diplomatic style in a letter, May 27, 1613, to King James:

> [He is] the ablest minister by many degrees that hath been employed unto you from this state . . . and will omit nothing that can be effected by industry or money, and therefore it will be fit he be the better looked unto. He hath a plain free fashion, differing from his nation, but his plainness is accompanied with much art and

[46] Lockyer, *Buckingham*, p. 104.
[47] Ibid., pp. 110–11.

skill. There is no gentleman of Spain better esteemed or of greater reputation.[48]

Gondomar's success derived from the relationship he established with King James, who liked his "plain free fashion" and admired his learning. In an age when few diplomats and even fewer sovereigns had a fluent command of conversational Latin, both ambassador and king could speak it with ease.[49]

Gondomar was indeed influential with the king, though less so than historians of an earlier time assumed. The king thought for himself, and he kept his deepest secrets to himself. Yet he and Gondomar were often in agreement on courses of action to be taken, even when they differed in their ultimate objectives. The ambassador desired the Spanish match for Charles and thought it practicable; he believed that it might bring toleration for English Catholics and that toleration would result in a return of the nation to Catholicism.[50] James believed that the projected marriage would induce the king of Spain to pressure his kinsman, the emperor, to restore the Palatinate to Frederick. James's intentions were widely misunderstood by his subjects.[51]

★

When Spínola invaded the Palatinate, his army met only minor resistance from troops of the German Protestant Union, the Dutch Republic, and the English regiment commanded by Vere. Frederick was in Bohemia, where in November 1620 the army of the German Catholic League supported by Spanish troops defeated his Bohemian army so rapidly and decisively that he was compelled to flee with his family, first to Branden-

[48] Digby to James I, May 27, 1613. P.R.O. SP 94/19, fol. 372 verso (reference made available to me by Professors Paul H. Hardacre and J. Kent Clark).

[49] See Garrett Mattingly, *Renaissance Diplomacy* (London: J. Cape, 1955), pp. 236–37.

[50] Ibid., pp. 266–67.

[51] On the relationship of King James and Gondomar, see Charles Howard Carter, "Gondomar: Ambassador to James I," *The Historical Journal* 7 (1964): 189–208; and Carter, *Secret Diplomacy of the Habsburgs*, pp. 120–33.

burg and then to The Hague, where he found refuge under the protection of English soldiers in the service of Prince Maurice, his uncle. For a time he could do nothing to try to regain the Palatinate. Although the English regiment remained there, the Protestant Union, confronted by the Spanish army, dissolved in the spring of 1621. Spínola returned to the Netherlands late in April 1621, but he left Gonzalo Fernández de Córdoba in command of the Spanish forces.[52]

During the autumn Protestant leaders with large numbers of troops came to the Palatinate, giving Frederick grounds to hope that he might regain it. The margrave of Baden-Durlach, fearing Spanish encroachment in his own principality, brought 11,000 men. Prince Christian of Brunswick, moved by love of war as well as by religious principle, brought about the same number.[53] The count of Mansfeld, a mercenary who usually fought on the Protestant side, brought an even larger force. In what proved to be an unsuccessful effort to form a united army from the separate groups, Frederick returned to the Palatinate in the spring of 1622.[54]

The Protestants soon suffered major reverses, and Frederick lost heart. He faced formidable enemies: the Spanish troops led by Gonzalo de Córdoba and the army of the Catholic League led by the count of Tilly, who was the field commander employed by the duke of Bavaria. On May 6, in the Battle of Wimpfen, the two Catholic leaders attacked Baden-Durlach, destroying a large number of troops. On June 20, in the Battle of Höchst, they inflicted heavy losses on Prince Christian's army. Christian carried on, however, and joined forces with the count of Mansfeld. The losses at Wimpfen and Höchst were too much for Frederick, who had received less assistance from Prince Maurice than he had anticipated. Early in July he

[52] Egler, *Die Spanier*, pp. 60–61.

[53] E. A. Beller, "The Thirty Years War," in *New Cambridge Modern History*, 4:316–17.

[54] Lope, *A Paleographic edition of . . . La nueva victoria de D. Gonzalo de Córdova*, ed. Henryk Ziomek (New York: Hispanic Institute of the United States, 1962), p. 47.

dismissed Mansfeld and Christian from his service and left the Palatinate.

Mansfeld and Christian had to look to their own devices for the support of themselves and their troops.[55] Mansfeld made overtures to the Catholic powers, the Austrian Habsburgs, the Spanish, and the French, with a view toward changing sides. He was rebuffed, but only after some hesitation by the French.[56] Christian, a younger and more principled man, was firmly attached to the Protestant cause.[57] With Mansfeld he decided to join Prince Maurice in the Netherlands; they turned westward with their troops. In their search for support, they found a valuable ally in the French Huguenot Henry, duke of Bouillon, who was living on his estates at Sedan, in the border area between France and the Spanish Netherlands. Twenty years before he had taken part in Byron's conspiracy against Henry IV and, rather than risk that king's mercy, had fled the court.[58] Now, Mansfeld and Christian received reinforcements from him and continued their march.

Catholic leaders throughout Europe became alarmed by reports of this Protestant army, including Huguenots as well as Germans— predators living on the land, marching westward toward an unknown destination. King Philip gave Gonzalo de Córdoba orders to lead his troops in pursuit.[59]

★

Lope chose this march and the battle that came at its climax as the subject of a play: *La nueva victoria de Don Gonzalo de Cór-*

[55] Frederick wrote a formal letter of dismissal of Mansfeld, Christian, and their men, dated July 3, 1622, which Mansfeld used in his effort to find employment: CODOIN, 54 (1896), 282–83.

[56] See the letter of September 8, 1622, written by the marquis of Bedmar from Brussels to King Philip IV. Printed in Antonio Cánovas del Castillo, *Estudios del reinado de Felipe IV*, 2 (Madrid: Imprenta de A. Pérez Dubrull, 1888), 411–15.

[57] His attachment was strengthened by his affection for his first cousin, the queen of Bohemia, Frederick's wife. See Markham, "*The Fighting Veres*," p. 410 n. 1.

[58] Sully, *Mémoires sages et royales*, 1:400, 420–22.

[59] See CODOIN, 54:287–90.

doba. Lope's title refers to a battle fought at Fleurus, fifteen miles from Brussels, on August 29, 1622. News of it reached Madrid on September 19; Lope signed his completed autograph on October 8.[60] He took advantage of the interest that Madrid and most of Europe evinced in a tense and, for the Catholic powers, potentially dangerous sequence of events. He wrote with incomplete information about Gonzalo de Córdoba's campaign, apparently using as his principal sources letters written by the general to his family in Spain.[61]

To Spaniards of Lope's era, the name of the title character was significant in itself: it recalled the revered name of Don Gonzalo's ancestor, the "great captain," Gonzalo Fernández de Córdoba (1453–1515), the founder of the house of Sessa, who had served in the army of Ferdinand and Isabel.[62] Apart from the timeliness of his subject and his customary pride in Spanish achievements, Lope had a personal reason for celebrating the exploits of Don Gonzalo: the general was the brother of Lope's patron, the fifth duke of Sessa.[63]

In successive scenes of the first act, Lope introduces the leaders of the opposing armies: Mansfeld and Brunswick, on the northeast border of France, uncertain of the route to take in their march to join the Dutch army; Gonzalo de Córdoba, Francisco de Ibarra, and, unhistorically, Tilly in pursuit of them. The Protestant generals confer with the duke of Bouillon, from whom they learn that a French general at the head of an army will block them if they attempt to enter France.

[60] Ed. Acad., 13:xxxv.

[61] Some of the letters are published in CODOIN, 54.

Lope apparently did not make use of either of two early printed narratives of the battle, one in Spanish and the other in Italian. The Spanish narrative, *Relacion certissima de la Felicissima Vitoria que ha tenido D. Gonçalo de Cordova* (B.L., T90*[9]), is dated from Brussels, September 7, 1622; the Italian narrative, *Relatione vera . . . Delle battaglie seguite, e la vittoria ricevuta da Don Consalvo di Cordona* (B.L., G.5484[7]), was printed in Italy at Bracciano with merely the date 1622. It was printed from a report sent from Brussels to the infanta Isabel's ambassador in Rome.

[62] Lope, *La nueva victoria*, ed. Ziomek, pp. 65–70. See also Ed. Acad., 13:xxxv n 2.

[63] Ed. Acad., 13:xxxiv–xxxv.

I. VICENTE CARDUCHO, *Battle of Fleurus* (Madrid, Prado)

2. DIEGO DE VELÁZQUEZ, *Surrender of Breda* (Madrid, Prado)

3. JUAN BAUTISTA MAINO, *Recapture of Bahía* (Madrid, Prado)

4. FRANCISCO DE ZURBARÁN, *Defense of Cádiz* (Madrid, Prado)

France is Catholic, Bouillon reminds them, and her king is the brother-in-law of the king of Spain. Philip IV's sister was indeed queen of France, but in 1622 relations between the countries were not so cordial as the duke implies. Bouillon advises Mansfeld and Brunswick to take a route northwest of Sedan through the border villages of Tiraza and La Chapelle.[64]

The Catholic leaders in pursuit acknowledge the courage of Mansfeld and Brunswick, and they refer to the superiority in numbers of the Protestant army.[65] But Gonzalo de Córdoba is specific and severe in his moral judgment: he blames atheism for the Protestants' cruelty to peasants, whose houses and means of livelihood the army destroys. Referring to the seventeen-year-old Philip IV, Ibarra adds that the young king experiences his first triumphs in Don Gonzalo's accomplishments.

The second act, an interlude before the armies meet, includes narrative accounts of earlier battles. Either from misinformation or from a desire to accentuate the achievements of his protagonist, Lope conveys the erroneous impression that Tilly, the field commander of the Catholic League's army, accompanied Gonzalo de Córdoba to Fleurus. In August 1622, he was not with Don Gonzalo but in the Palatinate, where he besieged fortified cities that included among their defenders Englishmen of Sir Horace Vere's regiment.[66] Don Gonzalo describes battles in which both he and Tilly had indeed participated, but as the commanders of independent though allied forces.

---

[64] See Lope, *La nueva victoria*, ed. Ziomek, p. 124n.

[65] The Spanish battle narrative of September 7, 1622, states that the Protestants had 7,000 cavalry and from 8,000 to 9,000 infantry; and that Gonzalo de Córdoba had 2,200 cavalry but a superior force in infantry: *Relacion certissima*, p. 2. The Italian narrative places the Protestant cavalry at 6,000 and the infantry at 4,000; Gonzalo de Córdoba's cavalry at 2,000 and his infantry at 8,000: *Relatione vera*, pp. 1–2.

An anonymous, contemporary letter, written in Spanish, estimates the Protestant cavalry as more than 5,000, their infantry as 4,000; and Don Gonzalo's cavalry as 2,000, his infantry as 8,000. Printed in Cánovas, *Estudios del reinado de Felipe IV*, 2:417.

[66] Gindely, *Thirty Years' War*, 1:342.

In the play, Don Gonzalo refers to letters he has written about the battles. Lope apparently had access to one describing Wimpfen:[67] he includes much more detail about it than about Höchst. Although Lope's Gonzalo de Córdoba does not say so, Tilly took the initiative in the troop movements that led to the Battle of Wimpfen, fought in early May 1622 near a small town of that name on the Neckar River. Alarmed by the numerical superiority of the opposing army commanded by Baden-Durlach, Tilly sent an urgent request to Don Gonzalo to join him. Don Gonzalo responded promptly, attacking Baden-Durlach unexpectedly. The Spanish attack was decisive; the Protestant army retreated soon afterwards in defeat.[68] Lope's Gonzalo de Córdoba correctly refers to heavy enemy losses. It should be added, however, that the Catholics too had many casualties, so many that Tilly was unable to pursue the retreating army.[69]

Although Lope devotes only a few lines to the Battle of Höchst, he conveys a vivid and accurate impression of a distinctive aspect of it, the slaughter of Protestant troops as they attempted to cross the Main River:

> . . . quedó degollada
> La infantería entre fuego
> Y agua, la margen del río.   (Ed. Acad. 13:130a)

The infantry was cut down between fire and water, on the bank of the river.

In this engagement, on June 20, 1622, Tilly's and Gonzalo de Córdoba's combined armies defeated Christian of Brunswick's large force of about 20,000 men, of whom more than half were casualties.[70]

Errors and omissions notwithstanding, Lope conveys a just

---

[67] Letter of Gonzalo de Córdoba to his wife, written May 7, 1622, the day after the battle. In CODOIN, 54:178–81.

[68] The duke of Bavaria, the employer of Tilly's army, wrote a letter of thanks to Don Gonzalo, May 13, 1622. In CODOIN, 54:184–85.

[69] See the Memoir of Tilly in the *Allgemeine Deutsche Biographie*, 38:321.

[70] *Allgemeine Deutsche Biographie*, 38: 322.

impression of the prosperous fortunes of the Catholic powers as they would have been perceived in Madrid when he completed his play in October 1622. Bohemia had been recovered; the Palatinate had been captured; Spanish and Imperial generals were winning battles.

After the respite in Act II, with Don Gonzalo's recollections of past victories to animate his men, Lope turns in his final act to the Battle of Fleurus. Don Gonzalo overtook Mansfeld and Brunswick on the southeasterly border of Brabant, fifteen miles from Brussels, at twilight on August 28. The battle began at dawn the following day and continued until almost noon.[71]

Lope includes few details about the battle, presumably because the information he had about it was limited. The opposing generals address their troops; the troops engage; Francisco de Ibarra is fatally wounded, exclaiming that he dies for the church and his king; Prince Christian is wounded. The stage battle ends abruptly, with the Spaniards heard shouting in victory. We learn little about the fate of the Protestants except that many were killed: 4,000 according to Lope's Mansfeld.[72]

Indeed, many of them were killed, more than of the Catholics. But the historical Battle of Fleurus ended indecisively, both sides claiming victory with some plausibility. The Spaniards claimed it because they inflicted heavy losses on a force that was numerically stronger and because they prevented a potential attack on Brussels. The Germans claimed it because despite their heavy losses they broke through the Spanish lines and ultimately reached their objective in the Netherlands. The survivors joined the army of Prince Maurice, providing

[71] See Gonzalo de Córdoba's letter written September 4, 1622, describing the battle: CODOIN, 54:307–10.

[72] Lope includes no reference to (and may not have known about) a sequel to the primary action of the morning of August 29. After sunset on that day, Don Gonzalo sent his cavalry in pursuit of the enemy. They found and killed all—or nearly all—the Protestant infantry and captured their artillery, munitions, and baggage (Gonzalo de Córdoba, Letter, [September 4], CODOIN, 54:308).

needed reenforcements. On October 2, the prince's army
forced Spínola to raise the siege of Bergen-op-Zoom.[73]

It is pointless now to try to say who won the Battle of Fleurus. Certainly the Spaniards fought gallantly. Lope's tribute to
them was deserved.

★

The brevity of the passages devoted to military action enables
Lope to place the campaign that provides his subject in its historical context. He employs his protagonist as his spokesman
in a retrospective account of the multinational war up to August 1622.

Don Gonzalo makes no reference to the occurrences in Bohemia in 1618 that led the Protestant nobility to reject Ferdinand, nor to their invitation to Frederick to accept the crown.
Don Gonzalo is silent as well about Spínola and the invasion of
the Palatinate, even though the historical Gonzalo de Córdoba
had served as his second-in-command until Spínola was sent to
the Netherlands. Lope could thus avoid a deflection of interest
from his protagonist and at the same time avoid reference to
events that could be interpreted as Catholic aggression.

Don Gonzalo establishes a secular reason consistent with
Spanish "just war" doctrine[74] for Spain's participation in the

---

[73] See Israel, *The Dutch Republic*, pp. 100–02. Israel refers to the Battle of
Fleurus as a Spanish victory, as Spaniards of the era, including Don Gonzalo
himself, regarded it. See Don Gonzalo's letter of September 4 describing the
battle, written on the day the infanta reviewed his troops: CODOIN, 54:307–10.
However, the nineteenth-century biographer of Mansfeld considered the victory his and furthermore believed that the reenforcements Mansfeld supplied
to Prince Maurice were decisive in the Dutch victory at Bergen-op-Zoom:
Ludwig Wolf Sigismund, Graf Ütterodt zu Scharffenberg, *Ernest Graf zu
Mansfeld, 1580–1626* (Gotha: F. A. Perthes, 1867), p. 513. This is implicitly the
interpretation of E. A. Beller, who refers to Wimpfen and Höchst, passes si-
lently over Fleurus, and states that the survivors of the Protestant army enabled Prince Maurice "to save the fortress of Bergen-op-Zoom from capture":
"The Thirty Years War," in *New Cambridge Modern History*, 4:316–17.

[74] See Bernice Hamilton, *Political Thought in Sixteenth-Century Spain: A
Study of the Political Ideas of Vitoria, De Soto, Suárez, and Molina* (Oxford: Clarendon Press, 1963), p. 140; and James Turner Johnson, *Ideology, Reason, and*

Thirty Years' War, though he comments on the difference in religion that separates his troops from their enemies. In his account, Frederick, the usurper of Ferdinand's crown, is the aggressor; Spain fights to repel usurpation. Don Gonzalo denounces Mansfeld. (The historical Mansfeld, although a brave and able general, was an unprincipled mercenary with a record of vacillation in allegiance. His troops, compelled to live by pillage, were notoriously destructive.)[75] Don Gonzalo contrasts the two sides: the Catholics are guided by religious faith; the "Lutherans" by greed, ambition, and heresy.

Don Gonzalo refers to the "Caesarean monarchy," meaning the Holy Roman or German empire. The phrase reminds us that Lope writes about a campaign in the German rather than in the Netherlands war, even though the climactic battle is fought not far from Brussels. The distinction between the wars cannot be sharp, as this play illustrates, though the pattern of military action differed from one to the other. After the Twelve Year Truce expired in the Netherlands, both sides occupied carefully fortified positions. Warfare largely took the form of sieges, and the opposing armies found it to their mutual advantage to refrain from attacks on noncombatants, from devastation of crops, and from pillage of captured strongholds.[76] The war in Germany, by contrast, was one of motion: fierce fighting at close range and devastation of large areas. Calderón's *El sitio de Bredá*, in which the besiegers starve the garrison out, exemplifies the war in the Low Countries; *La nueva victoria*, the war in Germany.

The Battle of Fleurus was given a place among the twelve victories that were commemorated by paintings placed in the

the *Limitation of War: Religious and Secular Concepts, 1200–1740* (Princeton: Princeton University Press, 1975), pp. 163–71, 205–06.

[75] The historical Gonzalo de Córdoba was not himself innocent of pillage. S. R. Gardiner describes the destruction wrought by his troops in the Lower Palatinate in the early summer of 1622. Gardiner notes, however, that Don Gonzalo's destruction, unlike Mansfeld's, stopped when his military objective had been attained (*History of England, 1603–1642*, 4 [1883], 321).

[76] Israel, *Dutch Republic and Hispanic World*, pp. 96–97.

new palace, the Buen Retiro, built in the 1630s.[77] The painting
of Fleurus, by the Italian artist Vicente Carducho, includes an
equestrian portrait of Don Gonzalo in the foreground and, on
a plain below him, the two armies engaged in battle, with col-
umns of infantry firing at one another at close range. Stylized
as a painting in the heroic idiom must be, it nevertheless captures the ferocity of Fleurus.

Lope's play like Carducho's painting should be regarded
as commemorative. Mansfeld and Brunswick's marauding
army, at large in the Spanish Netherlands, represented a threat
that required urgent action. Don Gonzalo responded to his orders promptly and with professional competence. The play
celebrates the gallant and successful completion of his mission.
Read without attention to the emergency to which he responded, the play can seem chauvinistic. Within its historical
context, its commemorative nature becomes apparent.

At the time of its first performance the play had also the
quality of a dramatic gazette.[78] In the nineteenth-century,
Franz Grillparzer commented on the near-contemporaneity of
the play and the historical events it depicts. He concluded several paragraphs of appreciative criticism of *La nueva victoria*
with an exclamation: "How remarkable that audiences of the
era could see enacted in colorful poetic drama events that were
taking place [almost] at the same time!"[79] The nature of the
play was conditioned by the haste in which Lope wrote and by
the incomplete information available to him about Don Gonzalo's campaign. Instead of a detailed portrayal of the Battle of
Fleurus, we have Don Gonzalo's retrospective account of
Spain's reasons for entering the war and his recollections of
Wimpfen and Höchst. There are gains as well as losses from
Lope's haste: along with the historical errors and awkward
omissions, we have an enlarged range of subjects including a

[77] Jonathan Brown and J. H. Elliott, *A Palace for a King: The Buen Retiro and
the Court of Philip IV* (New Haven: Yale University Press, 1980), p. 164.

[78] For informed comment on drama portraying very recent events, see Herbert Lindenberger, *Historical Drama*, pp. 20–21.

[79] Grillparzer, *Werke*, Part XIII ("Studien III: Zur Literatur"), ed. Stefan
Hock (Berlin: Deutsches Verlagshaus Bong, 1887), p. 234.

Spanish interpretation of the first phases of the Thirty Years' War. On balance, we can be pleased that Lope was willing to write journalistic drama without waiting until sources should become available that would enable him to write an accurate history play.

★

The protagonist of *La nueva victoria* explains—with historical accuracy—that the invasion of the Lower Palatinate was undertaken on behalf of the emperor. Yet the king of Spain and his ministers, knowing that their truce with the Dutch would soon expire, were aware that the region would acquire increased importance as a link in the military route to the Netherlands if war with the Dutch were resumed. At the time Spínola launched his attack, in August 1620, the peaceable Philip III still reigned, but Lerma had fallen and the war party had an influential spokesman on the Council of State, Don Baltasar de Zúñiga. Decision to renew the truce or resume war, of necessity bilateral in nature, had not yet been made either in Spain or in the United Provinces. In both countries much would depend on the individuals in power at the critical time, April 1621.

An English play, *Sir John van Oldenbarnevelt*, performed in London by the King's Men in August 1619, portrays events that determined who would make the decision for the Dutch: Maurice, prince of Orange, captain-general of the army, rather than Maurice in consultation with Oldenbarnevelt, who, for thirty years prior to his execution in May 1619, was his country's leading statesman.

In history, the trial and execution of Oldenbarnevelt were closely associated with the truce—with the negotiation of it, the impact of it in different parts of the republic, and the prospects for its renewal. Oldenbarnevelt had consistently favored the truce; Maurice had opposed it. The prince's concern lest the country be divided and weakened by dissension between the factions led by himself and by Oldenbarnevelt prompted him, it would appear, to take the actions that led to his opponent's death. Maurice's motive may have been patriotic; but the result bordered on judicial murder.[80]

The circumstances of the play's performance suggest its controversial nature. In a letter written from London, August 14, 1619, to the English ambassador at The Hague, a correspondent states that the players had made all preparations for bringing the play on stage only to be forbidden by the bishop of London to perform it. Yet on August 27 he wrote again to the ambassador: the "players have fownd the meanes to goe through with the play of Barnavelt, and it hath had many spectators and receaved applause."[81] It is not known how the players found the means to go forward. Although the Master of the Revels marked a number of passages for change or deletion, he licensed the play. The censors of the press apparently did not, with the result that it dropped out of sight until 1883 when A. H. Bullen published it from the manuscript prompt copy.

It is easy enough to understand why the play, which includes repeated reference to "the old Tirrany / that *Spaine* hath practisd"[82] in the Netherlands, should have been regarded as dangerous in 1619, a time when King James was pursuing his long-projected plan for a marital alliance with Spain. Furthermore, James disliked Oldenbarnevelt, having quarreled with him over the appointment to the University of Leiden of a professor, Conradus Vorstius, whose theological opinions James considered to be heretical.[83] Opposition on theological positions, dramatized in the play, became associated with the antagonism between Prince Maurice and Oldenbarnevelt: the former supported the Calvinist predestinarians; the latter, the Arminians, who were committed to the belief that all men

---

[80] Jan den Tex, *Oldenbarnevelt*, 2:664–66.

[81] Quoted from Gerald E. Bentley, *The Jacobean and Caroline Stage: Plays and Playwrights*, 3 (Oxford: Clarendon Press, 1956), 415.

[82] John Fletcher and Philip Massinger, *The Tragedy of Sir John Olden Barnavelt*, ed. Wilhelmina P. Frijlinck (Amsterdam: H. G. van Dorssen, 1922), p. 3 (1.i).

[83] Frederick Shriver, "Orthodoxy and Diplomacy: James I and the Vorstius Affair," *English Historical Review* 85 (1970): 449–74; Jan den Tex, *Oldenbarnevelt*, 2:526–33.

possess free will and may by their own good works achieve salvation.[84]

The play, attributed on internal evidence to Fletcher and Massinger,[85] is not without dramatic and—as propaganda—historical importance. Yet it is inadequate in depicting the stature and complexity of its protagonist; it is still more inadequate in representing the issues of national and European importance that led to Oldenbarnevelt's death.[86]

Despite his age and the honors that have come to him, the Oldenbarnevelt of the play remains ambitious and has become jealous of Maurice and resentful of what he regards as ingratitude to himself. "This ingrateful Cuntry," he exclaims (I.i.),

> shall first with horror
> know he that could defeat the Spanish counsailes,
> and countermyne their dark works, he that made
> the State what 'tis, will change it once againe
> ere fall with such dishonor.   (*Barnavelt*, ed. Frijlinck, p. 2)

He plans a rebellion against the prince. In his effort to win support he declares himself an Arminian, in defiance of the Calvinist Maurice; and he urges local autonomy of the provinces, again in opposition to Maurice, who supports the central authority of the States-General. He is easily overcome by the prince, veteran of many campaigns against the Spaniards, to whom the army and the English soldiers serving in the Low Countries remain loyal.

Maurice praises the Englishmen (IV.ii):

> I have sent Potents out for the choicest Companies
> hether to be remov'd: first Collonell *Veres*

[84] For the political implications in England of these theological positions, see Nicholas Tyacke, "Puritanism, Arminianism and Counter-Revolution," in *The Origins of the English Civil War*, ed. Conrad Russell (New York: Barnes and Noble, 1973), pp. 119–43; Peter White, "The Rise of Arminianism Reconsidered," *Past and Present* 101 (Nov. 1983): 34–54.

[85] *The Plays and Poems of Philip Massinger*, ed. Philip Edwards and Colin Gibson, 1 (Oxford: Clarendon Press, 1976), xx-xxi.

[86] On the sources used by the dramatists, see *Olden Barnavelt*, ed. Frijlinck, pp. xxiv–lviii.

from *Dort*, next Sr *Charles Morgans*, a stout company.
                              (*Barnavelt*, ed. Frijlinck, p. 52)

Both Sir Horace Vere (1565–1635) and Sir Charles Morgan
(1575?–1643?) had long served in the Dutch army. (Sir Charles
appears as a prominent character in *El sitio de Bredá*, Calderón's
play about the Spanish siege of that city in 1624 and 1625.)

Oldenbarnevelt is captured and tried. His eloquent defense
of himself, which merely glances at the offenses for which he
is on trial, assumes the form of a review of his career. Both his
defense and Maurice's rebuttal recall the years when they
worked together to unify the country and repulse the Spaniards. Oldenbarnevelt refers to embassies he has led to England and France: to Queen Elizabeth and King James and to
King Henry IV.[87] His defense, based in part on the historical
figure's *Apology*, suggests the heroic dimensions of his earlier
career. Found guilty and sentenced to die, he faces the executioner with dignity.

This is the dramatists' version of what led to Oldenbarnevelt's death, a version accurate in some details. But the representation of a revolt led by the old man is radically misleading.
Troops were raised in some of the industrial towns, but for the
purpose of preserving order at a time of unrest among artisans,
not for an attempt to overthrow the government or to undermine the authority of Prince Maurice as stadholder. The economic impact of the truce was variable from one region to
another, and variable too among occupational groups. Merchants in Amsterdam prospered from the removal of restraints
on foreign trade. But some of the common folk suffered. The
resumption of exports of grain to the Spanish Netherlands
raised the price that had to be paid for it by the Dutch. Furthermore, artisans in the manufacturing towns of the North
were forced into competition with those in Brabant and Flanders, whose industries were stimulated by the removal of the
Dutch naval blockades.[88] As early as 1610 occasional disturb-
ances occurred; by 1617 they had become serious enough in a

[87] Ibid., pp. 61–63.
[88] See Israel, *Dutch Republic and Hispanic World*, pp. 50–60.

number of the manufacturing towns for town councils, uncertain of the loyalty of their local militias, to employ professional soldiers to keep order.

Although there was ample precedent for the governing bodies of the towns to employ the soldiers,[89] doing so in this instance brought on a crisis. Maurice interpreted what was intended as a defensive measure to be grounds for intervention in the internal affairs of the province of Holland. In August 1618, he arrested Oldenbarnevelt. With troops to support him, he then travelled through the province and dismissed from the town councils those members who supported Oldenbarnevelt or Arminianism. Jonathan Israel describes Maurice's actions as a coup, adding that it was an attack not merely on a political faction, but also on the truce.[90]

Oldenbarnevelt illustrates the difficulty one encounters in evaluating an historical drama that is grossly inaccurate in authorial judgments as well as in factual detail.[91] Here is not merely rearrangement of time scheme, omission of irrelevancies, interpretation of characters about whom documentary evidence is inconsistent, but misrepresentation of a man, executed three months before the play was performed, who for over thirty years had been one of the most influential statesmen in Europe. Until Oldenbarnevelt and Maurice were alienated by the truce in 1609, the former, as civil leader of Holland, the

[89] Fletcher and Massinger, *Olden Barnavelt*, ed. Frijlinck, p. cxxviii.

[90] Israel, *Dutch Republic*, p. 62. For a comprehensive account of the circumstances leading to Oldenbarnevelt's arrest, see Jan den Tex, *Oldenbarnevelt*, 2:605–45.

[91] A corrective to the misrepresentation of Oldenbarnevelt's later career by Fletcher and Massinger may be found in a Dutch play by Joost van den Vondel, *Palamedes oft Vermoorde Onnooselheyd (Palamedes or Innocence Murdered)*, published in October 1625. For the transparent allegory used to cloak his audacious political matter, Vondel turned to an episode of the Trojan War recounted by Ovid in *Metamorphoses*, 13. Palamedes, the innocent man who is murdered, represents Oldenbarnevelt; Agamemnon, the Greek king responsible for his death, represents Maurice.

The play, with annotations, appears in Vondel, *De Volledige Werken*, ed. Hendrick C. Diferee, 1 (Amsterdam: Vennootschap Letteren en Kunst, 1910), 194–221. For comment on it, see W.A.P. Smit and P. Brachin, *Vondel, 1587–1679* (Paris: Librairie Marcel Didier, 1964), pp. 17–18.

wealthiest province in revolt, had supported the general, providing resources for his successful offensives in the 1590s and later. In partnership they had prepared the way for the achievements of Dutch civilization in the mid-seventeenth century. The historical Oldenbarnevelt was innocent of the charges of which he is accused in the play,[92] including the gravest of them—that of conspiring with Spain to overthrow the Republic.[93] His attitude toward the truce made him vulnerable to charges of collusion with the enemy; but his motives in favoring the truce, and even peace with Spain, were patriotic.

Historical inaccuracy in this play must be regarded as a fault.[94] We respond to *Oldenbarnevelt* with all our faculties and all our knowledge. Suspension of disbelief cannot be invoked on behalf of a play, accurate in many passages, that gains strength from the principal characters' references to events in the long Dutch war, including some in which Englishmen had a part.

It has been well suggested that the execution of Oldenbarnevelt, on stage, would have aroused memories of the execution the previous year of Sir Walter Ralegh.[95] In each instance a great patriot grown old, long a determined enemy of Spain, is executed by the leader of his nation. Both men could have been regarded as victims of judicial murder. Their experiences, however, were not closely parallel: James I, responsible for Ralegh's death, differed profoundly in his attitude toward Spain from Maurice; and Ralegh, unlike the Oldenbarnevelt of the play, was consistently heroic. But by play's end Oldenbarnevelt can be seen as essentially heroic throughout his career. His threat of restoring Spanish tyranny is best interpreted as an

[92] Fletcher and Massinger, *Olden Barnavelt*, ed. Frijlinck, p. 61.

[93] Jan den Tex, *Oldenbarnevelt*, 2:658–66.

[94] Attention to details Felix E. Schelling cited in support of his high praise of *Oldenbarnevelt* in 1910 suggests that evaluation of a history play about events in the recent past must take fidelity to the truth of history into account. Records of the era undermine Schelling's evaluation, which assumes that the play is historically accurate: *Elizabethan Drama, 1558–1642*, 1 (Boston and New York: Houghton Mifflin, 1910), 440.

[95] Bentley, *Jacobean and Caroline Stage*, 3:417.

expression of an old man's petulance. His defense of himself at his trial rests largely on reminding the court of his service to the country in opposing Spain. Neither he nor any other character expresses doubt that the rule of Spain was tyrannical and should have been resisted.

The death of the historical Oldenbarnevelt in May 1619 did not mean that the Dutch would necessarily refuse to renew the truce in April 1621. But it meant that they would be less likely to agree to terms for renewal which would be acceptable to the Spanish government. Much would depend upon who was appointed by the king of Spain to negotiate with Prince Maurice.

★

In 1619, in the interval between the beginning of the Thirty Years' War and the accession of King Philip IV, Gondomar and Francis Bacon, each perceiving the turn of events toward war, wrote analyses of their respective nation's military capabilities. Both men were acute and well-informed observers who, unlike the dramatists, had access to governmental sources of information. Their comments provide insight into the relative strengths of Spain and England at a time when war between the two countries began to seem a possibility.

When Bacon wrote "A Short View to be Taken of Great Britain and Spain" in the spring of 1619,[96] he was Lord Chancellor. Like Gondomar he was an elder statesman, a veteran of many years service to his government; like him, he possessed remarkable powers in the analysis of issues. It is not surprising that they reached a number of similar conclusions.

Bacon emphasizes the importance to England of her alliance with the Dutch, whom he describes as having the strongest navy in the world. He refers to Spain's naval weakness, the consequence, in his opinion, of the inadequacy in both numbers and ability of her seamen. Despite the truce, the nation's wealth has declined; overtaxation, Bacon writes, has taken its toll on revenues. Were it not for the shipments of treasure from

[96] The date is based on internal evidence alone. See Bacon, *Works*, ed. Spedding et al., 14:22.

America, which he believes have diminished, the king of Spain
would be the poorest sovereign in Europe. He cannot afford to
maintain the garrisons needed to defend his widely separated
dominions. Because of England's improved position in Ireland, she is less vulnerable to Spanish attack than previously:
Ireland is no longer a "back-door . . . open in the assistance of
our enemies."[97]

Bacon's analysis of Spain's weaknesses resembles Gondomar's in its tenor and some of its details. The ambassador's
statement, in a letter to Philip III, March 28, 1619, includes an
unflinching account of problems both in the administration of
government and in foreign relations.[98] Reading his pungent
criticism, we wonder how Olivares succeeded two years later
in mounting the offensive that came to a climax in 1625.[99]

Gondomar provides detail about conditions in Spain that
give force to the description of the nation as "decadent," referring to "the loss of population, the poverty, and the suffering
in the Spain of today."[100] He attributes these conditions to
overtaxation. But he writes as a diplomat concerned with
Spain's relations with foreign powers rather than as a human-
itarian. The perilous condition of the German empire can have
grave consequences. If Catholic control of the empire should
be lost, the king of England, in Gondomar's opinion, would
throw over negotiations for a marital alliance with Spain and
enter the conflict on the Protestant side. In assessing European
politics, Gondomar, like generations of Spanish diplomats before him, gives emphasis to France and England. France is im-
mobilized by internal dissension, but if her domestic affairs
permitted, he writes, France would stir up opposition to Spain
as she has always done, "more than the heretics themselves."[101]
The potential enemies with which he is chiefly concerned are

---

[97] Ibid., 14:23.

[98] The letter is printed in DIE, 2 (1943), 131–47.

[99] Gondomar was but one of many in Spain who advocated reform before
1621. See John H. Elliott, "El movimiento reformista en Castilla al adveni-
miento de Felipe IV," in *Felipe IV: Historia*, 25:335–42.

[100] Gondomar, in DIE, 2:135.

[101] Ibid., 2:133.

England and the United Provinces, both with large navies manned by experienced seamen.

He addresses two major issues that will soon require decision: the expiration of the truce and the projected English marriage. Although he does not overtly recommend renegotiating the truce or forwarding the marital alliance, nevertheless Gondomar, by his references to the wealth and the strength of both the Dutch and the English and his pessimistic analysis of conditions in Spain, implies that to do so would be advantageous. Spain is surrounded by enemies, one of them France, a major power and potentially a grave threat. The course of events in the German empire is unpredictable and ominous. Spain, it would seem to follow from his exposition, should avoid war if its aims can be achieved by diplomacy and by a diplomatic marriage. Yet he is aware that the English marriage probably will not take place and that Spain's "deception" of the English king cannot be continued for long.[102]

Gondomar criticizes the leaders of government with an audacity that would not have been tolerated in the Spain of the king's father nor in the England of Queen Elizabeth or King James. That he could do so suggests the strength the movement for reform had gained by 1619.

★

When Philip III died, on March 31, 1621, Philip IV, his sixteen-year-old heir, at once appointed a new chief minister, Baltasar de Zúñiga, who was the uncle of the count of Olivares. The truce expired within days of Philip IV's accession, and final decision, on the Spanish side, to renew it, to attempt to negotiate terms, or to resume war fell to Zúñiga—or, more likely, to Zúñiga in consultation with Olivares.[103] Despite his own doubts that total victory over the Dutch could be achieved, Zúñiga chose to resume the war.[104] Olivares too be-

---

[102] Ibid., 2:141.

[103] On relations between uncle and nephew, see John H. Elliott, *Felipe IV: Historia*, 25:343.

[104] See Israel, *Dutch Republic*, pp. 70–71, 84–85.

lieved that war should be resumed. Already a trusted friend and advisor of Philip IV, Olivares succeeded his uncle as *privado* when Zúñiga died on October 7, 1622; and for over twenty years Olivares, from 1625 the "count-duke," shaped Spanish policy.[105] Utterly different from Lerma, Olivares was a militant adherent of the Castilian imperial tradition.

★

The decision to resume the Dutch war, after the nation had already entered the war in Germany, seemed to Tirso de Molina an act of folly. Spain's resources were overstrained, its people overtaxed. An economic depression exacerbated by a plague of locusts and crop failures intensified the ills of those who would now be called upon to supply men and money to support the Army of Flanders.[106] Tirso expressed his opinions on these matters in a remarkable history play, *La prudencia en la mujer*,[107] which is, among other things, a satirical commentary on the court of Philip IV at the beginning of his reign. Through a comparative examination of the play and problems confronting Spain in 1621 and 1622, Ruth Lee Kennedy has demonstrated that Tirso completed it about the summer of 1622 with the intention of providing in it

> a *de regimine principum* in dramatic form. It is but one of the various mirrors for princes that were written with Philip IV in mind—done in this case by a man who was, for various reasons, deeply hostile to the new regime and its guiding forces.[108]

The play, though aimed at seventeenth-century problems, portrays medieval Spain; Tirso follows with fidelity his

[105] On the institutional aspects of the position of *privado*, see Carter, *The Secret Diplomacy of the Habsburgs*, pp. 67–71; and Francisco Tomás y Valiente, *Los validos en la monarquía española del siglo XVII* (Madrid: Siglo Ventiuno Editores, 1982).

[106] On the condition of Spain at the time the truce expired, see J. H. Elliott, *The Revolt of the Catalans: A Study in the Decline of Spain (1598–1640)* (Cambridge: Cambridge University Press, 1963), pp. 182–93.

[107] It is often described as the best "historical drama" of the Spanish Golden Age. See Ruth L. Kennedy, "*La Prudencia en la mujer*," p. 1131 and n. 1.

[108] Ibid., pp. 1131–90.

sources, the chronicle of King Fernando IV of Castile (1295–1312) and Mariana's *History*.[109] In his first two acts, Tirso portrays the heroic and successful effort of María de Molina, mother of the child-king Fernando IV and regent of Castile and León, to defend and preserve the kingdom for her son until he reaches maturity. She repels self-interested flatterers, detects corrupt officials in her court who have stolen royal funds, thwarts an attempt to poison her son. In all this she is the epitome of a *prudent* ruler, an example to whom a young king could look for guidance.

In the opening scene of the final act, María de Molina resigns her authority as regent to Fernando, who has reached the age of seventeen. (Philip IV reached that age on April 8, 1622.) On leaving him she offers advice on how he should conduct himself as king—advice relevant to the conduct of Philip IV (III.i):

> *Nunca os dejéis gobernar*
> *de privados, de manera*
> *que salgáis de vuestra esfera,*
> *ni les lleguéis tanto a dar*
> *que se arrojen de tal modo*
> *al cebo del interés,*
> *que os fuercen, hijo, despúes*
> *a que se lo quitéis todo.*   (Ed. Blanca de los Ríos 3:936b)

Never allow yourself to be led by *privados* in such a manner that you abandon your own authority. Do not be so liberal with them that they throw themselves at the bait of self-interest, forcing you later, my son, to take away from them all they have acquired.

Be equally generous with all the great nobles, she counsels him, so that no one should have cause to complain. Remember the old friends of the royal house; attend the sessions of the Cortes.

---

[109] On Tirso's sources, see Tirso, *La prudencia en la mujer*, ed. Alice Huntington Bushee and Lorna Lavery Stafford (Mexico, D. F.: Mexico City College Press, 1948), pp. xxiii–xxxv; and Tirso, *Obras dramáticas completas*, ed. Blanca de los Ríos, 3 (Madrid: Aguilar, 1958), 893–98. Tirso introduces only a single episode anachronistically taken from an account of a later reign.

In her advice at parting with her son, she counsels him to give attention to his troops (III.i):

Sea por vos estimada
la milicia en vuestra tierra,
porque más vence en la guerra
el amor que no la espada.   (Ed. Blanca de los Ríos 3:936b)

You must honor the soldiers of your country, for in war love conquers more than the sword.

She has earlier revealed her concern for the soldiers. Her remarks in reply to their commander's proposal that she levy new taxes have relevance to the Spain of 1621 and 1622. When she refuses, referring to the poverty of the people, the commander answers that without money the soldiers, who are guarding the frontiers against the Moors, will not fight. She explains her refusal in a metaphor taken from farming (II.v):

Ni hay tampoco huerta agora,
por más fértil que la vean,
que dé fruto a cada hora.
Cada año una vez le echa:
no le pidáis cada instante;
que descansada aprovecha,
y los vasallos, Infante,
también tienen su cosecha.   (Ed. Blanca de los Ríos 3:923b)

There is no garden, however fertile it may appear, that bears fruit every hour. It yields [its crop] once each year: do not make demands of it every moment, for it gains strength from rest. And subjects also, my Prince, have their harvest time.

But the troops must be paid. One town alone remains of the property that made up her dowry. Let that be sold, she tells the commander, who answers that the sale will yield money to pay the soldiers' wages for a year. (Tirso would seem to suggest an alternative means by which the government could raise money.)

María de Molina has scarcely left her son before he acts contrary to her advice. Just as Philip IV, Zúñiga, and Olivares moved swiftly to discharge from office and in some instances to punish severely Philip III's principal officers, Fernando, acting on the advice of his evil uncle, Don Juan (who earlier had attempted to usurp his throne), imprisons three loyal noblemen who in a time of urgent need had enabled his mother to retain control of León. Don Juan, having become his *privado*, arouses his suspicions toward those who had been most loyal to him. He requires even his mother to give an accounting of royal funds. He dismisses the Cortes so that he may go hunting.

All this bears a chilling resemblance to the Spain of 1621-1622—the Spain called upon to provide men and money for a major Spanish offensive. The war for the Palatinate continued at heavy expense. A maritime war with the Dutch to protect Spanish and Portuguese colonies in the East and West Indies had to be sustained.[110] Yet King Philip, in July 1621, sent 900,000 ducats to Antwerp and informed Albert that 300,000 ducats would be sent each month for the support of the Army of Flanders.[111] (Albert died in July; his widow, the infanta Isabel, remained as ruler of the Spanish Netherlands, no longer as titular sovereign, but as governess.)

★

Philip Massinger resembles Tirso in his audacity, in his willingness to examine within the medium of drama what he regards as important issues, even when the issues are sensitive politically. He includes in *The Maid of Honour* (*c.* 1621–1622) a passage that should be read as comment on King James's alleged failure to assist Prince Frederick in regaining the Palatinate; in *The Bondman* (1623) he portrays situations that should be interpreted as comment on England's unpreparedness for war; and in *Believe As You List* (1631) he creates a protagonist resembling Prince Frederick, one who is a royal exile suffering from the neglect of his natural allies and from the persecution of a powerful state—nominally the Rome of antiquity, intended to be identified as the Spain of Massinger's time. To be

---

[110] See Lynch, *Spain under the Habsburgs*, 2:76–77.
[111] Israel, *Dutch Republic*, p. 85.

sure, the political interpretation of Massinger's plays remains, in some respects, controversial; but the differences in opinion turn largely on details. His political audacity can be documented in records kept by the Master of the Revels.[112]

Since 1876, when S. R. Gardiner published a paper on "The Political Element in Massinger,"[113] critics of the dramatist have attempted to determine how much of what appears to be political comment in his plays was in fact so intended by the dramatist; how much the result of overingenious projection of meaning that is foreign to the dramatist's intention. Gardiner wrote that in several plays "Massinger treated of the events of the day under a disguise hardly less thin than that which shows off the figures in the caricatures of Aristophanes or the cartoons of *Punch*."[114] Asserting that Massinger wrote with the political bias of the Herberts (William, earl of Pembroke, and his brother Philip, earl of Montgomery), Gardiner describes what he assumes to be the political burden of *The Maid of Honour*, *The Bondman*, and *Believe As You List*.[115] Massinger's father had been in the service of the Herbert family, and Lord Montgomery, if not his older brother, seems to have assumed the role of the dramatist's patron.[116] The larger number of critics who have written about the plays have in varying measures accepted Gardiner's argument, with the qualification that Massinger's plays bear the impress of his literary sources as well as of political affairs. But there has been dissent by authorities whose opinions compel consideration.

Massinger's latest editors, Philip Edwards and Colin Gibson, are skeptical. About *The Maid of Honour*, which with good reason they date 1621–1622 (a decade before the date assumed by Gardiner), they assert that "The impartiality with

[112] *Dramatic Records of Herbert*, ed. Adams, pp. 19, 33 n. 4.

[113] *The New Shakespere Society's Transactions*, 1875–76, pp. 314–31. (First published in the *Contemporary Review*, August 1876, pp. 495–507.)

[114] Ibid., p. 316.

[115] In addition, Gardiner found in *The Great Duke of Florence* what he took to be glancing allusions to persons and events, notably a passage (v.ii) that can be interpreted as critical of James's lavish grants of honors and titles to Buckingham. Gardiner, "Political Element in Massinger," pp. 319–20.

[116] Thomas A. Dunn, *Philip Massinger: The Man and the Playwright* (London: Thomas Nelson and Sons, 1957), pp. 21–24.

which Massinger handles the motives and responses of the personalities, the expediency of the proposals, and the principles involved, make the idea that he was conducting political propaganda an absurdity."[117] If we substitute "commenting on political affairs" for "conducting political propaganda" and look closely at the play with attention to the preoccupations of well-informed Englishmen in 1621 and 1622, a political reading of portions of it becomes a necessity, I believe, rather than an "absurdity." The editors are less dogmatic in rejecting a political interpretation of certain passages in *The Bondman* (licensed December 3, 1623).[118] And in writing about *Believe As You List* (licensed 1631),[119] although they object reasonably enough to an interpretation of the play as systematic allegory, they agree with other critics "that the playwright was at least willing to exploit English sympathy for the fortunes of Frederick."[120]

Earlier, G. E. Bentley wrote aptly about the political aspect of Massinger's plays:

> Perhaps Massinger did have in an unusual degree the tendency common to most playwrights to see historic scenes in terms of his own time and country; but that he was so forgetful of his own social position and that of the actors as to presume to "make suggestions" to the King, as if he were writing an editorial in a modern newspaper, I cannot imagine. If in *The Bondman* he hinted at popular objections to certain royal policies or royal favourites (as in the apparent suggestion of Buckingham in 1.i; . . .), he can scarcely have done more than titillate the knowledgeable. Any consistent and obvious attack on powerful persons and their policies . . . would have been too easily stopped by a word from James or Buckingham to the Master of the Revels.[121]

This provides an accurate account of what we find when we read the plays with a knowledge of English history in the 1620s and 1630s. Massinger did indeed "have in an unusual degree

---

[117] *Massinger*, ed. Edwards and Gibson, 1:105–06.

[118] Ibid., 1:303; Bentley, *Jacobean and Caroline Stage*, 4:766.

[119] Bentley, *Jacobean and Caroline Stage*, 4:762.

[120] *Massinger*, ed. Edwards and Gibson, 3:298.

[121] Bentley, *Jacobean and Caroline Stage*, 4:769. See also Bentley, "Regulation and Censorship," in his *Profession of Dramatist*, pp. 145–96.

the tendency . . . to see historic scenes in terms of his own time and country."

Although Gardiner believed that *The Maid of Honour* was written nine or ten years later than 1621–1622, the date now regarded as probable,[122] he associated it with events of 1620. Recalling James's disapproval of Frederick's acceptance of the crown of Bohemia, we encounter in *The Maid of Honour* (1.i) a conversation between the king of Sicily and an ambassador sent to him by the duke of Urbino. The ambassador speaks:

> Your Majesty
> Hath beene long since familiar, I doubt not,
> With the desperate fortunes of my Lord, and pitty
> Of the much that your confederate hath suffer'd
> (You being his last refuge) may perswade you
> Not alone to compassionate, but to lend
> Your royall aydes to stay him in his fall
> To certaine ruine. Hee too late is conscious,
> That his ambition to incroach upon
> His neighbours territories, with the danger of
> His liberty, nay his life, hath brought in question
> His owne inheritance.   (Ed. Edwards and Gibson 1:125)

The king replies that the duke's misfortunes are a just retribution for his act of aggression. The king's account of the terms of his alliance with the duke, Gardiner writes, is an "exact description of the interpretation put by James upon the treaty which bound him to the Princes of the Union" of Protestant German States.[123] "The league proclaim'd between us," the king says,

> Bound neither of us farther then to ayde
> Each other, if by forraigne force invaded,
> And so farre in my honour I was tied.
>   (Ed. Edwards and Gibson 1:126)

He justifies his policy by reference to the welfare of his subjects; he wishes to be known as "the father of our people."

[122] Gardiner, "Political Element," p. 320.
[123] Ibid., p. 327.

The applicability of this passage to James's response to his son-in-law's urgent need for military assistance seems inescapable. Yet in reading it, one can also understand Edwards and Gibson's observation that in the play Massinger portrays impartially "motives and responses" of characters who make expedient and principled proposals.[124] We may interpret this passage in isolation as politically neutral, as expressing neither approval nor disapproval of King James's attitude toward Frederick, but we can scarcely refuse to recognize the relevance of the passage to Frederick's plight. An English audience of 1621 or 1622, knowing that Catholic powers had seized the patrimony of Princess Elizabeth's husband, would have provided their own interpretation of the "King of Sicily's" response to the ambassador.

The Maid of Honour exemplifies Massinger's method of commenting on affairs of state. He does not write sustained and consistent allegory. Rather, he establishes parallels that enable his audiences to recognize similarities to historical persons and events. But instead of maintaining the parallels he dissolves them in the fictions of the play.[125]

★

The historical King James I made a more vigorous effort to regain the Palatinate for Frederick than would appear from the contemporary drama. The improved understanding of James that has come in the last twenty-five years enables us to perceive more clearly the difficulties that confronted him and to understand more fully the reasons for his actions in his efforts to aid Frederick.[126] From the end of 1621, at least, he knew that an effort to regain the Palatinate by force of arms would meet

[124] *Massinger*, ed. Edwards and Gibson, 1:106.

[125] A century later John Gay in *The Beggar's Opera* employed a similar method in commenting on political affairs. See John Loftis, *The Politics of Drama in Augustan England* (Oxford: Clarendon Press, 1963), pp. 94–95.

[126] See Marc L. Schwarz, "James I and the Historians: Toward a Reconsideration," *Journal of British Studies* 13 (1974): 114–34; and Maurice Lee, Jr., "James I and the Historians: Not a Bad King After All?" *Albion* 16 (1984): 151–63.

Chapter Five

PRINCE CHARLES'S SPANISH COURTSHIP

AND THE PALATINATE

Carlos Estuardo soy	I am Charles Stuart, who, with
Que, siendo amor mi quía,	love as my guide, comes to the
Al ciel de España voy,	heaven of Spain to see my star,
Por ver mi estrella María.	María.

Sometimes attributed to LOPE DE VEGA

C HARLES'S and Buckingham's journey to Madrid, incognito and on horseback, in March 1623, came as the climax to James I's protracted negotiations for a Spanish match. Made precipitously and with the king's reluctant permission, the journey must be interpreted with attention to the English effort to restore the Palatinate to Frederick. The earl of Bristol (Digby), in Madrid as a special ambassador, had been sending reports to James of Philip's willingness to proceed with the royal marriage and to assist the English in procuring the restitution of Frederick's territories. Yet, events in Germany, where Catholic troops were consolidating their conquest of the Palatinate, seemed to belie the Spanish promises.[1] Both James and Charles, the latter influenced by his desire to marry the infanta, wanted to believe Bristol's reports. In fact, however, Charles and Buckingham arrived in Madrid in pursuit of impossible objectives. The Spanish court in which they were received was that which Tirso had satirically depicted the year before in *La prudencia en la mujer*. Olivares ruled the seventeen-year-old Philip IV as well as the nation, and he brought the king to his own opinion: that there should be no change in Spanish policy and no marriage.

In any event, in March 1623, concession by Spain on the Palatinate—to the English the more important issue—was im-

---

[1] Lockyer, *Buckingham*, pp. 125–35.

possible. A Spanish army had indeed invaded the territory in 1620 and Spanish troops continued to occupy a portion of it. But the Palatinate was in the empire, and in February 1623, the emperor had deposed Frederick and conferred his electorate on Maximilian, duke of Bavaria. The emperor had taken this action, of doubtful constitutionality, despite the objections of most of the princes of Germany and even of King Philip IV. The duke, the ruler of a large and wealthy state, employed and commanded the mercenary army of the Catholic League, which now occupied a major part of the Palatinate. This army gave Maximilian a power that Olivares as well as the emperor had to acknowledge. Confronted by Maximilian's overwhelming military strength, Ferdinand could not deny him the electorate.[2]

On December 8, 1622, Olivares addressed a *memorial* to King Philip, in which he described the insurmountable difficulties inherent in an effort to return Frederick's inherited lands to him.[3] The document reveals that Olivares was well informed about King James's motives in the marriage negotiations. Gondomar had returned to Spain the preceding year and had no doubt given full reports to the king's chief minister. The English king, Olivares writes, has two closely related objectives: one, to arrange a Catholic marriage for his heir; the other, and to James the more important, to secure the restitution of the Palatinate. Charles's marriage to the infanta would assure his father of the allegiance of English Catholics and

[2] Wedgwood, *The Thirty Years War*, pp. 158–63.

[3] The *memorial* is included in the count of La Roca's *Fragmentos históricos de la vida de d. Gaspar de Guzmán, Conde de Olivares, Duque de S. Lúcar la Mayor*, written with the authorization of Olivares in 1627 and 1628. Olivares made documents from his personal files available to Roca. First published in Antonio Valladares de Sotomayor, ed., *Semanario Erudito*, 2 (Madrid: Imprenta . . . de Alfonso López, 1787), 145–296. The *memorial* appears on pp. 193–96. Reprinted in translation, with minor variations, in F. Francisco de Jesús, *Narrative of the Spanish Marriage Treaty* [1629], ed. and trans. Samuel Rawson Gardiner, 101 (Camden Society: 1869), 192–96.

On Roca's biography, see Olivares, *Memoriales y cartas del Conde Duque de Olivares*, ed. John H. Elliott and José F. de la Peña, 1 (Madrid: Ediciones Alfaguara, 1970), 5–6; hereafter referred to as Olivares, *Memoriales*.

crypto-Catholics, and it would give the Stuarts an alliance with the Habsburgs. King James, Olivares writes, has even stronger reasons to seek the return of Frederick's patrimony, for along with considerations of prestige goes a concern for the welfare of his grandchildren.

Olivares describes the nature of the negotiations with England carried on in Philip III's reign. It was never the intention of that king, he writes, that there be a marriage unless the prince should become a Catholic. However, Philip III prolonged consideration of the subject to keep the friendship of the English king, which was advantageous to Spain when the wars in Flanders and Germany were in the uncertain state of that time. Friendship with England remains desirable, Olivares adds, saying that he believes King Philip shares Philip III's opinions on the subject. The infanta refuses to marry Prince Charles; she has resolved to enter a convent if her brother presses her to do so. Although he opposes a marital alliance, Olivares wishes to avoid giving offense to the English.[4]

These then were the thoughts of the most influential man in Spain not long before Charles and Buckingham arrived in Madrid unexpectedly on March 7/17, 1623. Most Spaniards were at first delighted by the turn of events, assuming that Charles would not have come unless he intended to announce his conversion to Catholicism as a preliminary to marriage. And they assumed that his conversion signaled the beginning of the end of heresy in England and an alignment of the nation with Spain and against the other Protestant powers of northern Europe. Luis de Góngora and Antonio de Mendoza, among other poets, expressed the joy Charles's arrival occasioned.[5]

---

[4] In the *memorial* Olivares suggests alternative marital alliances that could in time achieve King James's objectives. Let Prince Charles marry the elder daughter of the emperor Ferdinand (who, he and King Philip have learned from the imperial ambassador, would welcome the marriage). And let the heir of Prince Frederick marry the emperor's second daughter. (The grant of the electorate to the duke of Bavaria was limited to his lifetime.) The problem of Frederick's patrimony could thus be resolved in the following generation. See Roca, *Fragmentos históricos*, p. 196.

[5] On the Spanish literary response to the event, see Carl Justi, "Die span-

Góngora wrote a sonnet (Number 52), "Undosa tumba da al farol del día." In this poem, which turns on an identification of María with the sun and with Venus, Charles comes seeking beauty so intense that only a royal eagle can gaze upon it. The metaphors lead to the expression of a hope that their chaste love will rekindle the divine light of the true faith in the North.[6] Mendoza wrote *décimas* (ultimately published in 1631 following María's marriage to a Habsburg king), addressed "To the Queen of Hungary, When the Prince of Wales Was in Madrid." Again the poem expresses hope, confident hope, that the projected marriage will lead to a return of England to Catholicism. Mendoza refers to the appropriateness of the infanta's name.

> *No en vano la Iglesia os fía*
> *de redimir el oficio,*
> *que tan glorioso ejercicio*
> *empieza siempre en María.*[7]

The Church entrusts you, not in vain, with the task of liberation, for such glorious employments always begin with a Mary.

The intensity of devotion to Catholicism revealed in these poems suggests the inevitability of failure in Charles's mission. Yet despite its disastrous effect on diplomatic relations, the prince's six-month sojourn in Spain had the consequence of introducing the prince himself and other prominent Englishmen who joined him in Madrid to Spanish court ceremonies and dramatic entertainments. Charles had only a limited knowledge of Spanish, a circumstance that conditioned the entertainment provided for him, primarily dances and elaborate spectacles.[8] Not all the performances he saw were secular: with

---

ische Brautfahrt Carl Stuarts im Jahre 1623," in his *Miscellaneen aus drei Jahrhunderten spanischen Kunstlebens*, 2 (Berlin: G. Grote, 1908), 310–18.

[6] Luis de Góngora, *Sonetos completos*, ed. Biruté Ciplijauskaité, 5th edn. (Madrid: Editorial Castalia, 1982), p. 117.

[7] *Obras poéticas de don Antonio de Mendoza*, ed. Rafael Benítez Claros, 1 (Madrid: Gráficas Ultra, 1945), 249–50.

[8] A number of pamphlets published in both Spain and England describe the entertainments. See, for example, *A True Relation . . . of The Manner of The Arrivall, and Magnificent Entertainment, given to the . . . Prince Charles . . . at Madrid* (London: 1623) (B.L., G.6174).

the king and queen, he sat at a window of the palace as Corpus Christi plays were performed in an adjacent square. Along with other Englishmen, he saw plays of a nature not performed in England since the Reformation. Knowing that the prince and other "English heretics" were watching, the players staged these religious dramas with unprecedented magnificence.[9]

The accounts of the entertainments provided for the prince are too numerous and repetitious to be described at length. Reference to one, a description of a spectacle on a mythological subject, will suggest the frivolity of many of them. The earl of Bristol acted as interpreter for the prince. The events depicted are not inappropriately compared to "The famous actions of *Amadís de Gaule*, and *Lisuart* of great Britany," as the following passage from a "cartell" will reveal:

> The Knight of the Forrests who is tied by the order of his Knighthood, to travell over the mountaines, and trace wild biests, serving the great Prince of both the Spaines, to make knowne, that in the rusticity of the Country, there is found the Courtly urbanity of Love.[10]

The incongruity of such performances with the harsh reality of the Thirty Years' War, in which Charles was unwillingly playing the role of a pawn, must have become apparent to him.

★

Like other Spaniards, Olivares assumed from Charles's unexpected arrival that he had been converted.[11] In one of his first

<hr />

[9] [F. Pedro de la Hoz], *Noticias de Madrid, 1621–1627*, ed. González Palencia, pp. 63, 65. Reference from Shergold, *History of the Spanish Stage*, p. 433 and n. 2.

Accounts of the prince's journey published in English pamphlets do not, as far as I have been able to determine, mention the Corpus Christi plays.

[10] Andrés de Mendoza, *Two Royal Entertainments, Lately Given to . . . Charles, Prince of Great Britaine . . . Translated* (London: 1623), p. 15 (B.L., 643.C.68).

[11] Lockyer, *Buckingham*, p. 143; Roca, *Olivares*, pp. 197–98. Roca provides an account of Charles's sojourn in Madrid as it was perceived by the *privado*: *Olivares*, pp. 196–214. The most detailed and informative of the Spanish accounts is that of Father Francisco de Jesús, *El hecho de los tratados del matrimonio*

conversations with Buckingham, Olivares spoke of proceeding with the marriage without waiting for the papal dispensation, only to learn from Buckingham's response that nothing had changed. Since Olivares had not altered in his opposition to the marriage except on condition that Charles become a Catholic, he then purposely contrived delays in the negotiations, believing that frustration, reinforced by religious instruction, could lead the prince to a conversion. He sent a messenger to Rome, requesting that the dispensation be withheld, but it had already been granted and could not be changed. However, in response to his request, the conditions for its delivery by the papal nuncio in Madrid were made more stringent: rather than merely a suspension of the penal laws affecting English Catholics, which King James was prepared to grant, full freedom of conscience for them was required.[12] This was a demand that the English Parliament would not have accepted.

The events of the months that followed, and the persons having the principal roles in them, give the English sojourn in Spain the aspect of a medieval morality play, with the two *privados*, Buckingham and Olivares, contending for the soul of Charles, and with Olivares offering the beautiful infanta as a reward for the prince's conversion to Catholicism. Charles was indeed tempted, as the Spaniards perceived, and they intensified their efforts to convert him. In April, Charles heard Philip IV's confessor argue the Catholic position, though with Buckingham present to remind him of his duty.[13]

Charles did not yield, and negotiations remained at an impasse. In May his position assumed a more ominous aspect:

---

pretendido por el Príncipe de Gales con la sereníssima Infanta de España María, written in 1629. It was first published, in Spanish with an English translation (*Narrative of the Spanish Marriage Treaty*), by Gardiner in the 1869 Camden Society edition.

[12] Lockyer, *Buckingham*, pp. 140–44. In much of my discussion of events in Madrid, I am indebted to Lockyer's well-documented account of them: pp. 140–65.

[13] Buckingham created a disturbance to break up Charles's meeting with the priest: Francisco de Jesús, *Spanish Marriage Treaty*, p. 211.

when Charles requested permission from King Philip to return to England so that he might personally discuss the required concessions to Catholics with his father, he was told, May 24/June 3, he could not leave. Father Francisco de Jesús is unambiguous on this subject—important for understanding Charles's and Buckingham's subsequent actions—though the priest mentions a promise Charles had earlier made to Philip IV to remain in Madrid until he, Charles, could communicate with his father and receive his orders.[14] With good reason Charles felt himself to be imprisoned.[15]

Spanish members of Charles's staff while he resided in Philip IV's palace apparently recognized his ambiguous position as both honored guest and royal prisoner. This is implied by Luis Vélez de Guevara in an autobiographical sonnet entitled "Luis Vélez, When He Was Made Door Keeper to the Prince of Wales."[16] Vélez's self-mocking tone, topical allusions, and colloquialisms combine to make the poem difficult to understand. Yet if his precise meaning in certain lines is open to question, his reference to himself as the Cerberus of the prince and his use of words associated with prisons can scarcely be irrelevant to Charles's position in the summer of 1623. The sonnet merits close attention:

> Luis Vélez, cuando le hicieron portero del de Gales
>
> ¡Cancerbero del Príncipe de Gales!
> ¿En qué pecó mi padre ni mi agüelo?
> ¡Aquí del Conde de Olivares, cielo,
> Que me como de herejes garrafales!
>   Don Gaspar de Guzmán, si no me vales,
> A los catorce artículos apelo
> Y en el martirologio tomo un suelo
> Que caiga el calendario en las canales.

---

[14] Ibid., p. 241

[15] Charles's anxiety would have been intensified if he knew that in the reign of Philip II, the Spaniards had taken captive the eldest son of William I of Orange and had held him prisoner in Spain for many years.

[16] The sonnet was printed for the first time by Francisco Rodríguez Marín: "Cinco poesías autobiográficas de Luis Vélez de Guevara," *Revista de Archivos, Bibliotecas y Museos*, 3rd ser., 12 (June to Dec., 1908): 67.

Yo alargo la cadena á pinta y presa,
Que es lo que ha de venir del hospedaje,
Aunque Meneses pierda la interpresa.

  No tengo á nitis brut *por buen lenguaje;*
Sáqueme Dios desta empanada inglesa
Y deme para España buen viaje.

Luis Vélez, When He Was Made Door Keeper to the Prince of Wales

  Cerberus of the Prince of Wales!
What was the sin of my father or my grandfather [which merits this punishment]? May the count of Olivares help me, heavens, for I'm being eaten up by enormous heretics.

  Don Gaspar de Guzmán, if you don't help me, I shall appeal to the fourteen articles [of the marriage treaty].[17] And I'll take a position in the book of martyrs when the calendar hits the dog days [dog days?].

  I lengthen the [prisoner's] chain in this card game of captives,[18] for that's what this hospitality will result in, even though Meneses[19] loses his enterprise.

  I don't consider *nitis brut* [no (good) rascal?][20] proper language; may the Lord get me out of this English meat pie,[21] and favor my return trip to Spain.[22]

---

[17] A junta of theologians on September 5/15, 1617, formulated fourteen "necessary concessions with which it will be possible to treat for the marriage." See Francisco de Jesús, *Spanish Marriage Treaty*, pp. 298–303.

[18] Vélez presumably refers to the game of cards "pinta y presa" because of the meaning of *presa* as "prisoner."

[19] Meneses was Francisco de Meneses, another member of the prince's palace staff (Rodríguez Marín, "Cinco poesías," pp. 67–68).

[20] These syllables sound more like German than English. Their context suggests, however, that they are an approximation of a term of disparagement used by the prince or some other Englishman.

[21] The Spanish word *empanada* ("meat pie") has a figurative and an adjectival meaning, both of which contribute to its connotations: figuratively, it refers to the "action and effect of concealing [something in] or fraudulently complicating a transaction"; as an adjective, the word is used to describe "an apartment of a house that is surrounded by other rooms [or apartments] and that does not have direct light or ventilation" (*Dictionary of the Royal Academy of Spain*, 20th edn. [1984]).

Gardiner refers to the quarters given the prince: "The rooms assigned to the Prince in the royal palace were few and small, and it had been arranged that his

If the poem existed in isolation from other evidence that Charles was—temporarily, at least—a prisoner, its apparent meaning might be doubted. In fact, however, there is corroboration by the prince himself,[23] by John Chamberlain, and even by Father Francisco.

When the Spaniards refused Charles's request to confer with his father, they suggested that he send Buckingham to do so: they knew that the English *privado*, as they called him, was a barrier to the prince's conversion.[24] Instead, Charles sent his secretary, Sir Francis Cottington, to inform his father of his altered position. John Chamberlain conveys a sense of the urgency felt in England on Cottington's arrival. "Till yesterday," Chamberlain wrote, June 14/24, "we had no newes out of

[English] attendants should sleep at the other end of the town, with the evident intention of making their stay as inconvenient as possible" (Gardiner, *History of England, 1603–1642*, 5 [1883], 43).

[22] I gratefully acknowledge Professor Willard F. King's assistance in my effort to translate this difficult sonnet. Much of the language is hers, though she admits to extreme dubiety about the translation of ll. 7–11. The conjectural portions of the translation are my own. I alone am responsible for any mistakes there may be.

[23] Charles's state of mind late in June (o.s.) is suggested by a message he sent his father. Lockyer describes it. Charles told King James "that he was still a virtual prisoner," and asked "for permission 'to depart from Madrid as secretly as he came thither,' if he was not allowed to leave of his own free will. Should this attempt fail, he urged James to think no more about him, but to 'reflect . . . upon the good of his sister [Elizabeth] and the safety of his own kingdoms'" (*Buckingham*, p. 157).

[24] His faults of character and errors in judgment in other situations notwithstanding, Buckingham seems to have served King James and Prince Charles well during the months he spent in Madrid.

While there he received a letter from John Donne, in which the dean of St. Paul's, by cautious indirection, warns him not to be deceived by the Spaniards. Donne approaches the subject of his letter by praising Spanish intellectual achievement: "I can thus far make myselfe beleeve, that I ame where yor Lordship is, in Spaine, that in my poore Library, where indeed I ame, I can turne mine Ey towards no shelfe, in any profession, from the Mistresse of my youth, Poetry, to the wyfe of mine age, Divinity, but that I meet more Autors of that nation, than of any other. Their autors in Divinity, though they do not show us the best way to heaven, yet they thinke they doe. . . ." For the letter in full and comment on it, see R. C. Bald, *John Donne: A Life* (New York and Oxford: Oxford University Press, 1970), pp. 446–47.

Spaine this moneth or five weekes, for the King had found a way to have advertisement thence without notice of anybody the packets beeing sent to our ambassador in Fraunce. . . . But now Sir Fraunces Cottington and Greisly are come together. . . ."[25] He wrote again on July 26/August 5: "The Lords of the counsaile were sent for to Tiballs the 16th of this moneth, to be made acquainted with the articles concerning the Spanish match, where (yt is saide) there was some sticking upon points of religion . . . ; but yt was aunswered that yt was not now to be disputed what was of convenience but what of necessitie the Prince beeing in their hands, and the Kings children [Frederick and Elizabeth] dispoyled of their patrimony. . . ." Chamberlain adds that several days later the king at Whitehall, in the presence of the Spanish ambassador, "tooke his oath to observe all the articles agreed upon."[26] In August, when the Spanish ambassador's message that James had sworn the oath required for delivery of the dispensation reached Madrid,[27] negotiations could move to the final stage.

Despite all, Charles seemingly still wished to marry the infanta and take her home with him. King Philip determined otherwise. The couple were formally betrothed and were to be married within ten days after the arrival from Rome of the pope's "approbation." (The "approbation" was required because Pope Gregory XV, who had given the dispensation, had died and been succeeded by Pope Urban VIII.) However, María was not to accompany Charles to England (unless he would remain in Madrid until Christmas) but was to follow him there in the spring of 1624.[28] Resisting the Spaniards' attempt to persuade him to remain while Buckingham returned to England, Charles prepared to leave on August 29/September 8. He and King Philip took oaths to observe the articles of marriage agreed on, and Charles gave the earl of Bristol a doc-

---

[25] *The Letters of John Chamberlain*, ed. Norman Egbert McClure, 2 (Philadelphia: The American Philosophical Society, 1939), 503.

[26] Ibid., 2:509–10.

[27] Lockyer, *Buckingham*, p. 161.

[28] Francisco de Jesús, *Spanish Marriage Treaty*, p. 248.

ument, valid until Christmas, authorizing him to proceed with the marriage by proxy.[29]

Nothing was said in the articles or the oaths about the restitution of the Palatinate. Charles had indeed discussed the subject with Olivares, who had told him the blunt truth: that the duke of Bavaria would relinquish neither the electoral title nor Frederick's former territories.[30] Charles still did not understand the military realities of central Europe. He overestimated both the influence of the king of Spain with the emperor and the power of the emperor—had he been so disposed—to force a decision on the duke of Bavaria.

But Charles had learned that Spanish ministers of state were not to be trusted, and he remembered that he had promised his sister not to marry María unless Frederick were restored to his former position in the Palatinate. Presumably, considerations such as these, among others, led him to a maneuver that had the effect of preventing his marriage to the infanta. While en route northwards to the coast where he was to board ship for the voyage home, he sent a servant back to Madrid with instructions to remain at Lord Bristol's house until he learned that the pope's approbation for the marriage had arrived. At that time the servant was to give Bristol a letter from the prince ordering him not to proceed with the marriage until he had obtained assurance that María would not enter a convent after her marriage to him by proxy. The letter required Bristol to communicate with Charles in England before authorizing the marriage, a requirement that ensured the prince of time to change his mind after talking with his father.[31]

★

[29] Lockyer, *Buckingham*, pp. 162–63.

[30] Ibid., p. 162.

[31] Gardiner prints the letter: *History of England, 1603–1642*, 5:118. Gardiner attributes the letter to Charles's desire "to take revenge for the slights which he had received": Ibid., 5:119. Yet the "slights" had included denial of Charles's request to return to England to consult his father about concessions to Catholics that Charles knew could not be granted.

Charles's state of mind on leaving Spain was such that there was little chance of his marrying the infanta. Soon after his return to England, he supported Buckingham in denouncing the treaties he had signed—under duress—in Madrid and even in urging war with Spain. King James agreed to break the treaties, but he did not break diplomatic relations. Sir Walter Aston, the resident ambassador, remained in Madrid, though the earl of Bristol, the special ambassador, came home. The king's primary objective in foreign policy was the restoration of the Palatinate, and if Philip IV would not or could not help him reach that goal, James hoped at least to separate Philip from the emperor, thus reducing the difficulty of regaining Frederick's inherited lands, even if force was required.[32]

When James summoned the Parliament of 1624, one of his reasons for doing so was to use it as a bargaining chip in his negotiations with Philip.[33] In March of 1624 the Parliament voted supplies for a war against Spain. Unlike the House of Commons of 1621, that of the current Parliament was without firm conviction on the issue. Some members were understandably perplexed by the division between the king, who opposed war, and his heir. But the prince and the duke, in alliance with the House of Lords, prevailed, and the House of Commons somewhat reluctantly voted the needed subsidies.[34] Yet James remained king, in control of foreign policy, and he refused to make war on Spain.

Before the year was out, an army of some twelve thousand men, ill-trained, many of them new conscripts, and under the command of the German mercenary, the count of Mansfeld, was mustered to be sent for service in the Palatinate. James insisted that they be used only there, not against the Spaniards in the Netherlands. By January this foredoomed expeditionary force had been transported to the Continent, suffering heavy casualties from shipwreck during the winter voyage and later

[32] Robert E. Ruigh, *The Parliament of 1624: Politics and Foreign Policy* (Cambridge, Mass.: Harvard University Press, 1971), pp. 386–87.

[33] Ibid., p. 384.

[34] Conrad Russell, *Parliaments and English Politics, 1621–1629* (Oxford: Clarendon Press, 1979), pp. 189–90.

from disease and starvation. It was not until after King Charles succeeded his father in March that Mansfeld led some of the survivors to the besieged Dutch city of Breda.[35]

★

The jubilation expressed by Londoners at Charles's return without a Spanish bride is legendary. It found expression in drama. So also did popular resentment of King James's inability to give effective aid to his son-in-law.

For a time Parliament and leading members of the court were allied in distrust and resentment of Spain. During this period of unity, Jonson and Inigo Jones prepared a masque celebrating Charles's safe return, *Neptune's Triumph for the Return of Albion*, intending it for performance at court on Twelfth Night, 1623/24. Although a quarto edition of it was printed bearing a statement that it was "celebrated" as intended, the masque was not in fact performed because of a dispute over precedence between the Spanish and the French ambassadors. A year later, however, Jonson revised its central scene, using it in *The Fortunate Isles and Their Union*, the last Twelfth Night masque of James's reign.[36]

Attention to *Neptune's Triumph* reveals that Jonson was well informed about Prince Charles's journey to Madrid. The poet, speaking the argument in the opening scene, explains that Neptune—King James in Jonson's allegory—recently sent Albion (Charles), with Hippius and Proteus (Buckingham and Cottington) as companions, on a journey of "discovery" through *Celtiberia* (that is, through France to Spain). A need to discover the Spaniards' true intentions in the protracted negotiations for a marital alliance was indeed one of the motives that led Buckingham, and perhaps Charles as well, to undertake the journey.[37] (In Middleton's *Game at Chess*, written later in 1624, discovery of the Spaniards' intentions again provides the motive for the journey.) The reason for Buckingham's

---

[35] Gardiner, *History of England, 1603–1642*, 5:323.

[36] Graham Parry, *The Golden Age restor'd*, p. 55.

[37] Buckingham's motives are better known than Charles's: see Lockyer, *Buckingham*, p. 140.

prominence in the masque is obvious; that for Cottington's
prominence and his role of "divine *Proteus*, Father of disguise,"
is not. His mythological name may have been prompted by episodes such as his posing as the "master" on the outward journey when there was danger from bandits, Charles and Buckingham riding before him as his "servants." He knew the
language and customs of Spain well, having lived there upwards of ten years as a member of the embassy staff. At the
time of the journey, he was secretary to the prince, who sent
him back to London with the confidential message to King
James about the true nature of affairs in Madrid.[38]

Jonson refers to the Spaniard's efforts to prolong Charles's
residence in Madrid and to convert him to Catholicism:

> . . . what the arts were, usde to make him stay,
> And how the *Syrens* woo'd him, by the way,
> What Monsters he encountred on the coast,
> How neare our generall Joy was to be lost,
> Is not our subject now.[39]

The mythological reference to sirens tempting Charles gains
force when we recall that marriage to the infanta María would
have been his reward for becoming a Catholic. The prince's
sojourn in Madrid (which resulted in the frustration of King
James's long-held desire for an alliance with Spain) is not the
poet's subject; rather, the subject—appropriate for a celebration—is the deliverance of Charles from very real danger and
his safe return to England. In the masque the squadron that
brings Charles and his retinue home is represented as a moving
cloud.

Comment on the journey to Madrid is subordinate to the
pervasive tone of rejoicing that the prince had made discovery
of Spanish intentions without succumbing to Spanish guile.
King James, as Neptune, rules as the champion of peace.[40]

---

[38] Stephen Orgel notes that Cottington "had served as a secret agent": *The
Illusion of Power: Political Theater in the English Renaissance* (Berkeley: University of California Press, 1975), p. 72.

[39] *Ben Jonson*, ed. Herford, Percy and Evelyn Simpson, 7:686.

[40] Three recent critical studies of *Neptune's Triumph* elucidate its significance

In February 1626 Jonson cautiously and merely by innuendo referred again to Charles's courtship of the infanta. His *The Staple of News*, performed by the King's Men, is a moral allegory about the power of money to corrupt individuals and institutions. Yet the play glances at the courtship. The subject was sensitive, requiring caution. It has been well argued that Jonson planned the play some four years before its performance, at a time when the Spanish match was an intensely controversial subject, but delayed the completion of it until the time for performance was propitious.[41] In a masque of 1621, *News from the New World*, Jonson describes briefly a plan for a Staple of News—that is, an organization for gathering and disseminating foreign and domestic news. In writing *The Staple of News*, he drew on many of his earlier plays and masques, but on no other so fully as the masque he wrote for Twelfth Night, 1623/24, *Neptune's Triumph*.[42] When *The Staple of News* was performed, first in public and then at court, the Spanish adventure was safely in the past and the prince was king, married to a French princess. Although the subject still required delicate treatment, Charles's Spanish courtship could be a subject of indirect reference.

A character in the play is identified in the *dramatis personae* as "Pecunia, *Infanta of the* Mynes." She is described in I.vi as a "*Cornish* Gentlewoman" and hence ostensibly infanta of the tin mines of Cornwall. But both in I.vi and in the Second Intermean she is called Aurelia Clara Pecunia, names which resemble not those of María but of her aunt, Isabel Clara Eugenia, daughter of Philip II and, at the time of the play,

---

as an expression of James's conception of himself as king and peacemaker: Orgel, *The Illusion of Power* (1975), pp. 70–77; Parry, *The Golden Age restor'd* (1981), pp. 55–56; and Jonathan Goldberg, *James I and the Politics of Literature: Jonson, Shakespeare, Donne, and Their Contemporaries* (Baltimore: Johns Hopkins University Press, 1983), pp. 71–72.

[41] Jonson, *The Staple of News*, ed. De Winter (New York: Henry Holt, 1905), pp. xviii–xx. Quotations from the play follow *Ben Jonson*, ed. Herford, Percy and Evelyn Simpson, 6 (1938).

[42] De Winter, op. cit., pp. xxxiii.

governess of the Spanish Netherlands.[43] With the Spanish general Spínola, she had planned the siege of Breda, captured in 1625, after heroic resistance in which English and Scots had taken part. Jonson seemingly intended the infanta of the play to be associated with both aunt and niece, the former long one of the most prominent women in Europe.[44] In early 1626 England and Spain were at war, in part at least because of Charles's and Buckingham's resentment of the treatment they had received in Madrid. The allusions to Gondomar and to Middleton's *A Game at Chess* (III.ii) of 1624, known to all as a satirical review of the climactic events in the negotiations for a Spanish match, imply that Jonson had the niece as well as the aunt in view. The heiress of the play, personifying money and its power to corrupt, pursued by many suitors, resembles the infanta María just as her three names bring to mind the governess of the Spanish Netherlands.[45]

Since 1616 Jonson had received a pension granted by King James "in consideracion of the good and aceptable service done and to be done unto us." The "service" to which the king referred was primarily the writing of court masques.[46] Thereafter Jonson would have been disinclined to oppose the king's policies.

★

Other dramatists were more audacious, though all of them had to take into account the official censorship by the Master of the Revels. Plays were performed that reveal attitudes criti-

---

[43] See De Winter's note on lines 26–27 of the Second Intermean, "in the styling her Infanta, and giving her three names": De Winter, op. cit., pp. 172–74.

[44] In the French succession crisis that followed Henry III's death, she had been her father's choice to become France's sovereign; Catholic propagandists had asserted her claim to the English throne in succession to Queen Elizabeth; before her husband's death without heir in 1621, she had been sovereign of the Spanish Netherlands for over twenty years.

[45] Lope devotes the final scene of *La nueva victoria de Don Gonzalo de Córdoba* to Isabel's review of the Spanish troops after the battle of Fleurus. The title character refers to the infanta as "La divina Isabel Eugenia Clara" (Ed. Acad., 13:143a).

[46] Bentley, *Jacobean and Caroline Stage*, 4:609. Quotation from Bentley.

cal of the crown's policies: in addition to Middleton's *A Game at Chess* and several plays by Massinger, other plays with political voltage appeared. Most of them were acted in the popular outdoor theatres, such as the Red Bull and the Fortune, rather than in the fashionable indoor theatres, the Blackfriars and the Phoenix. Some have not survived, if indeed they were ever published, and are known only from records of censorship, suppression, or prosecution of offending persons.[47] Some of the surviving plays are quasi-literary in quality: *The Duchess of Suffolk*, for example, and *Albertus Wallenstein*.

The Master of the Revels licensed *The Duchess of Suffolk*, January 2, 1623/4, writing in his office book that the play "being full of dangerous matter was much reformed by me; I had two pounds for my pains: Written by Mr. Drew."[48] The author was perhaps the actor Thomas Drew.[49] Herbert charged twice his usual fee for licensing, a circumstance confirming his statement that he made substantial revisions. Not published until 1631, the play as it has survived may incorporate Herbert's revisions: it is impossible to determine.[50]

The play portrays the sufferings of the duchess during the Marian persecutions. She is forced to flee for her life, first in England and later on the Continent, pursued by agents of the Counter-Reformation. The "dangerous matter" to which Herbert referred is presumably the intense anti-Catholicism that permeates the play. It would have had political meaning a few months after Prince Charles returned from Spain. An episode in which the duchess is saved by the palsgrave (the elector Palatine) might well have put the audience in mind of the misfortunes of Frederick's wife, the titular queen of Bohemia.[51]

Henry Glapthorne's *Albertus Wallenstein*, acted at the Globe at some time between 1634 and 1639,[52] carries a political bur-

---

[47] Heinemann, *Puritanism and Theatre*, pp. 200–36.

[48] *Herbert*, ed. Adams, p. 27.

[49] Bentley, *Jacobean and Caroline Stage*, 3:280–81.

[50] Heinemann, *Puritanism and Theatre*, p. 209.

[51] Ibid., pp. 205–09.

[52] Bentley, *Jacobean and Caroline Stage*, 4:478. The topicality of the play would suggest an early date between these limits.

den in the restricted sense that it would have appealed to the widely held sympathies in England for the Protestants engaged in the war in Germany. The play is inadequate to its subject: the events leading to the death of the overwhelmingly successful, though unpredictable general, Wallenstein. Nominally in the service of the emperor Ferdinand, Wallenstein commanded the imperial army in the Battle of Lützen, November 6, 1632, in which the Protestant hero, King Gustavus Adolphus of Sweden, was killed. Subsequently, however, Ferdinand, who had reason to doubt Wallenstein's loyalty, sent soldiers to kill him. In the play he is murdered on stage.[53]

★

Not long after Prince Charles and Buckingham returned from Madrid urging war with Spain, Sir Henry Herbert licensed a new play by Massinger in which there are passages that can—I think, should—be read as comment on England's unpreparedness for war. *The Bondman: An Ancient Story*[54] has a locale in the Syracuse of antiquity, which is threatened by Carthage.

---

[53] The vicissitudes of Wallenstein's career were of intense interest in Spain. Both Lope and Calderón, the latter in collaboration with Coello, wrote *comedias* about events in Wallenstein's career. Neither play survives (presumably because Wallenstein disappointed Habsburg expectations of him and died in disgrace), though contemporary reports of performances of both plays provide insight into their natures. On Lope's *La muerte del rey de Suecia*, which Philip IV and Olivares saw in a public theatre, January 26, 1633, see Brown and Elliott, *A Palace for a King*, pp. 63 and 263, n. 40. On Calderón and Coello's play about Wallenstein, performed in Madrid early in 1634, see Václav Černý, "Wallenstein, héros d'un drame de Calderón," pp. 179–90.

In a surviving *auto sacramental* (*c.* 1634) by Alvaro Cubillo de Aragón, *La muerte de Frislán*, Wallenstein (duke of Friesland) has the role of *El Demonio*. See the edition prepared by Marie France Schmidt (Kassel: Edition Reichenberger, 1984).

La muerte de Frislán—and Spanish attitudes toward Wallenstein at different times—are well described in a critical study of Cubillo by Shirley B. Whitaker, *The Dramatic Works of Alvaro Cubillo de Aragón* (Chapel Hill: University of North Carolina, Department of Romance Languages, 1975), pp. 159–65. (I am indebted to Professor Whitaker for calling my attention to the Spanish plays on the subject and for providing information about them.)

[54] Licensed December 3, 1623: Bentley, *Jacobean and Caroline Stage*, 4:766.

Having no competent leader of their own, the Syracusans have turned to their ally Corinth for assistance. Archidamas, the Syracusan "*Pretor*," speaks (i.iii):

> So carelesse we have beene, my noble Lords,
> In the disposing of our owne affaires,
> And ignorant in the Art of government,
> That now we need a stranger to instruct us.
> Yet we are happy, that our neighbour *Corinth*
> (Pittying the unjust gripe *Carthage* would lay
> On *Siracusa*) hath vouchsafed to lend us
> Her man of men *Timoleon* to defend
> Our Country, and our Liberties. (Ed. Edwards and Gibson 1:319)

Archidamas regrets the shame implicit in his country's inability to "produce / One fit to be our Generall," even though Syracuse is "a populous Nation, / Ingag'd to liberall nature, for all blessings / An Iland can bring forth."[55] In addressing the senate upon assuming his command, Timoleon rebukes the Syracusans for preferring private profit to the public good. "Yet in this plenty" (i.iii), he adds,

> And fat of peace, your young men ne're were train'd
> In Martiall discipline, and your ships unrig'd,
> Rot in the harbour.   (Ed. Edwards and Gibson 1:325)

The criticism of the Syracusan navy had an obvious relevance to that of England. The disrepair into which the fleet had fallen would become apparent in the autumn of 1625, when Sir Edward Cecil led an ineffectual attack on Cádiz.[56]

Massinger also wrote other plays that can be associated with the English response to the Spanish invasion of the Palatinate: *The Maid of Honour* and *Believe As You List*. Yet at least one of his plays, *The Renegado*, and arguably two others, *The Virgin Martyr* (written with Dekker) and *The Maid of Honour*, reveal a veneration for the ceremonies and uses of Catholicism so

---

[55] Massinger, *Plays and Poems*, ed. Edwards and Gibson, 1:319.

[56] On the deterioration of the navy, see Menna Prestwich, *Cranfield: Politics and Profits under the Early Stuarts* (Oxford: Clarendon Press, 1966), pp. 211–19; Lockyer, *Buckingham*, pp. 273, 284.

strong as to imply that he, if not himself a Catholic, was sympathetic to the faith.[57] It would seem that in Massinger's mind Spain and Catholicism were not necessarily associated.

Massinger's audacity, veneration for Catholicism, and originality of mind are particularly revealed in *The Renegado*, which was licensed in April 1624,[58] only a month after the House of Commons had voted supplies for a war against Spain. The play is based on writings by Cervantes, principally on his play, *Los baños de Argel*,[59] about the experiences of a group of Christians who are held as slaves by the Moors of North Africa. With the ministrations and guidance of a saintly Jesuit priest, Francisco, they withstand their captors' oppression and make an escape by sea. Massinger, like Cervantes before him, emphasizes Christian and specifically Catholic piety and fortitude. The Jesuit priest controls much of the action. With his counsel and the holy relic he has given her, Pauline (a beautiful young woman) withstands attempted seduction and rape by her Muslim owner. The priest's admonitions transform her brother, Vitelli, from a worldly young man into a devout Christian, willing to die a martyr's death and possessing an eloquence sufficient to convert the sultan's niece, Donusa. When both of them face imminent death, Vitelli, although a layman, baptizes Donusa. She experiences a religious ecstacy. A pirate, Grimaldi, after having confessed his sins to Francisco and undergone a period of penitence, is transformed in a St. Paul-like conversion; the sin that had most deeply troubled him was a calculated act of sacrilege, committed at the altar of St. Mark's in Venice on a holy day.

---

[57] Massinger's modern biographer, T. A. Dunn, comments on his religious beliefs: "While I have inclined more to the view that Massinger had Roman Catholic sympathies, probably to the degree of being a Romanist, the question is still arguable. What does seem to emerge quite clearly from the plays is that, Anglican or Roman Catholic, Massinger had a respectful tolerance in matters of faith rare in his century" (Dunn, *Philip Massinger*, p. 191).

On the subject, see also Louise George Clubb, "*The Virgin Martyr* and the *Tragedia Sacra*," *RD* 7 (1964): 103–26; and Peter F. Mullany, "Religion in Massinger's *The Maid of Honour*," *RD*, n.s., 2 (1969): 143–56.

[58] Licensed April 17, 1624: Bentley, *Jacobean and Caroline Stage*, 4:812.

[59] See below, Appendix.

All this is surprising indeed to find in a play performed in the spring of 1624, a year when England was preparing for war against Spain. Massinger presumably wrote the play not long after Prince Charles returned from Madrid without the dreaded Spanish bride, to be greeted by public celebrations. We must wonder how Massinger's patron, the earl of Montgomery, a Protestant,[60] responded to *The Renegado*. Massinger's play provides a reminder that there was some measure of religious toleration in England.

Believe As You List, although performed in the following decade (1631),[61] should be considered with other plays by Massinger. The most audacious politically of those that survive,[62] it did not pass the Master of the Revels' reading in its original form. It was then a play based on the story of Don Sebastian of Portugal, who, in the midsummer of 1578, led an expeditionary force on a crusade into Morocco. In a battle at Alcacer-el-Kebir, his army, made up of many of Portugal's most able men, was lost, and he was killed. But Massinger—like Dryden in *Don Sebastian* (1689), the best play in English on the subject—uses a poet's license in assuming that the king survived. The historical consequence for Portugal of losing not only its foolhardy king but so many of its leading men was a fierce contention for the crown. Philip II, who along with others had a dynastic claim, settled the matter in 1580 by annexing Portugal. A play based on this sequence of events could have been interpreted as an accusation that a Spanish king usurped a kingdom—Frederick's Palatinate represented by Sebastian's Portugal—and that King Charles abetted the usur-

---

[60] See Heinemann, *Puritanism and Theatre*, pp. 167–68, 214–15.

[61] Licensed May 6, 1631: Bentley, *Jacobean and Caroline Stage*, 4:762.

[62] His *The King and the Subject* (1638) may have been even bolder. King Charles himself read the play in manuscript and marked a passage, about a king's raising money by unconstitutional means, for deletion. Sir Henry Herbert describes the episode, noting "that the poett makes it the speech of . . . Don Pedro, king of Spayne. . . ." After requiring this omission and other changes including an alteration of the title, Herbert licensed it. The play is not known to have survived, but because the title was changed, it may exist without having been identified as Massinger's: *Herbert*, ed. Adams, pp. 22–23; Bentley, *Jacobean and Caroline Stage*, 4:794–96.

pation.[63] In the autumn of 1630 Charles had signed a peace treaty with Philip IV that did not require the restitution of the electorate. English interest in the fate of Frederick was heightened in 1630 by Gustavus Adolphus's entry into the German war. The Swedish king had stated that he intended to restore the Palatinate to him.[64]

Massinger revised his play, replacing Don Sebastian as protagonist with Antiochus of Syria, finding in the fortunes of Antiochus (and also of Hannibal after his defeat) unhistorical parallels with those of the Portuguese king.[65] In history, Don Sebastian was killed in the Battle of Alcacer-el-Kebir; in a legend about him upon which Massinger drew, he survived and vainly attempted to regain his kingdom.[66]

"The Sebastian cult . . . ," Philip Edwards writes, "has been one of the most long-lived versions of the myth of the 'sleeping hero' ": the myth, that is, that a hero from a nation's past (in England, King Arthur, for one) would return, drive out corrupt leaders, and restore the standard of conduct that had made the nation great. In an illuminating essay on *Believe As You List* and John Ford's *Perkin Warbeck*, Edwards suggests that the royal pretenders in the two plays, both of them embodiments of kingly virtue, provide a studied contrast with the reigning sovereign, Charles I. In this reading, the idealized Antiochus of Massinger's play provides a cautious reminder of the personal inadequacies of Charles and of the failures of his government, among them his alleged neglect of his dispossessed brother-in-law, Frederick.[67]

---

[63] Massinger, *Believe As You List*, ed. Charles J. Sisson (Malone Society Reprint: 1927), p. xviii.

[64] Wedgwood, *Thirty Years War*, p. 277.

[65] On the revisions, see Sisson's Malone Society reprint, pp. v–xxvi, and *Plays and Poems*, ed. Edwards and Gibson, 3:293–94.

[66] On the sources, see *Plays and Poems*, ed. Edwards and Gibson, 3:294–97. This should be supplemented by David Bradley, "A Major Source of Massinger's *Believe As You List* (1631)," *Notes and Queries*, n.s., 29 (1982): 20–22. (The source is Edward Grimeston's translation and continuation of Louis Turquet de Mayerne's *The Generall Historie of Spaine* [1612].)

[67] Edwards, "The Royal Pretenders in Massinger and Ford," *Essays and Studies*, n.s. 27 (1974): 18–36 (quotation on pp. 35–36).

To some extent Massinger found parallels between the experiences of Antiochus and Frederick. In a prologue of unknown authorship, we are invited to see resemblances between the wanderings of Antiochus and those of Frederick. The speaker asks pardon for the author's ignorance of cosmography,

> . . . yf you finde what'e Roman here,
> *Grecian*, or *Asiaticqe*, drawe to nere
> a late, & sad example.[68]

The interpretative problem turns on how closely we choose to see Antiochus's experiences as an allegorical comment on Frederick's. An association of the Rome of the play (the persecutor of Antiochus) with Spain (the persecutor of Frederick) is inevitable. But the detailed commentary on contemporary history that Gardiner found,[69] in which—among other correspondences—the king and queen of Bithnia represent Charles I and Henrietta Maria, is needlessly specific. Massinger would not have ventured the disrespectful portrayal of the sovereign and his consort these correspondences entail. He made his point in subtler fashion.

★

Thomas Middleton, in one play at least, was even more audacious than Massinger. His *A Game at Chess* (August 1624) is the boldest political play that appeared on the London stage before 1642, and perhaps the only play of the era that caused a foreign ambassador to threaten to leave the country. The Spanish victories of 1625 were in the future when Middleton wrote his play, but he and other Englishmen knew by the preceding year that the accession of King Philip IV and the rise to power of the count of Olivares—the count-duke from January 1625—marked the beginning of a new era in Spanish affairs.

In the third act of *A Game at Chess*, the Black Knight, a character representing the count of Gondomar, refers in soliloquy

[68] Massinger, *Plays and Poems*, ed. Edwards and Gibson, 3:305.
[69] Gardiner, "Political Element in Massinger," pp. 320–25.

to what contemporary Protestant propagandists call the Spanish master plan to attain a "universal monarchy" (III.i.80–84):

> But let me a little solace my designs
> With the remembrance of some brave ones past
> To cherish the futurity of project
> Whose motion must be restless, till that great work
> Called the possession of the world be ours.[70]

The character describes the aspect of Spanish policy that most deeply troubled Englishmen: the Spanish desire for territorial aggrandizement.

"The possession of the world," a universal monarchy: the phrases, reminiscent of Sir Epicure Mammon's, are so grandiose that to a modern reader they are likely to seem empty hyperbole, having little relationship to the historical reality of Spain in 1624. Yet however extravagant the Black Knight's reference to a "great work / Called the possession of the world" may now seem, Middleton in 1624 had reason to fear Spain's master plan to achieve, if not a universal monarchy, then world hegemony.

Neither the Spanish ambassador nor any other well-informed person who saw, read, or heard about the play, performed by the King's company at the Globe nine times consecutively beginning August 6, 1624, could fail to know that it was vehemently hostile to Spain and the Catholic church. They would have known as well that it included reference to Prince Charles's recent journey to Madrid and a harsh portrayal of Gondomar. No earlier play had achieved a longer run nor had attracted more comment. Structured as a game of chess with the rules of the game modified to serve satirical ends,[71] the play remains entertaining despite its burden of topical allusion. An understanding of the primary thrust of Middleton's allegory, embodied in the main plot, requires only such knowledge of recent events as his audiences were likely to

[70] Middleton, *A Game at Chess*, ed. J. W. Harper (New York: Hill and Wang, 1967), p. 44. All quotations from the play will follow this edition.

[71] Paul Yachnin, "*A Game at Chess* and Chess Allegory," *SEL* 22 (1982): 317–30.

have had or as a modern editor can easily supply. The pawns' allegory, comprising the underplot, now seems obscure; perhaps it did not seem so to contemporaries. It may include reference to Frederick's loss of the Palatinate.[72]

The unprecedented success of the play owed much to its timeliness. Performed in the interval between March 1624, when Parliament voted supplies for a war against Spain, and the commencement of hostilities in October (o.s.) 1625, it appeared at a time when the nation was united in attitude toward Spain. In writing his dialogue, Middleton drew upon the anti-Spanish propaganda of Protestant pamphleteers.

Middleton wrote the play quickly. One of his important sources, Thomas Scot's *The Second Part of Vox Populi*, was not published until May 1624.[73] Even so, he interpolated later passages, perhaps in the interval between licensing and performance: nearly two months, June 12 to August 6. He made important changes after the impeachment in April 1624 of Lionel Cranfield, earl of Middlesex, who as lord treasurer had been alone among the lords of the Privy Council in opposing the recommendations of Charles and Buckingham for war with Spain. Middlesex knew what the financial consequences would be. An early manuscript of the play includes neither the lines that associate the treacherous White King's Pawn with Middlesex (III.i.266–68) nor the role of the Fat Bishop, who is a caricature of Marco Antonio de Dominis, archbishop of Spalatro.[74]

In retrospect it seems surprising that the play was performed. Why, we may ask, did Herbert license it despite its representation of modern Christian sovereigns (disguised as chessmen, to be sure), one of whom was King James himself?

---

[72] On this subject, see Middleton, *A Game at Chesse*, ed. R. C. Bald (Cambridge: Cambridge University Press, 1929), pp. 12–13 and 13n; *A Game at Chess*, ed. Harper, p. xiv. For a recent interpretation of the underplot see Jane Sherman, "The Pawns' Allegory in Middleton's *A Game at Chesse*," *RES*, n.s., 29 (1978): 147–59.

[73] Heinemann, *Puritanism and Theatre*, p. 158.

[74] R. C. Bald, "An Early Version of Middleton's 'Game at Chesse,' " *MLR* 38 (1943): 177–80.

Herbert was customarily cautious in the performance of his duties. Why did the King's company wait nearly two months before performing the play? Why did the lords of the Council wait for an order from the king, not then in London, before suppressing the play? The king acted in response to a protest from the Spanish ambassador. The players and Middleton himself were admonished and punished, though apparently not severely. Probably the lords of the Council found the play an amusing expression of opinions that, in the summer of 1624, were not uncongenial to them. The players made a large sum of money from *A Game at Chess*. Some five months later they again had trouble with the authorities, this time over a play with the suggestive title *The Spanish Viceroy*.[75] It has not survived. Yet they would scarcely have ventured on a play with that title had their earlier experience been costly or painful.

The performance of *A Game at Chess* retains an element of mystery that is unlikely to be resolved except by the discovery of unknown documents. It has been argued that Herbert was emboldened to license the play and the actors to perform it by the intervention of a powerful sponsor: J. Dover Wilson suggests Buckingham with the support of Prince Charles;[76] Margot Heinemann suggests the third earl of Pembroke, who as lord chamberlain was the superior of Sir Henry Herbert, Master of the Revels, as well as his kinsman and patron.[77] Both arguments are attractive; yet neither is fully convincing. Bentley and others have identified problems with Dover Wilson's suggestion.[78] I find Heinemann's argument unconvincing because it assumes that Pembroke, though a powerful nobleman who shared Middleton's hostility to Spain, would have taken the needless risk of associating himself with a play in which the king, the prince of Wales, and Buckingham, who was an even

[75] See Bentley, *Jacobean and Caroline Stage*, 1 (1941), 14–15.

[76] Wilson in a review of R. C. Bald's edition, *Library*, 4th Ser., 11 (1930): 110–11.

[77] Heinemann, *Puritanism and Theatre*, pp. 166–69.

[78] Bentley, *Jacobean and Caroline Stage*, 1:11n. Cf. *A Game at Chess*, ed. Harper, p. xv.

more powerful nobleman, were represented on stage, the latter in a not altogether favorable manner.[79] The play withholds its secrets: we must be content with uncertainty.

Gondomar's successor as ambassador in England, Don Carlos Coloma, wrote a detailed report of *A Game at Chess*, August 10 (O.S.), to Olivares. Coloma's letter reveals his indignation over the play, which he saw in performance; the letter provides as well a contemporary's account of what passed on the stage.[80] Since his last letter, Coloma writes, the English have given new offense to Spain. The King's Men continue to act a play so popular that at least 3,000 persons have attended each performance:

> The subject of the play is a game of chess, with white houses and black houses, their kings and other pieces, acted by the players, and the king of the blacks has easily been taken for our lord the King, because of his youth, dress and other details. The first act, or rather game, was played by their ministers, impersonated by the white pieces, and the Jesuits, by the black ones.[81]

Coloma mistakenly thought that a new game of chess began in each act and that, like Spanish plays, this one had only three acts.[82]

> . . . the Count of Gondomar . . . [was] brought on to the stage in his little litter almost to the life, and seated on his chair with a hole in it (they said), confessed all the treacherous actions with which he had deceived and soothed the king of the whites, and, when he discussed the matter of confession with the Jesuits, the actor disguised as the Count took out a book in which were rated all the prices for

[79] See *A Game at Chess*, ed. Harper, p. xv.

Referring to a committee of five peers (including Buckingham and Pembroke) appointed by Charles I to give advice on foreign affairs, Samuel R. Gardiner writes that "Pembroke was the only one who had ventured to differ from Buckingham, and even he had never differed from him for any length of time": Gardiner, *History of England, 1603–1642*, 5:323.

[80] Edward M. Wilson and Olga Turner, "The Spanish Protest Against 'A Game at Chesse,'" *MLR* 44 (1949): 476–82. They print both the Spanish letter and an English translation of it. I quote below from the translation.

[81] Ibid., p. 480.

[82] Ibid., p. 479.

which henceforth sins were to be forgiven. . . . In these two acts and in the third . . . they hardly shewed anything but the cruelty of Spain and the treachery of Spaniards. . . .The last act ended with a long, obstinate struggle between all the whites and the blacks, and in it he who acted the Prince of Wales heartily beat and kicked the "Count of Gondomar" into Hell, which consisted of a great hole and hideous figures.[83]

With his report Coloma included a copy of the letter of protest he had sent to King James: he would leave England, he had stated, if the dramatist and the actors were not punished.[84] Coloma remarks in closing that he thinks war with England will come, commenting on Spain's need to delay it.[85] He had obviously been instructed to try to keep England from entering the Continental war as long as possible.

Coloma's summary account of the play may be supplemented by attention to Middleton's climax: the representation of Prince Charles's and Buckingham's sojourn in Spain. Here it becomes apparent that the Black Knight's (Gondomar's) primary objective has been the entrapment of the White Knight (Prince Charles) (cf. III.i.247–48). The former boasts to his king of what he regards as the master stroke of his embassy: his negotiations for the White Knight and the White Duke (Buckingham) to make the journey to Madrid (IV.iii.137–39). He expects to achieve his objective, the reconversion of England to Catholicism, through the conversion of the White Knight. By their "discovery" of the Black House's intentions, the White Knight and Duke win the game of chess.

If Middleton was free to depict Gondomar's carefully nurtured plan to lure the prince to Spain, he was not free to depict the hopefulness with which the prince and Buckingham arrived in Madrid, if indeed he knew much about their expectations. As they are portrayed, the prince and duke have had foreknowledge of the Spaniards' intended double dealing and have come to outwit them, as they do at play's end. "What a

[83] Ibid., p. 480.
[84] Ibid., p. 481.
[85] Ibid., p. 482.

pain it is," the White Knight remarks to the White Duke upon their arrival, "For truth to fain a little" (IV.iv.17–18).

But they "feign" very successfully, leading the Black House to attempt openly to convert the White Knight. In doing so, the Black Knight reveals their territorial ambition, the goal to be reached by their master plan. In his temptation of the White Knight, he refers to the "universal monarchy" (v.iii.80–93):

> . . . Your ambition, sir,
> Can fetch no farder compass than the world?

WHITE KNIGHT:
That's certain, sir.

BLACK KNIGHT:
> We're about that already;
> And in the large feast of our vast ambition
> We count but the White Kingdom whence you came from
> The garden for our cook to pick his salads;
> The food's lean France larded with Germany,
> Before which comes the grave chaste signiory
> Of Venice, served in capon-like in whitebroth;
> From our chief oven, Italy, the bake-meats,
> Savoy, the salt, Geneva, the chipped manchet;
> Below the salt the Netherlands are placed,
> A common dish at lower end a' the table
> For meaner pride to fall to; . . .[86]

All this, before he describes the second course. The White Knight and Duke lead him to acknowledge the heinous crimes long attributed to Catholics by their Protestant foes. Believing that he has succeeded in converting the White Knight, the Black Knight overreaches himself (v.iii.158–61):

> Now y'are a brother to us; what we have done
> Has been dissemblance ever.
> WHITE KNIGHT:

---

[86] The politico-gastronomic delights of the Black Knight's imagined feast attracted enthusiastic comment by one member of Middleton's audiences: see Geoffrey Bullough, " 'The Game at Chesse': How It Struck a Contemporary," *MLR* 49 (1954): 158.

There you lie then
And the game's ours—we give thee checkmate by
Discovery, King, the noblest mate of all.

The Spanish ambassador's indignation at all this is intelligible and even to an extent defensible. Middleton's representation of Philip IV, made more effective by the youth, dress, and mimicry of the actor who played the role, violated not only a royal order (mentioned by James in his letter to the Privy Council) forbidding the representation of modern Christian kings but also a sense of propriety that at the time transcended national boundaries. However, Middleton addresses more important issues that were justifiable concerns of the English.[87] The actor portraying Gondomar, Don Carlos Coloma wrote, "confessed all the treacherous actions with which he had deceived and soothed the king of the whites." Gondomar's influence with King James has often been exaggerated.[88] But the ambassador had understated the obstacles to a Spanish match for Prince Charles. Coloma refers to the "Black Knight's" soliloquy in III.i.79–117. Several of Gondomar's accomplishments mentioned in these lines can be substantiated: he had persuaded the king in 1620 to send an English fleet into the Mediterranean to fight the Turks; during the negotiations for a marital alliance, the king on Gondomar's recommendation had released Catholic priests from prison; at the same time he had forbidden Protestant preachers to refer to Anglo-Spanish affairs.[89]

★

Middleton drew upon none of his literary sources more fully than upon Thomas Scot's *Vox Populi . . . Which may serve to forewarn both England and the United Provinces how farre to trust*

---

[87] Christopher Hill writes that the fears aroused in England by Prince Charles's journey to Madrid "were justified, for this marriage implied concessions to English Catholics which would have been utterly unacceptable to Parliament": *The Century of Revolution, 1603–1714* (Edinburgh: Thomas Nelson, 1961), p. 58.

[88] See Carter, *Secret Diplomacy of the Habsburgs*, pp. 120–23.

[89] See *A Game at Chesse*, ed. Bald, pp. 148–50; *A Game at Chess*, ed. Harper, pp. 44–45.

to Spanish Pretences (1620), a purported translation of an account written by Gondomar of his embassy to England, and *The Second Part of Vox Populi . . . wherein are discovered . . . [Gondomar's] treacherous & subtile Practises to the ruin as well of England, as the Netherlandes.*[90] Middleton follows Scot in the Black Knight's soliloquy about collecting naval intelligence (IV.ii. 60–68):

> But more to inform my knowledge in the state
> And strength of the White Kingdom! No fortification,
> Haven, creek, landing-place 'bout the White coast
> But I got draught and platform, learned the depth
> Of all their channels, knowledge of all sands,
> Shelves, rocks, and rivers for invasion proper'st;
> A catalogue of all the navy royal,
> The burden of the ships, the brassy murderers,
> The number of the men, to what cape bound.[91]

[90] On Scot's career, see Louis B. Wright, "Propaganda against James I's 'Appeasement' of Spain," *Huntington Library Quarterly* 6 (1942–43): 149–72.

It is worth noting, in view of the frequency with which characters in the *comedia* talk about the size of Spain's empire, that Scot had some knowledge of Spanish drama, acquired presumably in the Netherlands. The subject is obscure. When King James's anger over Scot's *Vox Populi* of 1620 placed Scot in danger of arrest, he went to the Netherlands, where in 1623 he became the chaplain of the English garrison at Utrecht. In one of his pamphlets of 1624, *Vox Regis*, he argues that the drama could be effectively used in controversy: "And might I not borrow a *Spanish* name or two, as well as *French*, or *Italian*, to grace this Comedie with stately Actors? Or must they onely be reserved for Kingly Tragedies? Why not *Gondomar*, as well as *Hieronymo* or Duke *d'Alva*? And why not *Philip*, as well as *Peter*, or *Alfonso*, or *Caesar*? Or might not I make as bold with them, as they with our *blacke Prince*, or *Henry* the eighth, or *Edward* the sixth, or Queene *Elizabeth*, or King *James,* or the King and Queene of *Bohemia*? If this be censurable for being fiction, it is surely for lacke of a foole, which (they say) Comedies should not be without" (*Vox Regis*, p. 10. Cited by Heinemann, *Puritanism and Theatre*, p. 157).

This paragraph includes internal evidence that Scot's remarks are not pure fabrication. His statement that "comedies should not be without" "a fool" has little meaning if applied to English comedy, but it is an appropriate allusion to the *gracioso*. Scot obviously knew that representations of recent historical sovereigns were controversial. His references to English sovereigns have the appearance of factual reporting.

[91] Commenting on this passage, Mattingly writes that neither Gondomar nor anyone employed by him collected the kind of naval intelligence the Black

In *The Second Part of Vox Populi*, Gondomar speaks:

> During the time of abode in *England* . . . I had [from "well-affected friends" and from travel in the summer] perfect knowledge of the state of the whole Land: for there was no Fortification, Haven, Creeke, or Landing-place about the Coast of *England*, but I got a platforme and draught thereof, I learned the depth of all their Channels, I was acquainted with all Sands, Shelves, Rocks, Rivers that might impeach or make for invasion. I had perpetually in a Role the names of all the Ships of King *James* his Navy Royall, I knewe to a haire of what burthen every ship was, what Ordinance she carried, what number of Saylors, who were the Captaines, for what places they were bound.[92]

Don Diego in Tirso's *No hay peor sordo* of 1625 (III. vii) refers to reports that Catholics in England are rising in rebellion.[93] Spanish hopes for a successful invasion turned largely on the expectation that the invaders would receive major assistance from English Catholics and Catholic sympathizers. Middleton's Black Knight has sounded the political temper of Englishmen throughout the island (IV.ii.69–74):

> Again, for the discovery of the inlands,
> Never a shire but the state better known
> To me than to the best inhabitants,
> What power of men and horse, gentry's revenues,
> Who well affected to our side, who ill,
> Who neither well nor ill, all the neutrality.

Knight refers to. Gondomar had English informants who told him what he wanted to know. "If he wanted the latest strength of the English navy or the movements of Dutch and English ships in the narrow seas," Mattingly writes, "Sir William Monson, since 1604 commander of the Channel fleet and since 1604 also recipient of a handsome Spanish pension, was glad to oblige": *Renaissance Diplomacy*, pp. 258–59.

Gondomar's collection of information was supplemented by that of the Flemish ambassador, Jean-Baptiste van Male, who was in England from 1615 to 1629. Charles Howard Carter refers to him as a "spymaster." See Carter, *Secret Diplomacy*, pp. 134–52.

[92] Scot, *The Second Part*, p. 15. Quoted from Middleton, *A Game at Chesse*, ed. Bald, pp. 153–54.

[93] *Obras dramáticas*, ed. Blanca de los Ríos, 3:1056a.

Again, the dramatist follows Scot's Gondomar:

> I was no lesse diligent for the discovery of the Inland, then for the Shores and Sea-coasts: For there was never a Shire in *England*, but I better knew the estate, power and quality thereof then the Inhabitants, even the best of them themselves did. I could in particular relate . . . what power of men and horse they were able to raise . . . how they stood affected in Religion, who were Puritanes, and who Catholiques, and among Catholiques who stood for us, and who (for such there were) were indifferent or against us.[94]

Events were to prove that Middleton's fears of a Spanish invasion were justified. The spectacular Spanish victories of 1625, culminating in the repulse of the English attack on Cádiz, led Olivares to plan an invasion on a large scale.[95] In the summer of 1626, two years after *A Game at Chess* was performed, Englishmen again found themselves called on to defend their island.[96]

[94] Scot, *The Second Part*, pp. 16–17. Quoted from Middleton, *A Game at Chesse*, ed. Bald, p. 154.

[95] Lynch, *Spain Under the Habsburgs*, 2:80.

[96] Lockyer, *Buckingham*, pp. 338–39.

Chapter Six

PRELUDE TO THE DEFEAT OF SPAIN:

THE SPANISH VICTORIES

OF 1625

DON DIEGO:

veréis que nuestro rey, en años tierno, You will see our king, in his
triunfando de Bretaña, youth, conquering Britain and
nuevas coronas acumula a España. gaining new crowns for Spain.

DON JUAN:

Afírmase por cierto It is said as a certainty that he
que intenta en la isla [the king] intends to seize a port
  hereje tomar puerto in the heretic island with five
con cinco mil infantes, thousand infantrymen. If they
que si españoles son, are Spaniards, the number will
  serán bastantes be sufficient for Rome to tram-
para que pise Roma ple the apostate neck that Spain
la apóstata cerviz que España doma. rules.

TIRSO DE MOLINA, *No hay peor sordo* (c. December 1625)

IN 1624 Francis Bacon wrote a second assessment of Spain's
military capabilities in relation to England's: "Considerations Touching a War with Spain." Here he concludes that the
nation is a graver menace than he considered her in 1619. After
a long period of war, Bacon writes, the Spaniards, "being
brought extreme low by their vast and continual imbrace-
ments, . . . were enforced to be quiet that they might take
breath, and do reparations upon their former wastes." He refers to Philip III's reign—or to the part of it prior to the Thirty
Years' War. "But now of late," Bacon continues in a reference
to the offensive led by Olivares,

> things seem to come on apace to their former estate. Nay with far
> greater disadvantage to us. For now that they have almost contin-
> ued and (as it were) arched their dominions from Milan, by the Val-

toline and Palatinate, to the Low Countries; we see how they thirst
and pant after the utter ruin of those states. . . .

These details, "briefly touched," he writes, "may serve, as in a
subject conjectural and future, for to represent how just cause
of fear this kingdom may have towards Spain. . . ."[1] On balance, Bacon continues to believe, England is the stronger
power. But his darker tone and his detailed argument, much
more systematic than that in his paper of 1619, suggest that
Olivares had succeeded in making Spain feared in Europe as
she had been in the time of Philip II.

How had Olivares done it? What was his objective and how
did he propose to reach it?

In 1621, when he, with his uncle, Zúñiga, assumed leadership, he established a systematic and rigorous program directed at eliminating embezzlement, extravagance, and ineffi-
ciency in the government. He enacted sumptuary laws to
reduce private expenditure. Like Gondomar and many others,
he had been repelled by the waste of Spain's resources by the
dukes of Lerma and Uceda—the latter, Lerma's son and successor—as well as by their lazy inattention to grave issues requiring decision.

The movement for reform was broadly based.[2] A letter as
audacious in its criticism of the government as Gondomar's of
March 28, 1619, could have been written only if that experienced diplomat had known that the king and many of those
surrounding him would be receptive to it. Philip III's prema-
ture death made it possible for his sixteen-year-old son to en-
trust the management of affairs to a man he knew to be committed to a thorough-going reformation of the institutions of
government.

During the regime of Lerma, who had negotiated the truce,
Spain had been peaceable and had grown poorer and weaker.
The greatness of Spain had been achieved in earlier periods
when she was at war. Gondomar remarked in 1619 that all the

[1] Bacon, "Considerations Touching a War with Spain," in Spedding et al.,
eds., *Works*, 14:480–81.

[2] See Elliott, *Felipe IV: Historia*, 25:335.

king possessed had been won by conquest.[3] The renewal of war, in 1618 in central Europe and in 1621 in the Netherlands, can be associated with the reform movement. Influential persons thought of it as a means to invigorate Castile, to regain the ideals that in earlier times had brought greatness.[4]

Notwithstanding the poverty of the people, the purpose of the program of reform initiated by Zúñiga and Olivares and carried on by the latter was military: to strengthen Spain in order to wage war more vigorously; to regain for the nation the position of preeminence she had enjoyed in the reign of Philip II. Olivares described his objective and some of the means by which he planned to reach it in a document he addressed to the king, the *Gran Memorial*, dated December 25, 1624.[5] Much of this long treatise was intended to provide information to Philip about the nature of his dominions, about the ranks and privileges of his subjects, about the institutions of government, about potential threats to his authority. Of particular importance, Olivares included a proposal for the unification of the kingdoms and provinces that made up seventeenth-century Spain. Castile bore a disproportionate burden in taxation and in men recruited for military service; Olivares perceived that Spain could be strengthened if other provinces made a larger contribution.

He proposed that the king

undertake, as the most important business of your reign, the task of making yourself king of Spain: that is to say, señor, that your Majesty not content yourself with being king of Portugal, of Aragón, of Valencia, count of Barcelona, but rather that you work and think, assisted by confidential and mature council, with the objective of transforming these kingdoms into a unified Spain having the customs and laws of Castile, without regard to all that pertains to boundaries.

If the king accomplished all this, Olivares continued, he would be the most powerful prince in the world.[6] Olivares concluded

---

[3] DIE, 2:141.

[4] See Elliott, *Felipe IV: Historia*, 25:340.

[5] On the date, see Olivares, *Memoriales*, 1:38–39.

[6] Ibid., 1:96.

the *Gran Memorial* with a statement that, though phrased piously, revealed the scope of his ambition. The king should desire the proposed augmentation of his power in order to be able to extend the boundaries of Catholicism and extirpate the enemies of the church.[7] The *privado*'s objective, that is, was to regain world hegemony for Spain.

It was an anachronistic objective, incompatible with Spain's place in the Europe of his time, and his prolonged military effort to achieve it led to disaster.[8] But for several years events seemed to promise success. The victories of 1625 were indeed impressive, and the mood of the nation was optimistic. Those victories were made possible by the arrival the preceding October of two treasure fleets with a combined cargo that was among the most valuable ever received.[9] But after the most spectacular—and expensive—of the victories, Spínola's capture of Breda in 1625, there was little money left for more than defensive operations. The people of Spain had military triumphs, but little else, to celebrate.

★

In the spring and early summer of 1624 it had become known throughout Europe that Spínola, with an army of eighteen thousand, was preparing an attack and that Breda was a likely target. Sir Horace Vere went to the Hague to join Prince Maurice,[10] under whose command he had served in many earlier campaigns. Other Englishmen followed his example. Each of four noblemen—the earls of Oxford, Southampton, and Essex, and Lord Willoughby— raised a regiment for service in support of Maurice.[11] Other Englishmen in Dutch service included Vere's contemporary and comrade in arms Sir Charles Morgan, whom Maurice sent to assume a command within

[7] Ibid., 1:99.

[8] Gregorio Marañón, *El conde-duque de Olivares (la pasión de mandar)*, rev. edn. (Madrid: Espasa-Calpe, 1945), p. 308.

[9] Lynch, *Spain Under the Habsburgs*, 2:78. See also Geoffrey Parker, "War and Economic Change: The Economic Costs of the Dutch Revolt,"in his *Spain and the Netherlands*, p. 187.

[10] Markham, *"The Fighting Veres,"* p. 423.

[11] Ibid., p. 424.

the walls of Breda. Again the English served gallantly but in vain.[12] After a siege of nine months, the garrison within Breda surrendered.

The importance of the siege of Breda in the Spanish offensive requires explanation. Apart from that of Antwerp by the prince of Parma in 1585, it was the most celebrated siege of the Eighty Years' War; for the Spanish, it was probably the most expensive. Spínola in consultation with the infanta Isabel decided to attack the heavily fortified city for several reasons, among them concern about the morale of his inactive troops and concern for his own prestige. After his well-executed capture of much of the Palatinate in 1620–1621, he had taken command of the Army of Flanders. His first years in the Netherlands were unimpressive. Along with minor victories, he lost a major battle to Prince Maurice, who in 1622 forced him to raise the siege of Bergen-op-Zoom, where several thousand of his men deserted, many to join the Dutch. The defeat was the more conspicuous because simultaneously Tilly, the duke of Bavaria's field commander, was winning victories in Germany. Yet Spínola was inactive in 1623 and in much of 1624, before he struck at Breda on August 28.

He struck decisively, quickly constructing his own siege fortifications outside the walls, before Maurice could take position to block him. Three moats surrounded Breda and made it impossible for the attacking army to reach its walls, either to mine or scale them; recognizing that the defenses were impregnable, Spínola blocked all approaches to the city and settled to the slow task of starving the garrison out. After many months, in early June 1625, the city surrendered in a ceremony made famous by Velázquez's painting *Surrender of Breda*.

Spínola's choice of his target occasioned criticism in

---

[12] The English were but one of the foreign contingents that fought alongside the Dutch. In a *memorial* to Philip IV of July 26, 1625, Olivares refers to the multinational forces that defended Breda: "In the Netherlands, Your Majesty's army having besieged Breda, armies raised by France, England, Denmark, and Sweden, as well as troops of other nationalities serving in the Dutch army, attempted to relieve it." In Olivares, *Memoriales*, 1:152.

On this subject, see also Antonio Rodríguez Villa, *Ambrosio Spínola, primer marqués de los Balbases* (Madrid: Tipográfico de Fortanet, 1904), pp. 427–28.

Madrid: from the outset it was apparent that a long and expensive siege would be required to capture the city and that, when it came under Spanish control, it would have limited strategic value in the effort to conquer the northern provinces. Yet the king and Olivares wanted Spínola to resume the offensive. Late in July 1624 they learned that a Dutch expeditionary force had captured Bahía de Todos Santos in Brazil, which had been a Spanish possession since the annexation of Portugal. Writing to the infanta Isabel on August 17, the king instructed her to take diversionary action in the Netherlands: ". . . for the chief reason why we decided to renew the war with the Dutch on the expiry of the Truce," he wrote, "was that our army should engage them on land so that they should not have the forces to attempt ventures such as this by sea."[13] He soon learned about the siege of Breda, undertaken without his prior knowledge.[14]

The siege came at a time when the Spanish empire was threatened or under attack in several parts of the world. In Calderón's *El sitio de Bredá*, the character representing Spínola mentions two principal areas apart from Flanders: Brazil and Italy. (I consider the attack on Bahía below.) Spain's troubles in Italy had their origins in France, in the foreign policy of Cardinal Richelieu, who in August 1624 became Louis XIII's chief minister. Although troubled as other French leaders had been before him by the aggressiveness of Spain, he was not prepared in the first years of his ministry to undertake open war against her. France had internal problems that required his attention: rebellion by Huguenots and dissension within the royal family. Yet Richelieu caused Spain trouble by encouraging and supporting the dissident duke of Savoy in attacking Spanish territories or those of her allies. Richelieu also sent French troops to the territories of the Protestant Grisons to occupy an Alpine pass, the Valtelline, of major importance to Spain as a link in her military corridor.[15]

The passages in *El sitio de Bredá* referring to Spain's multiple

[13] Trans. Jonathan Israel, *Dutch Republic*, p. 131. See also Charles R. Boxer, *The Dutch in Brazil, 1624–1654* (Oxford: Clarendon Press, 1957), p. 24.

[14] Rodríguez Villa, *Spínola*, p. 424.

[15] See Geoffrey Parker, *The Army of Flanders and the Spanish Road*, pp. 70–75.

military commitments, as well as those referring to the enormous cost of maintaining the siege itself, suggest the strain placed on the Spanish treasury. In historical retrospect the passages acquire an ironical dimension in that they reveal the overcommitment to military ventures that had grave consequence for Spain before the end of Philip IV's reign. But the Spínola of the play speaks exuberantly about the king's ability to wage war simultaneously in several places.

Early in act II the general reads from a gazette about current campaigns: in Lombardy twenty thousand Spanish troops are defending the Valtelline against an attack by the French; in Naples the duke of Alba has deployed all his troops; in Genoa (not a possession but an ally of Spain) Savoyard troops reenforced by the French are attacking.[16] King Philip, Espínola (Spínola) remarks with satisfaction, has two hundred thousand men in the field fighting in defense of the Faith. The general fails to note that Spain's enemies in Italy are also Catholic.[17]

Espínola grows even more exuberant about King Philip's ability to meet heavy military expense when he describes his deployment of the besieging army to the prince of Poland, pointing to a large drawing or map of the battle area.[18] The general refers to the enormous amount of money required to support the army, asking rhetorically if any other king could afford such expeditions. The prince of Poland responds as Espínola wishes: the king of Spain alone among kings rules; all other kings are but lifeless imitations of his preeminent greatness.

The historical figure who had to find the money to meet Spain's obligations, Olivares, was less sanguine about the

---

[16] In a *memorial* to King Philip written July 26, 1625, Olivares refers to the hostilities in Italy: "[The monarchy] is also under attack in Italy: in the Valtelline, in Genoa, in Milán; Naples is threatened. . . ." Olivares mentions also, as the Spínola of the play does not, the threat posed by England: "Spain expects at any time an attack by one hundred and thirty English ships; this fleet also threatens Spain's islands in the Atlantic." In Olivares, *Memoriales*, 1:152.

[17] Manuel Fernández Álvarez notes that little by little Spain's wars became dynastic ones: *Felipe IV: Historia*, 25:660.

[18] See Whitaker, "First Performance of *El sitio de Bredá*," pp. 526–28.

king's resources than the dramatic character Espínola. On June 2, 1625, a few days before the formal surrender of Breda, the *privado* wrote a somber report to the now elderly count of Gondomar about the condition of Spain. Despite his pride in the accomplishments of his regime, Olivares does not (as his modern editors observe) "neglect to express his conception, pessimistic enough, of the present situation and of the uncertain future of the country."[19] Olivares describes the improvements made in the conduct of government in the four years since the king's accession. However, he does not wish to imply, he writes, that these are happy times. He more than anyone else knows the contrary: all the king's territories are invaded or threatened by enemies. To Gondomar's recommendation that Spain make war on France, Olivares replies that to do so would be impossible; the additional armies that would be required could not be found.[20]

Despite its patriotic tone, *El sitio de Bredá* includes passages that can be interpreted as critical of Spain's war in the Netherlands. Like Lope in *El asalto de Mastrique*, from which Calderón took suggestions for his own siege play,[21] *El sitio* reveals a pride in Spain and Spanish heroes, on the one hand, and, on the other, a sensitive awareness of irrationalities in the war and its cost in human suffering. Unlike Lope, Calderón shows a concern for the "heretics" who were Spain's enemies.[22]

His critical spirit appears early in the play, in a passage parallel to one in *El asalto*, when Espínola addresses his commanders in a council of war. Like the prince of Parma, he offers a cynical reason for undertaking a siege: concern that his

[19] Olivares, *Memoriales*, 1:104.

[20] Ibid., 1:112–13.

[21] Vosters, "Lope y Calderón, Vázquez y Hugo, Maastricht y Breda," pp. 132–36.

[22] Calderón's sympathetic portrayal of the defenders of Breda reminds us of Cervantes' portrayal of the defenders of Numancia. See Anthony J. Cascardi, *The Limits of Illusion: A Critical Study of Calderón* (Cambridge: Cambridge University Press, 1984), p. 112.

Cervantes is implicitly critical of Spanish imperialism as Calderón in *El sitio* is not. See King, "Cervantes' *La Numancia* and Imperial Spain," pp. 200–21.

troops, if not engaged against the enemy, will mutiny. A siege
will keep them occupied and will offer them an incentive:

> *y no dudo*
> *que la esperanza del saco*
> *pueda sufrir con más gusto*
> *el grave peso a las armas,*
> *cuando el diciembre, que anuncio,*
> *molduras de escarcha y hielo*
> *labre en sus hombros robustos.*   (Ed. Valbuena Briones, 1:75a)

. . . and I do not doubt that the hope of looting [a city] will enable
them to endure in better spirits the heavy burden of bearing arms
when December, announced by formations of frost and ice, cuts
their strong shoulders.

The parallel passage in *El asalto de Mastrique* reflects Philip II's
financial difficulties: having recently undergone bankruptcy,
he could not pay his soldiers. When the besieged city was captured, Parma permitted his troops to sack it as compensation
for unpaid wages. Spínola could pay his soldiers. Although
mutiny had not been a serious problem in the years since the
truce,[23] desertion had been; the historical Spínola had cause for
concern about morale. Yet when Breda was captured, he forbade looting. In any event, the passage functions as a harsh
comment on the motives and cruelty of soldiers from the highest to the lowest ranks.

Again like Lope in *El asalto*, Calderón emphasizes the suffering caused by the war, though unlike the older dramatist he
reveals an impartiality in portraying the suffering of those
within and without the walls. More surprising in a Spaniard of
his era, he shows some sympathy in references to Dutch religious beliefs.[24] Lope keeps the attacking Spanish army firmly
in view, including only perfunctory glimpses of the defenders
of Maastricht. Calderón, in contrast, devotes almost as much

---

[23] In his letter to Gondomar of June 2, 1625, Olivares writes that there has
not been a mutiny in the army during the four years since the king's accession.
See Olivares, *Memoriales*, 1:111.

[24] See Johanna Rudolphine Schrek, ed., *El sitio de Bredá* ('s Gravenhage:
G. B. van Goor Zonen's, 1957), pp. 68–69.

attention to the Dutch and their allies as to Spínola's army, and he reveals concern for the Dutch, caught up in a long war, fighting valiantly for their own religious convictions.

El sitio exhibits a spirit of chivalric generosity to the conquered similar to that apparent in Velázquez's painting of 1635. The generosity is extended to the historical Welshman, Sir Charles Morgan, who is among those Calderón depicts as defenders of the city—the same Sir Charles Morgan mentioned admiringly by the dramatic character Prince Maurice in Fletcher and Massinger's *Oldenbarnevelt*.[25] In describing the organization of the defense of Breda, Calderón's Espínola praises Morgan to the prince of Poland. The French and Walloon troops, he explains,

> están a cargo
> de un coronel, que sustenta
> toda esa máquina en peso,
> que es hombre de inteligencia,
> muy altivo y ingenioso,
> y que si por él no fuera,
> se hubieran rendido, tanto
> los anima y los alienta;
> Morgan se llama, es inglés.   (Ed. Valbuena Briones, 1:93a)

. . . are under the command of a colonel, who keeps this force in order. He is a man of intelligence, high minded and resourceful. He enlivens and encourages them to such an extent that, were it not for him, they would have surrendered. His name is Morgan; he is English.

This is a magnanimous tribute from the enemy general, consonant with historical records pertaining to Morgan, such as a report about the siege written by the Venetian ambassador to the Netherlands, November 4, 1624, to the doge and senate:

The two princes of Nassau [Maurice and his younger brother Frederick Henry] alone have the leading commands. No one else has an important command except [Sir Horace] Vere. Among the subordinates, the Frenchman Altariva is at present out of the question, as

---

[25] *Barnavelt*, ed. Frijlinck, p. 52.

he is shut up in Breda, and so is Morgan, of the English, the best of them all.[26]

El sitio is a history play of a kind for which it would be impossible to find an English parallel: a dramatization of a major siege, written by an author of the first rank within six months of the event, including detailed information about the strategies and the troops of the opposing commanders. The nature of the play reflects the unusual circumstances under which it was written.

Calderón wrote *El sitio* for a palace performance before the king and the royal family; the performance took place a short time before November 5, 1625. Olivares planned the event—a victory celebration—as an entertainment for the king, and he, the count-duke, supplied Calderón with information about the siege presented in the play.[27] Antonio de Mendoza wrote a *loa* for the occasion that includes a number of topical allusions: to the queen's pregnancy, to the anticipation of an attack on Spain by an enemy fleet (the English attack on Cádiz), to members of Olivares' personal staff, and to Olivares himself. The allusions provide a means of establishing the place of performance, the approximate date, and the association with Olivares.[28] The play can be regarded as a form of self-congratulation by the count-duke, who as the king's chief minister set the course in Spain's wars. Calderón wrote a play consistent with Olivares' conception of the nation's destiny, placing the victory—in Shirley B. Whitaker's words—"within the mythology of imperialism."[29]

★

[26] *C.S.P., Venetian, 1623–1625*, 18:478.

[27] Whitaker, "The First Performance," pp. 515–31. Simon A. Vosters has written a rebuttal to Whitaker's arguments about the performance: Vosters, "Again the First Performance of Calderón's *El sitio de Bredá*," *Revista Canadiense de Estudios Hispánicos* 6 (1981): 117–34. I find the rebuttal unconvincing.

[28] Mendoza, *Loa que representó Don Pedro de Villegas en la comedia, que se hizo en palacio por las nuevas de Bredá*, in *Obras poéticas*, ed. Benítez Claros, 2 (1947), 10–14. See Whitaker, "The First Performance."

[29] Whitaker, "The First Performance," p. 525.

The play opens with Espínola's council of war, August 26, 1624, at Tournhout, a town about six miles from Breda. The general's greeting of his subordinate commanders, some like Don Gonzalo de Córdoba with famous names, resembles an epic catalogue of heroes. Like those in the service of the Dutch, the troops they command are multinational. They meet on orders from the infanta Isabel, Espínola tells them. He describes two places as objectives of a siege, Breda and the less important but also less heavily fortified town of Grave. The commanders differ on the choice of a target, though all agree that capturing Breda would be difficult because of its massive fortifications. In confident high spirits, they anticipate victory, one of them remarking (I.vi) that he intends to conduct "Un auto de inquisición" of heretics. After hearing them out, Espínola sends troops in the direction of Grave to induce the Dutch to send men and supplies there. But he leads the Spanish infantry toward Breda and orders the other troops to reverse the direction of their march and follow him. In the play, as in history, the stratagem succeeds.

The Dutch are introduced in a pastoral scene just before they learn that Breda rather than Grave will be attacked. In a valley a mile and a half outside the walls of Breda, Frederick Henry of Nassau (half-brother of Maurice) tries to comfort Flora, a fictional character who has the principal female role. The weeping Flora recalls her husband, who died in her arms of battle wounds. He died, she says, in defense of his religion. Colonel Morgan brings Frederick Henry (Enrique) a letter from Maurice, who is confined to bed by illness. Having written the day before, when it appeared that Espínola would attack Grave, Maurice has ordered Henry to lead troops to that town, leaving their brother Justin as governor of Breda. Henry instructs Morgan to send 2,000 of the 8,000 troops in Breda to Grave by fast river boats. Not long afterwards, Justin learns that they have been deceived. The first act closes with Espínola calling on Justin to surrender, and Justin, seconded by Morgan, defiantly refusing to do so.

Calderón arranges the scenes of the second act in three groups: the first, portraying Espínola's skill as a field commander; the second, placed within the walls, depicting the suffering of the defenders; the last, devoted to Espínola's account (in conversations with the visiting prince of Poland) of the fortification of Breda and of his own strategy and deployment of troops.

The act opens with Espínola writing reports to Spain. His aide, the *gracioso* Alonso Ladrón, expresses wonder that he can write despite the sound of gunfire and exposure to falling lead, shot from the city walls. In a series of short scenes, subordinates come to Espínola with reports. An engineer tells him that he has constructed twelve fire boats: small boats loaded with gunpowder and projectiles which can be sent on the river against Breda. One of his principal officers comes, with whom Espínola discusses plans for the reception of the prince of Poland. Another officer brings a report about a Dutch plan to divert the river so that it will flood the Spanish camp. Still another comes to tell him that Henry of Nassau, leading troops for the relief of Breda, is within sight of the Spanish camp. Espínola gives orders for blocking Henry's forces both by land and by the river, the latter a means of rapid transport for the Dutch. All this, reminiscent of Lope's portrayal of Parma in *El asalto*, conveys an impression of the general as superbly competent. Espínola closes this part of Act II with praise of the Spanish soldiers, with whose support he hopes to unite the two Habsburg empires (II.vii).

The defenders suffer from a pestilence and from hunger: Flora learns that Justin and Morgan, in an effort to conserve food, have ordered that all males under fifteen or over sixty years of age must leave, an order that affects both her father and son. When Justin determines that only one, her father or son, need go, Flora decides in favor of her father. In fact, as we soon learn, the Spaniards force all those whom Justin tries to send out back into the city.

Calderón devotes the third act to the closing days of the siege, in early June 1625.[30] The act opens with Justin and Mor

[30] A casual remark by Espínola in the third act that the siege has lasted two months must be the result of an oversight by Calderón or his copiest: the gen

gan listening to voices off-stage: peasants urging them to surrender. Flora enters and recites in moving detail the suffering
that war has brought to the people of the Netherlands. Breda,
she says, is a sepulchre for the living. Justin, expecting the arrival of his brother Henry with an army, asks for just one more
day. Outside the walls, Espínola too encounters complaints
from his troops, many of whom urge him to raise the siege.
He speaks in turn to the national groups that make up his
army. Addressing the Burgundians, Scots, and English,[31] he
offers the riches of Breda, soon to be captured. (In fact, he is
soon to countermand his offer of plunder by the generous
terms of surrender he grants to Justin of Nassau.) Only his
Spanish troops retain their zeal for conquest. Like Justin, Espínola expects the arrival of Henry: Prince Maurice has died,
he tells his officers. Henry (Frederick Henry) has succeeded to
the responsibilities and the title of prince of Orange.

Henry has been encouraged by the arrival of reinforcements,
Espínola explains; the arrival of Mansfeld[32] and other noblemen give the Dutch leader hope that, with thirty thousand
men deployed, he can enter Breda. Henry attacks a sector held
by Italians. Spanish officers describe the battle and the victory
won by the Italians, who force the Dutch to retreat with heavy
losses. Soon the Spaniards see a white flag raised above the
walls of Breda.

Morgan appears and tells Espínola that Justin, who is ill,

---

eral calls attention to the date, August 26, [1624], at his council of war just before the siege; Justin states that he will surrender Breda on June 6, [1625]. Historically, the city was surrendered on June 5.

[31] On the Scots and English, many of them Catholic rescusants, in the Spanish army, see Parker, *The Army of Flanders*, pp. 28–29.

[32] In his account of the siege, Hermannus Hugo implies that Mansfeld's
winter journey to England (undertaken according to Hugo on instructions
from Prince Maurice) was made specifically to recruit troops for service at
Breda. Apparently Mansfeld prevaricated both in England and France, where
he also raised troops, about his intended destination. Many Frenchmen serving under him deserted, Hugo writes, saying that Mansfeld had deceived them
by telling them that they would serve in the Palatinate. Hugo, *Obsidio Bredana
armis Philippi IIII* (Antwerp: 1626); *The Siege of Breda*, trans. Henry Gage
([Ghent]: 1627), pp. 50–51, 93–94, 109 (STC 13926).

wishes to surrender the city.[33] Two Spanish officers enter Breda and in conference with Justin and Morgan reach preliminary agreement on the terms of surrender: generous terms, including full pardon for all those within the walls. Espínola ratifies the agreement, and on June 6, as arranged, Justin ceremoniously gives him the keys of the city.

★

With the capture of Breda Spain regained some of her former military reputation. The feat of arms aroused admiration, in some quarters fear, throughout Europe. Cardinal Richelieu found the victory impressive. It was one of his considerations in deciding to end French aggression directed against Spanish positions in Italy. In 1626 he negotiated the treaty of Monçon, leaving Spain in control of the Valtelline.[34] Yet Breda was an expensive victory with negative consequences for Spain's war in the Netherlands.[35] The cost of it led to a change in strategy. A week after the surrender, King Philip ordered Spínola to direct his principal effort to war at sea, conducting only defensive war by land.[36]

★

[33] It tells much about Sir Charles Morgan's international reputation for military prowess and gallantry that Calderón should have given him so prominent a role. Hugo mentions him as having been sent with his company from Holland to reinforce the garrison at Breda, where he was given responsibility for guarding one of the gates (*Obsidio*, trans. Gage, pp. 9–10). But the historian says no more about him. Morgan's role as second in command to Justin of Nassau is without historical foundation. Hugo describes in detail an assault led by Sir Horace Vere (not mentioned by Calderón), who was in command of the English troops outside the walls. Probably Calderón knew the reputations of both Vere and Morgan but chose to give the latter the important role because he was within the walls and Vere was without.

[34] See Robin Briggs, *Early Modern France* (Oxford: Oxford University Press, 1977), p. 97.

[35] Manuel Fernández Álvarez refers to Breda as a Pyrrhic victory: *Felipe IV: Historia*, 25:685.

[36] Letter of Spínola to the king, June 3, 1626, in which the general refers to the king's order of the previous year. Cited in Rodríguez Villa, *Spínola*, p. 447.

King Philip's letter to the infanta of August 17, 1624, reporting the Dutch capture of Bahía de Todos Santos in Brazil and instructing her to intensify military operations in the Netherlands, emphasizes an important aspect of Spain's motive for continuing the war against the Dutch. The truce had not prevented the growth of Dutch trade in the East Indies and of Dutch surreptitious trade with Brazil and Portugal. Two months after the expiration of the truce, the States-General had granted a charter to the West India Company, organized on the pattern of the East India Company. Having institutional support and more operating capital, Dutch seamen and traders offered a bolder challenge to the Spanish claim to a monopoly of trade with America.

After smaller ventures, the new company undertook a major one in 1624, invading and capturing the Portuguese colony at Bahía de Todos Santos, the seat of the governor of Brazil. The governor had been warned from Madrid to expect an attack somewhere in Brazil; at Bahía he attempted to organize the planters as reinforcements of the small garrison, but in the weeks of anticipation the force dispersed. When the Dutch attacked on May 9, only a handful of men remained with the governor, too few for him to defend his capital city, Salvador de Bahía.[37] The Dutch had an easy time of it—but their good fortune was short-lived. When news of the event reached Portugal and Spain in late July, the leaders of government responded rapidly and vigorously. For the first time a foreign government had challenged Spain by establishing a colony, intended to be permanent, on the mainland of South America.[38] The king levied men and equipped ships in Castile, Andalusia, and Portugal for an expedition of reconquest. A large fleet—fifty-two ships bearing 12,500 men—commanded by Don Fadrique de Toledo y Osorio sailed from the Canary Islands on

[37] C. R. Boxer, *Salvador de Sá and the Struggle for Brazil and Angola, 1602–1686* (London: The Athlone Press, 1952), pp. 41–50; Boxer, *The Dutch in Brazil*, pp. 17–23; Israel, *Dutch Republic*, pp. 130–31.

[38] Diego Martínez Torrón, "Valores informativos en el teatro de Lope de Vega: la fuente de *El Brasil restituido*," in *Lope de Vega y los orígenes del teatro español*, ed. Manuel Criado de Val (Madrid: Edi-6, 1981), p. 152.

January 14, 1625, arrived off Bahía March 29 (the day before Easter), and after a siege of a month forced the Dutch to surrender.[39]

Although the Dutch surrendered Bahía on April 30, news of the victory did not reach Spain until early July, when a small ship sent by Don Fadrique on May 14 brought word to the king. Accounts of the Spanish conquest were published in eight different cities throughout Spain.[40] Don Fadrique himself did not leave Brazil until August 1, when he sailed with the main body of the fleet; delayed by adverse winds, he did not reach Málaga until October 24. Long before the return of Don Fadrique, Lope began to write a play about the reconquest, *El Brasil restituido*: he dated his autograph October 23, the censor approved the play October 29, and it was performed at court on November 6—the day after news reached Madrid that an English fleet had attacked Cádiz with little success.[41]

In licensing the play on October 29, the stage censor, Pedro de Vargas Machuca, wrote a commendation of it at the end of Lope's autograph.[42] He praises Lope's play, which, he writes,

> is accurate and is consistent with the best account we have of the expedition, vouched for by a qualified witness who served in this campaign and took from it honorable tokens [of his service] in his wounds. He is mentioned in the play as are many other gentlemen.[43]

The censor, in emphasizing Lope's accuracy, seems to imply (without precisely saying so) that Lope's source was the particular report of the expedition to which he, the censor, refers. However, no scholar has yet succeeded in identifying any one

[39] Boxer, *The Dutch in Brazil*, pp. 23–27.

[40] Marcos A. Morínigo, *América en el teatro de Lope de Vega* (Buenos Aires: Universidad de Buenos Aires, Instituto de Filología, 1946), p. 23.

[41] Juan de Valencia y Guzmán, *Compendio historial de la jornada del Brasil* (1626), CODOIN, 55 (1870), 170; Brown and Elliott, *Palace for a King*, p. 186.

[42] The manuscript is now in the New York Public Library. See *Lope de Vega's El Brasil restituido*, ed. Gino de Solenni (New York: Instituto de las Españas en los Estados Unidos, 1929), pp. i–ii.

[43] Ibid., p. 114.

report of the expedition among the large number of early ones published that satisfies all the criteria mentioned.[44]

Recalling the circumstances of the first performance of *El sitio de Bredá* at court a short time before November 5, we should at least keep in mind the possibility that Olivares made information available to Lope for *El Brasil* as he did to Calderón about the contemporary victory in the Netherlands. Lope could have written the play from published reports.[45] Contemporary records are silent, but it is possible that he received encouragement and assistance from Olivares.

★

Lope includes in *El Brasil restituido* lines similar to ones spoken by Espínola in *El sitio de Bredá* (II.i), expressing confidence in King Philip's ability to carry on wars simultaneously in different parts of the world. In an exchange between personifications of Brazil and the Catholic Religion—the former represented by an Indian matron, the latter by a Spanish one—Brazil speaks:

> *Sube á este monte y verás*
> *La fe y el valor de España,*
> *Y que á un mismo tiempo tiene*
> *Felipe cuarto sus armas*
> *En Indias, Italia y Flandes*
> *Para victorias tan altas.*   (Ed. Acad. 13:91a)

Climb this mountain and you will see the faith and the power of Spain. Philip IV has troops in the field at the same time in America, in Italy, and in the Netherlands to win important victories.

[44] Diego Martínez Torrón has argued that the account of the expedition referred to by the stage censor is Don Fadrique de Toledo's official report to the king, a copy of which was published in 1625. But the censor's phrasing, I believe, makes the argument unacceptable. To say that Don Fadrique took part in the campaign and is mentioned in the play would have been understatement so extreme as to have been offensive. See Martínez Torrón, "Valores informativos," in *Lope de Vega y los orígenes del teatro,* ed. Criado de Val, pp. 153–55.

[45] The most comprehensive study of Lope's potential sources for the play is a recent one by Robert Shannon, who has examined nearly all the narratives published early enough to have been used: "The Vision of America in Lope de Vega's Theater," Ph.D. diss., Bryn Mawr College, May 1984.

Espínola in Calderón's play refers to the same places:

Pues ¿qué temor, qué recelo
puede ocuparla, si sólo
el nombre de España ha puesto
terror al mundo, tocando
con sus manos sus extremos?
Díganlo Italia, el Brasil
y Flandes, que a un mismo tiempo
embarazados con guerras,
su poder están diciendo.   (Ed. Valbuena Briones 1:84a)

Then, what fear, what misgiving can disturb her [Spain], if the
name alone of Spain (whose power reaches to the most remote
places) has frightened the world? Italy, Brazil, and the Netherlands,
which at the same time are encumbered with wars, tell about her
power.

The dramatists could not know how severely the multiple
wars strained the nation's resources.

The nature of *El Brasil restituido*, as well as a record of its performance at court, November 6, 1625[46] (soon after it was written), suggests that Lope planned it for a palace audience. Like
El sitio de Bredá, performed at court a short time earlier, it is a
ceremonial play,[47] a celebration of a Spanish victory that Lope,
like Calderón, places within the context of the triumphant
opening years of the young king's reign.

Although both *El sitio de Bredá* and *El Brasil restituido* celebrate victories and the men who won them, the plays are very
different: *El sitio* is an episodically organized chronicle in
which narration rarely displaces dramatized action; *El Brasil* is
similarly a chronicle, but in it scenes of dramatized action alternate with scenes in which personified abstractions—for example, Brazil, the Spanish Monarchy, and the Catholic Religion—provide both exposition and commentary. In *El Brasil*,
panegyric, reinforced by stage spectacle and lyrical passages of

[46] N. D. Shergold and J. E. Varey, "Some Palace Performances of Seventeenth-Century Plays," *BHS* 40 (1963): 218.

[47] For discussion of the nature of ceremonial drama, see Herbert Lindenberger, *Historical Drama*, pp. 78–86.

description, is more consistently prominent than in *El sitio*. Lope is even more concerned with comprehensiveness and, in battle scenes, accuracy than is Calderón, but he achieves them by supplementing dramatization with narration. In one passage Apollo crowned with laurel appears on a mountaintop surrounded by muses and poets. At the request of the personified Brazil, he describes the progress of the battle of reconquest, naming the Spanish and Portuguese leaders as heroes deserving the attention of historians and poets. Lope was writing for an audience that would have recognized the names.

El Brasil has been subjected to criticism that fails to take sufficiently into account both the ceremonial nature of the play and the prominence of its nonrealistic conventions.[48] Lope frequently employs superlatives in describing the Spanish and Portuguese fighting men. Yet in a play of this nature he cannot be held strictly accountable to conventions of realism. In other commemorative literary forms—the pastoral elegy and the funeral oration, for example—literal accuracy is not esteemed. Let us recall that when Lope wrote about campaigns against the Dutch that were some twenty years in the past, in *Los españoles en Flandes* and *El asalto de Mastrique*, he was not uncritical of his countrymen.

Díez Borque's criticism of *El Brasil* for its passages of bravado should be reconsidered. "[The play] includes bravado," he writes, "sad ostentation in comparison with the chaotic reality of Spain."[49] The lines he cites are accurately described as "bravado":

FADRIQUE:
Que no le importa á mi Rey
Que os rebeléis, porque es cierto
Que tener más enemigos
Será gloria de su pecho.   (Ed. Acad. 13:105b)

---

[48] See, for example, José María Díez Borque's criticism of *El Brasil* in *Sociología de la comedia española del siglo XVII* (Madrid: Ediciones Cátedra, 1976), pp. 197–99.

[49] Ibid., p. 198.

It does not matter to my king that you rebel, for to have more enemies will certainly result in more glory to him.

But to say that the lines are incongruous boasting in view of
the chaotic reality of Spain is anachronistic; it assumes an assessment of the nation's strength that could not be made—by
dramatists, at any rate—until later in Philip IV's reign. Tirso,
like Lope and Calderón proud of the nation's victories of 1625,
wrote passages expressing a similar confidence in Spain's ability to take on all comers. (We are reminded of the "Armada idiom" apparent in the bastard Faulconbridge's lines closing
King John:

> Come the three corners of the world in arms
> And we shall shock them! Nought shall make us rue
> If England to itself do rest but true!)[50]

Menéndez y Pelayo places Lope's euphoric conception of
Spain's strength in historical perspective. The poet, he writes,
"who had the good fortune not to live to experience the dis-
asters of the second half of Philip IV's reign, shared the justified enthusiasm of his contemporaries aroused by the memo-
rable victories that coincided with the king's first years and
that seemed the promise of a new era of prosperity for the
monarchy."[51]

★

Although *El Brasil restituido* provides a generally accurate account of Spanish and Portuguese naval and military operations, portions of the first act, portraying events in the colony
before the arrival of Don Fadrique's fleet, are unhistorical. The
capture of Bahía occurs, in Lope's play, when the Jews living
there, fearing the severity of the Inquisition, secretly inform
the Dutch that the city is inadequately defended. Modern re-

---

[50] See Shakespeare, *King John*, ed. Honigmann, pp. xlvi and n. 2; 147, notes
to ll. 117–18.

[51] Marcelino Menéndez y Pelayo, *El Brasil restituido*, "Observaciones
preliminares," Ed. Acad. 13:xxiii. Manuel Fernández Álvarez describes the
reasons for euphoria in Spain in the early 1620s: *Felipe IV: Historia*, 25:698–99.

search has revealed that the Jews, though active in the Portuguese and Dutch sugar trade, were not responsible for the attack.[52] In other respects, Lope represents the arrival and the attack of the Dutch accurately. When the fleet appears, the Portuguese governor acknowledges that he has neither ammunition nor troops with which to defend Salvador. He nevertheless makes a brave stand. The Dutch seize the city quickly and turn at once to strengthening its defenses.

Lope employs personifications to provide a history of Brazil and to emphasize the rapidity with which the Spanish court in Madrid received news of the Dutch capture of Bahía. (The leaders of Portugal and Spain learned about the event a month before the Dutch.)[53] The Indian matron representing Brazil appears with a group of Indian warriors armed with bows and arrows. When one of them asks why she is sad, she recounts her history. She lived in pagan ignorance of the eternal day ("En noche eterna al sempiterno día") until a brave Portuguese found her—referring to Pedro Álvarez Cabral, who discovered Brazil in 1500 while leading an expedition bound for the East Indies. Here, as elsewhere, Lope scrupulously acknowledges the accomplishments of the Portuguese.[54] From them, Brazil continues, she learned the Christian religion. Her faith having grown strong, she has resisted persecutors who have attempted, with the support of the Dutch, to introduce error and apostasy and to bar King Philip from her shores. The Dutch have come and have taken the king's governor prisoner.

---

[52] C. R. Boxer writes that the charge, made by "runaway defenders of Bahía" and "echoed" in Lope's play, "receives no support from the accounts of trustworthy Jesuit eyewitnesses nor from the voluminous Dutch narratives" (*The Dutch in Brazil*, pp. 22–23).

[53] Israel, *Dutch Republic*, p. 130.

[54] The contemporary historian Matías de Novoa (1576?–1652?), after describing the events that led to the death of Don Fadrique de Toledo in 1634, praises him, enumerating his accomplishments, among them the recapture of Bahía. Novoa refers to the Portugueses' dislike of Castilians and low esteem for Castilian military leaders: they did not wish to go to Brazil under any commander except Don Fadrique; they said that "if Don Fadrique de Toledo went, there would be an army and victories; if not, there would be nothing" (Novoa, *Historia de Felipe IV*, in CODOIN, 69 [1878], 476).

A character representing Rumor promptly conveys Brazil's message to the Monarchy of Spain.

(Although the king's response was rapid, nearly eleven months elapsed between the Dutch attack and the arrival of the Spanish fleet. In the interval, Salvador became a formidable fortress.)

The second act portrays the early phases of Don Fadrique's siege of Bahía. He arrived on Easter Eve; Lope changes the date to Good Friday, one of his few departures from the historical record. After a preliminary reconnaissance of the fortifications, Don Fadrique deploys Spanish and Portuguese troops outside the walls. The Dutch make a single sortie, and are driven back into the city with severe losses on both sides. After the battle a character representing Heresy comes on stage to the sound of gunfire. Addressing Catholic Religion and Brazil, she taunts the latter, calling her attention to the bodies of Spanish and Portuguese soldiers lying on the battlefield. Brazil replies, referring to the Catholic faith that sustains her: soon Heresy will experience the power of King Philip.

The final act opens with an exchange between Don Fadrique and his kinsman, Don Enrique de Alagón, who has suffered a serious though not fatal wound. Don Fadrique speaks disparagingly of the enemy, who are, he says, of disparate nationalities. They fight desperately and with a strange valor, according to Don Fadrique, who attributes their bravery to their belief that reinforcements will soon arrive.[55] A deserter from the city soon afterwards identifies the nationalities of the defenders: in addition to the Dutch, he mentions German, French, and English troops.[56] Although they fight stubbornly to protect the treasure they have amassed, he reports, some of them wish to surrender. Don Enrique and Don Fadrique comment on the damage to the city's walls caused by the naval bombardment. The admiral adds that explosives have been placed in trenches beneath the walls: if the enemy has not sur-

[55] The Dutch surrendered on April 30, 1625; the fleet sent to reenforce them arrived on May 26. Boxer, *The Dutch in Brazil*, p. 27.

[56] In his *memorial* to King Philip IV of July 26, 1625, Olivares refers to still other nationalities. See Olivares, *Memoriales*, 1:152.

rendered by the day consecrated to Saint Philip and Saint James, he will ignite the explosives and charge through openings made in the walls.

This proves to be unnecessary. In a scene placed within the city, the Dutch colonel in command tells an assembled group that he believes the time has come for surrender. Assault is imminent; reinforcements are distant. All present agree except Bernardo, a Portuguese Jew who had taken a leading role in betraying Bahía.[57]

Soon the sound of a drum is heard on the walls and a soldier appears with a white flag. When a Dutch officer comes to him offering surrender on terms specified in a document, Don Fadrique tears it up without reading it; he will not consider conditions. Rather, he will submit the offer of surrender to King Philip,

> *aquel divino Monarca,*
> *Que cuanto es jüez severo*
> *Sabrá ser padre piadoso.*   (Ed. Acad. 13:104b)

That godlike monarch will know how to be a merciful father as well as he knows how to be a stern judge.

In the action that follows, we are reminded that this is a ceremonial drama in which the celebration of a victory frequently takes precedence over verisimilitude. Don Fadrique displays a portrait of King Philip, instructing the Dutch to kneel before it. He submits their petition to surrender to this emblem of royal authority. When the portrait is covered, Don Fadrique concedes a pardon in the king's name on condition that the garrison sail home, taking only the clothes they wear and a three-months' supply of food. The Dutch officer accepts the terms, the gates open, and those within the walls walk out to prepare for their voyage. The play closes with Brazil crowning Don Fadrique with laurel.

★

[57] Lope's references to Jewish treachery at Bahía are unhistorical.

The siege of Breda and the reconquest of Bahía, both resulting in brilliant victories, were very expensive ventures.[58] Yet the victory in Brazil proved to be no more productive of lasting consequences in Spain's war than that in the Netherlands. When in 1630 the Dutch renewed their offensive in Brazil, this time not at Bahía but north of it at Recife, Spain did not respond. By 1643 "the north coast to the mouth of the Amazon" had come under the control of the Dutch West India Company.[59]

Olivares made an abortive effort in 1633 and 1634 to send another fleet against the Dutch. This effort had tragic consequences for Don Fadrique de Toledo, the hero of the 1625 expedition. Don Fadrique refused to accept command, believing that he would be given a force of insufficient strength for the mission assigned. He quarreled angrily with Olivares in July 1634 and was imprisoned. He was saved from a harsh sentence only by death.[60]

★

Spain won still another important victory in 1625 in the repulse, with heavy enemy losses, of the maladroit attack on Cádiz led by Sir Edward Cecil in November (N.S.). To Spaniards, the defeat of the English provided yet another occasion for rejoicing. Tirso de Molina, his earlier satire in *La prudencia en la mujer* notwithstanding,[61] joined in celebrating the multiple victories. In *No hay peor sordo* (*It's Hard to Persuade Someone Who Won't Listen; c.* late 1625) characters speak with pride of Cádiz; in *Desde Toledo a Madrid* (1625–1626)[62] characters refer

---

[58] Jonathan Israel places the cost of the naval expedition at two million ducats: *Dutch Republic*, p. 131.

[59] John H. Parry, *The Age of Reconnaissance* (London: Weidenfeld and Nicolson, 1963), p. 261.

[60] Brown and Elliott, *Palace for a King*, pp. 172–73. Matías de Novoa provides a detailed account of events leading to Don Fadrique's death, though its accuracy is impaired by his hostility towards Olivares: *Historia de Felipe IV*, in CODOIN, 69 (1878), 467–78.

[61] Kennedy, "La prudencia en la mujer," pp. 1131–90.

[62] Ruth Lee Kennedy, "Tirso's *Desde Toledo a Madrid*: Its Date and Place of

to Breda and Brazil. In the latter play, Don Felipe answers Don Alonso, who has asked him why he is going to court:

soy mozo, y no sé perder
fiestas que ilustran hazañas
con que España alegre está:
convida a toros Bredá,
y el Brasil pone las cañas.   (Ed. Blanca de los Ríos 3:825b)

I am young, and I cannot miss fiestas that celebrate the triumphs that fill Spain with gaiety. Breda invites [me] to bullfights and Brazil to games of *cañas*.

Don Alonso replies, referring to the king as the defender of the faith; and when his companion answers that Spain is surrounded by enemies, Don Alonso, in a passage similar to one spoken by Espínola in *El sitio de Bredá* (II.i), refers confidently to the campaigns King Philip carries on in different parts of the world. The lion of Spain roars and destroys the wolves that attack her.

The attack on Cádiz came as the climax of one of the most discreditable expeditions in the history of the English navy.[63] Planned by Buckingham as Lord Admiral and commanded by Sir Edward Cecil (an able soldier but one without experience in warfare at sea), the expedition was inadequately prepared for and poorly executed. It was a joint venture with the Dutch, who contributed twenty of the total of one hundred ships, with about five thousand seamen and ten thousand troops aboard.[64] Most of the English ships were merchantmen whose captains served reluctantly. Their ships were manned by re-

Composition," in Kossoff and Amor y Vázquez, eds., *Homenaje a William L. Fichter*, pp. 357–66.

[63] For a detailed account of it, see Charles Dalton, *Life and Times of General Sir Edward Cecil, Viscount Wimbledon* (London: Sampson Low, 1885), 2:152–97. See also Lockyer, *Buckingham*, pp. 280–85.

Sir Edward Cecil's secretary, John Glanville, wrote a baldly factual account of the expedition. He provides a list of the ships that made up the fleet. Glanville, *The Voyage to Cadiz in 1625*, ed. Alexander B. Grosart (The Camden Society, n.s., 32 [1883]).

[64] Dalton, *General Sir Edward Cecil*, 2:139–40; Israel, *Dutch Republic*, pp. 115–16.

cruits. Many of the officers knew little more about sailing than their admiral. The fleet was so poorly provisioned that crews were placed on short rations from the beginning.

Hoping to intercept the Spanish treasure fleet, Cecil sailed into Cádiz Bay. He failed to sack the city or, owing to insubordination of captains of merchantmen, to sink ships in the harbor. Nor did he capture the treasure fleet. News of his intentions having reached the Spanish commanders in America, that fleet took a southerly route to the coast of Africa and made its way north to Cádiz, arriving not long after the English had departed. Frustrated in his objectives, Cecil was compelled by the condition of his ships and the illness of many of his men to return to England. His fleet was dispersed by storms on the homeward voyage, and the ships, many of them leaking, straggled back singly into British ports. Cecil's flagship went to Kinale in Ireland.

Spanish leaders had for some time expected an English naval attack, but they were unable to predict its time or location. In a letter to Gondomar, June 2, 1625, Olivares had mentioned the probability of an attack (which he regarded as less of a danger than did the ambassador), asserting that Spain was prepared to defend herself.[65] In the *loa* written for the court performance of *El sitio de Bredá* in the autumn of 1625, Antonio de Mendoza refers to a large enemy fleet approaching the shores of Spain.[66] It is difficult to know if Mendoza meant that the English were literally under way or merely expected to come soon. At any rate, in Cádiz on October 22/November 1 many sails were sighted, though not at once identified.[67]

---

[65] Olivares, *Memoriales*, 1:113–15.

[66] Whitaker, "The First Performance of Calderón's *El sitio de Bredá*, p. 519.

[67] Details are provided in a narrative written by an eyewitness: Luis de Gamboa y Eraso, *Verdad de lo sucedido con ocasion de la venida de la armada inglesa del enemigo sobre Cadiz*, dated by the author from San Lúcar, December 10, 1625 (Cordova: Salvador de Cea, 1626). For another contemporary account of the attack, see Andrés de Almansa y Mendoza, *Cartas: novedades de esta corte y avisos recibidos de otras partes, 1621-1626* (Madrid: Imprenta de Miguel Ginesta, 1886), pp. 310–13.

As soon as possible, Don Fernando de Girón, a member of the Council of State and governor of Cádiz, notified the duke of Medina Sidonia, the admiral responsible for the defense of the coasts of Andalusia, that Cádiz was under attack by an enemy fleet of 104 ships. The duke, in turn, sent messages of warning to appropriate officers with orders that troops and munitions be sent to Jerez from throughout Andalusia. At the time Cecil's fleet entered Cádiz Bay, fourteen galleons recently returned from Brazil were at anchor, but fewer than 300 soldiers were in the presidio. However, a very rapid build-up of forces followed.[68] Don Fernando Girón deployed troops for the defense of the city; the duke of Medina Sidonia directed naval operations from San Lúcar.

On entering the Bay of Cádiz, ships of Cecil's fleet approached and fired upon Fort Puntal. The naval gunfire forced the garrison, after a spirited defense, to surrender. From the afternoon of October 23/November 2 until the following morning, several thousand English troops debarked. They accomplished nothing, making little effort even to defend themselves. (English reports explain their inactivity: they had found casks of wine and become drunk.)[69] After days of frustration, the troops reboarded the ships, and the fleet sailed away on October 29/ November 8.[70]

In Tirso de Molina's *No hay peor sordo* (probably written late in 1625),[71] two gentlemen talk about the occurrences at Cádiz:

DON DIEGO:

¡Gracias a Dios, que ha dado
tan buen suceso a España! Derrotado

---

[68] Gamboa y Eraso, ff. 1–2.

[69] Lockyer, *Buckingham*, p. 283.

[70] Gamboa y Eraso, f. 8. News of the attack and its negligible results reached Madrid on November 5: [Fray Pedro de la Hoz], *Noticias de Madrid, 1621–1627*, ed. Ángel González Palencia (Madrid: Ayuntamiento de Madrid, 1942), p. 126.

[71] Ruth L. Kennedy, "Tirso's *No hay peor sordo*: Its Date and Place of Composition," in J. Homer Herriott et al., eds., *Homenaje a Rodríguez-Moñino*, I (Madrid: Editorial Castalia, 1966), 261–78.

dese modo el blasfemo,
Y Cádiz defendida, ya no temo
desdichas desta guerra.[72]   (Ed. Blanca de los Rios 3:1055b)

Thanks be to God, who has given such great success to Spain! Blasphemy [has been] defeated in this manner, and Cádiz defended. I no longer fear misfortunes from this war.

Graver ills are in store for England, Don Diego says, than the naval losses in the attack on Cádiz. Don Juan explains that they will come from the infanta Isabel, governess of Flanders, who will launch an invasion. Five thousand Spaniards will be enough, he says, to conquer the island of heretics. Don Diego adds that English Catholics, not frightened by the persecutions that since the reign of Henry VIII have made martyrs of many of them, are rising in rebellion. One Isabel, a bastard (Queen Elizabeth I), led England away from Catholicism, Don Juan says; another Isabel, "legítima española," will restore it to the faith.

★

For the English, the attack on Cádiz was at once the first and the last major action by King Charles's government in the war with Spain. A treaty of peace did not come until 1630, and in the intervening years there were hostilities, but they were small affairs, largely confined to privateering. Charles and Buckingham had not lost their will to make war on Spain, but to do so required money in amounts that Parliament would not provide. Relations between the king and Parliament deteriorated. The House of Commons in 1629—the year after Buckingham was assassinated—passed resolutions calculated to antagonize Charles, who not long before had shown his indifference to the wishes of the Commons. Confirmed in his distrust of Parliaments, the king turned increasingly to unconstitutional means of raising money, and he did not summon

---

[72] Tirso also refers to the attack on Cádiz in *Habladme en entrando* (*Obras dramáticas*, ed. Blanca de los Ríos, 3:1222b). Don Diego speaks briefly of the heavy losses sustained by the English.

another Parliament until 1640. By that time events were in train that led to the Great Civil War.

★

The Spanish did not attempt an invasion of England, though Olivares made plans for one[73] and Buckingham made plans for defense.[74] After a year of victories the Spanish people and their leaders were optimistic. But the leaders knew that the cost of war had been high.

The War of the Mantuan Succession (1628–1631),[75] fought in the high Alps, forced Olivares to give over long-range plans in order to meet current military needs. The count-duke did not foresee the vigorous response that would come from France when he took the occasion of a disputed succession to the dukedom of Mantua to send Spanish troops from Milan to take control of it. In the absence of a direct heir, the French duke of Nevers had the strongest dynastic claim to Mantua; and Louis XIII, encouraged and aided by Cardinal Richelieu, determined that Nevers should gain his inheritance. Not waiting for spring, Louis and the cardinal early in 1629 led French troops through snow in the Alps to Casale, which was under siege by troops commanded by Gonzalo Fernández de Córdoba. Faced by superior forces, Don Gonzalo was compelled in March to raise the siege and recognize Nevers as the duke of Mantua. This was a resounding defeat, perhaps the gravest suffered by the Spanish crown since Philip IV's accession.[76] The king and Olivares recalled Gonzalo de Córdoba, sent Spínola to replace him, and determined to fight on. Despite its lo-

[73] Lynch, *Spain Under the Habsburgs*, 2:80.

[74] Lockyer, *Buckingham*, pp. 338–39.

[75] On the events leading to the war and the first phase of it, see Manuel Fernández Álvarez, *Don Gonzalo Fernández de Córdoba y la guerra de sucesíon de Mantua y del Monferrato, 1627–1629* (Madrid: Consejo Superior de Investigaciones Científicas, 1955). The principality of Monferrato was subject to the duke of Mantua.

[76] M. Fernández Álvarez, in *Felipe IV: Historia*, 25:709. See also Victor-L. Tapié, *France in the Age of Louis XIII and Richelieu*, trans. and ed., D. Mc.N. Lockie (New York: Praeger Publishers, 1975), pp. 198–99.

cale in the Italian Alps, this was a war between France and Spain, one that was interpreted throughout Europe as having been caused by Spanish aggression. In confirming Richelieu's warnings about the Habsburgs, the Mantuan war can plausibly be interpreted as one of the reasons for France's declaration of war in 1635.[77]

With the reverses in Spain's fortunes, Olivares, never a popular figure, came under intensified criticism. But along with critics, he found defenders, among them Francisco de Quevedo, who in 1629 wrote a political statement in the form of a play, *Cómo ha de ser el privado* (*How a King's Chief Minister Should Conduct Himself*).[78] Of relevance here, Quevedo turned for his plot to Roca's account, in his biography of Olivares, of Prince Charles's sojourn in Madrid and the subsequent English attack on Cádiz.[79] Quevedo simplifies, making no reference to the complicating dimension provided by the Palatinate, and more than Roca he emphasizes the potential advantages to Spain of an alliance with England. The changes enable Quevedo to sharpen his focus on the motive that leads the king (nominally the king of Naples), who acts on the advice of Valisero (an anagram of Olivares), to reject the proposal of the heretic "Carlos, Príncipe de Dinamarca." The decision is the consequence of an unambiguous preference of religious principle to reasons of state.

The courtship and its aftermath in the unsuccessful attack on Cádiz provide continuity in the play. They are also vehicles for Quevedo's defense of Olivares. The *privado*'s critics included

[77] On the significance of the Mantuan war for the Spanish monarchy and for Olivares, see J. H. Elliott, *Richelieu and Olivares* (Cambridge: Cambridge University Press, 1984), pp. 86–112; and R. A. Stradling, "Olivares and the Origins of the Franco-Spanish War, 1627–1635," *English Historical Review* 101 (1986): 68–94. Emphasizing Olivares' anticipation of and preparation for war with France, Stradling provides a compact account of events leading from the Mantuan war to the beginning of Spain's open war with France.

[78] J. H. Elliott established the date of the play: Elliott, "Quevedo and the Count-Duke of Olivares," in James Iffland, ed., *Quevedo in Perspective* (Proceedings from the Boston Quevedo Symposium, October 1980) (Newark, Del.: Juan de la Cuesta, 1982), p. 235.

[79] Elliott, "Quevedo and Olivares," p. 236.

some who held him responsible for Spain's failure to gain an
alliance with England, particularly desirable because of English sea power. Quevedo's king gives first consideration to the
"Danish" navy in describing the reasons that lead him to en-
tertain Carlos's proposal. Valisero does not disagree with his
master on this issue. Rather, he insists on the primacy of religious principle. Subsequent events reveal that under Valisero's
skillful direction, his master has no need for an ally with a
strong navy. Among the victories won during Philip's early
years, the two that receive attention in the play are both related
to naval power: that in Bahía as well as that at Cádiz. (Quevedo
refers to the enemy in Brazil as "Islanders," that is, as English.)[80]

Yet in this play written in support of Olivares' policies and
decisions, Quevedo's defense of the decision against a marital
alliance with England invites objections. At the time of the negotiations, many Catholics, including Gondomar, had regarded the projected marriage as a means to strengthen Catholicism in England. The issue had not then seemed
necessarily to turn on religious principle. The emphasis in the
dramatic fable on the advantages of an English alliance under-
cuts the defense of Olivares' decisions. At the time Quevedo
wrote the play, Spain was suffering the consequences of a
grave loss to the Dutch navy. In the autumn of 1628 the Dutch
admiral Piet Heyn had captured the treasure fleet, the first
such loss Spain had experienced. Valisero reports it to the king
late in the play.[81] In 1629 an alliance with England would have
appeared much more desirable than it had appeared in the circumstances of 1623.

★

In the years after 1625, Spanish armies won only a few spectacular victories—one of them in 1634 at Nördlingen, where
Spanish and imperial troops, the former led by King Philip's

---

[80] See *Cómo ha de ser el privado*, in Quevedo, *Obra poética*, ed. José Manuel
Blecua, 4 (Madrid: Editorial Castalia, 1981), 200–01.

[81] Elliott, "Quevedo and Olivares," p. 235; *Cómo ha de ser el privado*, in *Obra
poética*, ed. Blecua, 4:219.

Chapter Seven

CONCLUSION

THE HISTORY portrayed in Spanish and English drama rests on religious premises that were accepted as acts of faith. If we remain within the customary boundaries of academic criticism in the United States, we cannot choose between the Catholic and Protestant interpretations of the past. Yet we can profitably examine some of the forces conditioning the dramatists' representations of history.

One of the strongest of these forces affecting the English plays was the systematic and long-continued denigration of Spain and the accomplishments of Spaniards known as the Black Legend.[1] We can begin to understand its force if we think of the plays considered in previous chapters with attention to the history of Spain in the sixteenth and early seventeenth centuries. The plays were written in the years from the 1590s to the 1620s, just after a period during which Spain's power and influence had been greater than that of any other Western nation since antiquity. When Spain's reverses began in the late 1580s, Philip II, at war in northern Europe, determined to fight on; his son and his grandson, Philip III and Philip IV, made similar decisions. In 1665 Philip IV's incompetent son, Charles II, inherited a demoralized and impoverished kingdom that had sacrificed reputation as well as men, wealth, and a place among world powers to her wars.

Bitter criticism of Spanish imperialism began late in Charles V's reign in the writings of a Spanish Dominican friar, Bartolomé de Las Casas, who in 1542 wrote a denunciation of the conquistadores' alleged brutality to the Indians of America. Las Casas' tract, its exaggerations notwithstanding, remained for a century and more after its publication in 1552 the most

---

[1] See Philip Wayne Powell, *Tree of Hate*, p. 11; and William S. Maltby, *The Black Legend in England: The Development of Anti-Spanish Sentiment, 1558–1660* (Durham, N.C.: Duke University Press, 1971), p. 3.

influential assessment of Spanish policy in America. Others wrote with more restraint about the conquistadores' cruelty, among them Francisco López de Gómara, who in 1552 described instances of Spaniards torturing Indians in efforts to find their gold. Criticism of Spanish colonial policy spread to northern Europe. Montaigne used Gómara's account of the Spaniards' cruelty as a source for an *essay*,[2] and through John Florio's translation of Montaigne (1603), the passage in Gómara reached an English audience. As early as 1583 Las Casas' tract was translated into English (in abridged form), and it was retranslated in the seventeenth century.[3] Meanwhile, the Revolt of the Netherlands provided Protestant writers with a motive for keeping the memory of Las Casas' accusations green.[4] The Revolt itself prompted a voluminous review of Spain's imperial policies; Dutch and English propagandists found subjects to match the atrocities alleged by Las Casas, among them the sack of Antwerp in 1576 by mutinous soldiers in Spain's Army of Flanders, who killed upwards of 8,000 persons.

A Larum for London, a play of the 1590s[5] by an anonymous propagandist, portrays the sack of Antwerp, then the financial center of western Europe. In the opening scenes, Sancho de Avila, historically the commander of the city's citadel at the time, plans the attack: he summons reinforcements from other parts of the Netherlands and suborns a leader of German mercenaries employed by the burghers of Antwerp. When the additional troops arrive, some of them led by the duke of Alba, the Spaniards charge, quickly overcoming the city's German defenders. In the following scenes the Spanish soldiers slaughter Netherlanders indiscriminately. Avila concludes this dra-

---

[2] Pierre L. J. Villey-Desmeserets, *Les Sources & l'évolution des essais de Montaigne*, 12th edn., 2 (Paris: Hachette, 1933), 298–99.

[3] Dougald MacMillan, "The Sources of Dryden's *The Indian Emperour*," *Huntington Library Quarterly* 13 (1950): 359 nn. 10, 11.

[4] See Philip Wayne Powell, *Tree of Hate*, pp. 62–65, 69.

[5] It was probably acted between 1594 and 1600: W. W. Greg, ed., *A Larum for London* (Oxford: Malone Society Reprints, 1913), p. v.

matic warning to London with a description of Antwerp in desolation.[6]

Comparison of the play with near-contemporary records reveals that the dramatist misrepresented Spanish leaders and the events that led to the sack. The duke of Alba had returned to Spain three years before. Avila was indeed in the citadel at the time, but his historical role was very different from that portrayed in the play. Modern opinion of Avila, based on research in primary sources, is expressed by D. W. Davies, who describes him as a "talented Spanish officer." When the mutinous Spanish troops "made a sortie from the Citadel," according to Davies, Avila could not stop them.[7] This version is consistent with that of the best contemporary Spanish historian, Bernardino de Mendoza, who served in the Army of Flanders.[8] George Gascoigne, who was in Antwerp at the time and wrote an account of the sack, names other prominent Spanish officers but makes no reference to Avila.[9] The English author of an early history of Antwerp implies that Avila and other officers attempted to restrain the men.[10]

A Larum for London, representative of Protestant propaganda of the era, evokes the fear of invasion long felt in England. Marlowe, Massinger, and Middleton all assumed—to judge by their plays—that Spain was aggressive, expansionist, and dangerous. The early scenes of *The Massacre at Paris* portraying the slaughter of Protestants have more than a casual re-

[6] Ann L. Mackenzie provides an account of a mid-seventeenth-century Spanish play, perhaps by Rojas Zorrilla, about the sack of Antwerp: "A Study in Dramatic Contrasts: The Siege of Antwerp in *A Larum for London* and *El saco de Amberes*," *BHS* 59 (1982): 283–300.

[7] D. W. Davies, ed., Sir Roger Williams, *The Actions of the Low Countries* (Ithaca, N.Y.: Cornell University Press, 1964), pp. 122–23.

[8] Mendoza, *Comentarios de las guerras de los Países-Bajos*. In B.A.E., 28:549a.

[9] Gascoigne's pamphlet was published anonymously, though his authorship of it has been established: "The Spoyle of Antwerpe. Faithfully reported, by a true Englishman, who was present at the same." In Gascoigne, *Complete Works*, ed. John W. Cunliffe (Cambridge: Cambridge University Press, 1910), 2:586–99.

[10] *An Historicall Discourse, or rather a tragicall Historie of . . . Antwerpe* (London: 1586; STC 691), Sig. E.iii.

semblance to the slaughter scenes that make up the latter part of *A Larum*. *The Bondman*, with its warning of the danger in military unpreparedness, and *A Game at Chess*, in which the Black Knight tells of gathering information useful to an invading army, both carry a burden of warning resembling the more blatant "larum" of the anonymous play.

In face of the record of Spain's attempts to invade England and Ireland, Englishmen's fear of that nation was rational, based on an accurate assessment of the enemy's intentions and capabilities. Yet hostility to Spain often led to distortion of the history portrayed in drama—in *Oldenbarnevelt*, among other plays.

Fletcher and Massinger's conception of their protagonist as a man who threatened to betray the Dutch Republic to Spain and who led a revolt to displace Prince Maurice was largely based on propaganda pamphlets hostile to Oldenbarnevelt. The pamphlets were translated and imported into England during 1617 and 1618. Although the dramatists drew from Oldenbarnevelt's *Apology*, they employed it primarily as a source for passages spoken by Oldenbarnevelt himself, with the result that what he wrote as a defense of his career becomes, in several passages of dialogue, unseemly boasting.[11] The Master of the Revels' concern to delete passages reflecting on Prince Maurice intensifies the partisanship revealed in the play.[12] Apparently the dramatists did not knowingly misrepresent Oldenbarnevelt and the events that led to his execution: when referring to episodes that occurred before the truce, they are accurate.[13] Englishmen of the time were easily persuaded to believe the worst of Spain. Presumably Fletcher and Mas-

[11] For a detailed study of the sources used by Fletcher and Massinger, see *Olden Barnavelt*, ed. Frijlinck, pp. xxiv-lviii. Israel describes pamphlets that were hostile to Oldenbarnevelt, *Dutch Republic*, pp. 62–63.

[12] On the deletions apparent in the manuscript, see *Olden Barnavelt*, ed. Frijlinck, pp. 84–85.

[13] There is, for example, a close correspondence between Oldenbarnevelt's account of the part taken by Sir Francis Vere in the Battle of Nieuport, July 2, 1600 (IV.v; ed. Frijlinck, p. 65) and the account written by the Veres's nineteenth-century biographer (Markham, *"The Fighting Veres,"* pp. 294–95).

singer assumed that the fall of Oldenbarnevelt, insofar as it was not the result of faults accentuated by old age, was but another consequence of Spanish intrigue.

Prejudice and fear combined to distort Englishmen's perceptions of Spain; pride, ambition, intolerance, and prejudice distorted Spaniards' perceptions of England. Other forces as well conditioned the history portrayed in Spanish and English drama.

In an earlier chapter, I referred to Franz Grillparzer's comment on the near-contemporaneity of Lope's *La nueva victoria de Don Gonzalo de Córdoba* and the events of August 1622 that it commemorates. Implicit in Grillparzer's remark is a recognition that good plays about very recent historical events are rare. The English sometimes wrote about recent events: Fletcher and Massinger in *Oldenbarnevelt*, for example, and Marlowe in *The Massacre at Paris*, in which the final scene portrays the accession of Henry IV, the reigning king at the time the play was first performed. But these plays are about the histories of foreign countries. The important English dramatists, unlike Lope and—in one play—Calderón, did not write literally about their recent national history. ". . . in the years of the Armada," David Bevington writes, "dramatists preferred to invoke memories of Crécy and Agincourt rather than deal face-to-face with the Armada victory itself."[14]

Only the Spain of the Renaissance produced such plays as Lope's *El Brasil restituido* and Calderón's *El sitio de Bredá*, good plays about major battles won within the preceding year, written by men who are in the first rank of world dramatists. Both *El Brasil* and *El sitio* were performed at court in the autumn of 1625. If due allowance be made for their commemorative purposes, for the flattery to be expected in court drama, and for the Catholic partisanship of their authors, both plays are accurate: that is, the dramatized history corresponds closely to contemporary records and narrative accounts of the two campaigns that have survived into the twentieth century. Both Lope and Calderón wrote from reliable sources. In contrast,

---

[14] Bevington, *Tudor Drama and Politics*, p. 301.

Lope's *La nueva victoria* is, in important details, inaccurate. In this play, Lope wrote with only limited information about his subject available to him.

Yet a conception of factual accuracy or inaccuracy is inadequate to an evaluation of these plays as a form of history. The dramatists, writing when they did, could not assess the significance of the campaigns they wrote about. Even in 1622 Spain's enemies did not consider the Battle of Fleurus a victory for Don Gonzalo because he failed to prevent the Protestant army led by Mansfeld and Christian of Brunswick from reenforcing Prince Maurice at Bergen-op-Zoom. In 1625 the Spanish capture of Breda and the recapture of Bahía seemed to all observers to be victories. In both *El sitio de Bredá* and *El Brasil restituido* characters refer to Spain's ability to wage war simultaneously in different parts of the world as evidence of her strength. Yet by the time of the plays' first performances the massive expenditures on multiple fronts had required the substitution of a defensive for an offensive strategy in the Netherlands.

Knowledge of the date of composition of these two plays by Lope and one by Calderón adds a dimension to our understanding of the plays and the conditions under which these two greatest of the Spanish dramatists worked. Knowledge of the date, or approximate date, when Calderón wrote *La cisma de Inglaterra* adds even more. Here the date of composition provides assistance in answering questions raised by the play. Why did Calderón write a play about events less than a century in the past that took place in a foreign country; why did he depart so markedly from the historical record known to his audiences; why did he close the play with Princess Mary's promise, spoken in an aside, to restore Catholicism in England? Why, indeed, if he did not have reason to hope that an invasion of England, planned in 1626, would lead to a fulfillment of that promise? *La cisma* was written, it would seem, in an effort to bring audiences to a determination to restore England to Catholicism. *La cisma* seems to be something rare: a good drama written as propaganda.

In most of the plays I have considered, including, emphatically, *La cisma de Inglaterra*, date of composition is a major determinant of the nature of historical representation or of topical comment. The England of the 1590s conditions Shakespeare's portrayal of King John's reign; the Spain of Philip IV's first years conditions Tirso's portrayal of the minority of King Fernando IV of Castile. Lope's disillusionment with Spain's war in the Netherlands, apparent in plays written not long before the Twelve Year Truce, is replaced by a vigorous militarism in a play written at the end of the truce. In most, but not all, of the plays, the date of composition bears an intelligible relationship to the nature of the play. Massinger's *The Renegado* provides an exception, the more striking when considered amid the pattern of conformity with the times provided by other plays. (As I have said, Massinger's audacious independence resembles that of Tirso.) Licensed in 1624, a month after the House of Commons voted supplies for war against Spain, *The Renegado* reveals a sympathy for, even an admiration of, Catholicism strong enough to have led critics and biographers of Massinger to believe that he was a crypto-Catholic. Despite Spain's militant Catholicism, it was not absolutely necessary to associate the nation and Catholicism, and Massinger's plays reveal that he did not associate them.

The history portrayed reflects the dramatists' sources, not in substantive matters alone but often in the texture of dialogue and in emphasis on episodes. Grimeston's *History*, for example, provided Chapman with phrasing for portions of the remarkable exchange between Byron and Montigny about King Philip II in *The . . . Tragedy of . . . Byron*. England's prolific pamphleteers contributed to the dramatic warnings about Spain and international Catholicism. *The Massacre at Paris* retains the acerbity present in the pamphlets from which Marlowe drew his history. The annotation R. C. Bald provided for his edition of *A Game at Chess*—a stylized history of Prince Charles's Spanish courtship—reveals dialogue deeply embedded in Protestant propaganda.

In Spain, another form of popular literature, a more important form, conditioned historical drama: the *romancero*, the collective term for the nation's store of traditional ballads (or romances). Of greater relevance to the drama than English folk ballads, "the Castilian 'romances,' " W. J. Entwistle wrote, "are unsurpassed in Europe for their number, vigour, influence, dramatic intensity, and veracity."[15] To Lope, the ballads provided at once a source for history plays and a determinant of his conception of Spain's past. Lope, like Shakespeare, used chronicles as sources, but even in doing so he shaped his materials in patterns familiar in the *romancero*. The Spanish ballads, Leicester Bradner notes, "accustomed both writers and public to see their national past as a series of spectacular successes or failures."[16] In Shakespeare's history plays, most of them based on chronicles, political and constitutional issues are of central importance; in Lope's, these issues are subordinate or absent altogether. Lope's history plays considered here conclude with "spectacular successes." In only two of them, *Los españoles en Flandes* and *El asalto de Mastrique*, are the victories qualified by doubts expressed earlier in the plays about national policy.

The institution of patronage left its impress on topical and historical drama in both countries. Gifts from patrons—of whom Lope's benefactor, the duke of Sessa, is a preeminent example—supplemented the dramatists' income from theatrical companies. There would seem to be no parallel in England to the long and close relationship between Sessa and Lope, who served as the duke's secretary (a relationship that had as one of its consequences the preservation of a large number of Lope's plays and letters in holograph).[17]

Lope's *La nueva victoria de Don Gonzalo de Córdoba* may be regarded as a fulfillment of an obligation to Sessa, Don Gonzalo's brother. The haste in which Lope wrote the play, before full and accurate information was available to him about the

---

[15] Entwistle, *European Balladry* (Oxford: Clarendon Press, 1939), p. 152.

[16] Bradner, "The Theme of *Privanza* in Spanish and English Drama, 1590–1625," in Kossoff and Amor y Vázquez, eds., *Homenaje a William L. Fichter*, pp. 97–98.

[17] On Lope and Sessa, see Augustín G. de Amezúa, ed., *Epistolario de Lope de Vega Carpio*, 4 vols. (Madrid: 1935–43).

Battle of Fleurus, was presumably intensified by his desire to serve the duke, who in turn wished to aid his brother in gaining recognition and reward for his achievement. The published correspondence of Don Gonzalo and the duke reveals the former urging his brother to intercede for him with persons in authority and the latter doing so.[18] Lope could honestly portray Don Gonzalo's conduct at Fleurus as heroic: the general and those serving in his command fought savagely against a determined enemy having numerical advantage in cavalry. But Don Gonzalo was not a selfless hero: he wished to have fitting reward for what he had done, and his letters written not long after Fleurus reveal bitterness at what he regarded as inadequate recognition of his achievement.

Sessa apparently assisted Lope in writing the play by making letters available to him that Don Gonzalo had written to members of his family about the war in Germany. Sessa's motive is clear: he wished to help his brother.

By contrast, the duke of Lerma's motive in commissioning Vélez de Guevara to write *El caballero del sol* is puzzling. We may assume Vélez would not have included reference to Prince Charles's Spanish courtship without the approval of Lerma. We may also assume that Lerma determined the time the play was performed as well as the time Sir John Digby arrived in the vicinity of the ducal palace. In 1617, before the beginning of the Thirty Years' War, the possibility of offending King James may not have seemed important to Lerma. Was he willing to offend the English for the sake of a theatrical jest—and did he, having second thoughts, arrange a stratagem to prevent Digby from seeing the play?

In Spain and England alike, dramatists wrote for the court as well as the public theatres. Royal patronage at times conditioned or determined dramatic interpretation of important events. Jonson's and Inigo Jones's *Neptune's Triumph* celebrates Prince Charles's journey to Madrid and his safe return; it also expresses King James's conception of himself as a mon-

[18] CODOIN, 54 (1869), 311–15, 319–21, 325–26, 334–37, 349–51, 359–62.

arch ruling in peace.[19] Lope's *El Brasil restituido* and Calderón's *El sitio de Bredá* celebrate Spanish victories; they also represent King Philip IV's conception of himself as a triumphant king, the most powerful of sovereigns.

Olivares, as the leader of King Philip IV's government, made a concerted effort to win the support of men of letters for his policies, and it was his good fortune that he did so when Lope, Calderón, and Quevedo were in full career.[20] Quevedo defended him from critics; Lope and Calderón wrote, respectively, *El Brasil restituido* and *El sitio de Bredá* about victories won under his direction, plays that were performed in the royal palace in the autumn of 1625. Olivares is known to have sponsored the performance of Calderón's play; possibly he sponsored that of Lope as well: surviving records do not permit us to say. In any event, the tone of celebration in these plays, as in much else that was written in Spain about the victories of 1625, is the result not solely of spontaneous euphoria but also of the policies of the count-duke.

King James gave Jonson a pension, but neither he nor Queen Elizabeth before him made a concerted effort to gain the support of men of letters. Each of them received a full measure of flattery, and as monarchs they had little to fear from public comment about themselves. But as previous chapters have revealed, King James's policies were not immune from indirect criticism.

Middleton's *A Game at Chess* comes close to direct criticism of James's pro-Spanish policy. Dissent in this instance was made less dangerous by the differences on the subject of Spain between the king and his heir and his favorite. Even so, the ex-

[19] "The theatre that was created by royal patronage," Stephen Orgel writes, "was the theatre of the masque, and it was uniquely responsive to the minds of its patrons" (Orgel, "The Royal Theatre and the King," in Guy Fitch Lytle and Stephen Orgel, eds., *Patronage in the Renaissance* [Princeton: Princeton University Press, 1981], p. 270).

[20] On Olivares' patronage, of painters as well as writers, see John H. Elliott, "Philip IV of Spain: Prisoner of Ceremony," in A. G. Dickens, ed., *The Courts of Europe: Politics, Patronage and Royalty, 1400–1800* (New York: McGraw-Hill, 1977), pp. 176–78.

istence of the play poses an unsolved problem in the operation of patronage. Would Middleton have written so audaciously without encouragement from someone in a position of high authority? If not, no scholar has succeeded in a convincing identification of that person or persons.

The royalism pervading political thought in England and Spain influences the portrayal of recent historical monarchs in both countries. The remoteness of Shakespeare's Henry VIII from perennial political problems and his providential role in shaping English history may be associated with King James's belief that kings were the agents of God. Even Calderón's Henry VIII has a regal dignity. The exemplary Queen Elizabeth of Coello's *El Conde de Sex* embodies the neoclassical conception of decorum in characterization. In this play probably more than in any other Spanish or English play of the seventeenth century, literary theory controls the representation of a major historical figure.

Government regulation as well as literary theory influenced the dramatists. Chapman's Henry IV of France appears in the Byron plays with the qualities appropriate to his rank. But a character portraying Henry IV's wife—to judge from a letter written by the French ambassador—appeared in a scene, cancelled in the printed text, quarreling with one portraying her husband's mistress. Chapman's offense in this instance, it has been suggested, may have prompted the English authorities to prohibit the representation of recent Christian monarchs.[21] King James cited the prohibition in his order forbidding further performances of *A Game at Chess*.

Yet the representation of them had been controversial in Queen Elizabeth's reign. When the English ambassador protested the planned performance in Paris in 1602 of a play that included a character portraying Queen Elizabeth, the French authorities forbade the performance. But on that occasion, the French recalled Marlowe's *The Massacre at Paris*, in which Henry IV was represented on stage. There was, it would appear, a re-

[21] Gildersleeve, *Government Regulation of the Elizabethan Drama*, pp. 105–07.

ciprocal relationship between literary theory and the attitudes of supervising officials.

The English dramatists often wrote about Spain; Spanish dramatists rarely mentioned England, though what they wrote about the imagined destiny of Spain had relevance to all the nations of Europe. The assumption that Spain was preordained to world hegemony was lethal. For decades it distorted the history portrayed by her dramatists. More seriously, it distorted the perceptions of her leaders who, like Gondomar in his letter of 1619 to Philip III and Olivares in his *Gran memorial* of 1624, urged domestic reform not to aid Spain's poor but to strengthen the nation's military power. Many Spaniards of the early seventeenth century, troubled by the decline in their nation's fortunes, attempted to account for the reverses that had plagued Spain since the 1580s. Seemingly, so it appeared to many, Spaniards had incurred the wrath of God, who had long favored them as His own people.[22] Their leaders shared their misgivings, but they fought on.

Nearly always the wars of the era had a religious dimension even though they were not fought primarily for reasons of religion. Spain's refusal to countenance toleration for Protestants made an early settlement of the Dutch Revolt impossible. Trade rivalry and pride prolonged it. Again, trade rivalry exacerbated the animosity in Anglo-Spanish relations during the reigns of Philip II and Elizabeth I. But it is impossible to doubt the intensity of English Puritan hatred of Spanish Catholicism, or, on the other side, the religious zeal that animated many of the Spaniards in their attempts to restore the heretic isle to the true faith.

Religious conviction, the most powerful of the forces shaping the history portrayed in drama, is more often the subject of dialogue in the Spanish than in the English plays. Shakespeare in *King John* represents antagonism between an English sovereign and a pope claiming authority—intrusively, it is made to appear—in England. Middleton in *A Game at Chess* repre-

[22] See John H. Elliott, "Self-Perception and Decline in Early Seventeenth-Century Spain," *Past and Present*, 74 (1977): 41–61.

sents the Spaniards' attempt to convert Prince Charles as the culmination of their treachery; Jonson in *Neptune's Triumph* celebrates Prince Charles's discovery of the Spaniards' intention: the intention, we may assume from the events preceding the masque, to convert him. Of the major dramatists I have considered, Marlowe alone, in *The Massacre at Paris*, portrays vigorously and at length an international Catholic alliance threatening England. At the other extreme, Massinger in *The Renegado* surprises by his sympathy for Catholicism; Chapman in *The Conspiracy and Tragedy of . . . Byron* surprises by his refusal to reveal religious conviction. For the most part the English dramatists assume, sometimes without becoming explicit, that Catholicism is a component of the threat represented by Spain.

The Spanish dramatists are more outspoken. The difference is to be expected: Lope and Calderón became priests; Tirso, a friar.[23] Their plays frequently include reflective passages on theological or philosophical subjects, they are ordinarily more chaste in dialogue and situation than contemporary English plays, and more often they illustrate a design in human affairs that reflects their authors' belief in divine providence.[24]

How can the dramatists' religious professions be reconciled with the attitudes toward Spain's wars their plays reveal? They do not, it should be noted, write about "holy wars": that is, wars undertaken to impose a religion on a foreign country. In the opinion of influential Spanish theologians who had written on the theory of warfare, notably Franciscus de Victoria (1492–1546) and Francisco Suárez, S.J. (1548–1617), the propagation of religion was not a cause for just war.[25] On the other hand, war to suppress rebellion of a king's subjects (as in *Los españoles en Flandes*, *El asalto de Mastrique*, and *El sitio de Bredá*),

[23] It is relevant to add that Tirso belonged to the Mercedarian order from youth, whereas Lope and Calderón were not ordained until they were past fifty years of age.

[24] Shergold comments on the consequences for their plays of the dramatists' religious professions: *The Spanish Stage*, p. 554.

[25] See James Turner Johnson, *Ideology, Reason, and the Limitation of War*, pp. 154, 163.

to regain a king's territories wrongfully seized (as in *El Brasil restituido*), or to fight against an enemy who had declared war (as in *Pobreza no es vileza*) was altogether consistent with just-war doctrine. It was perhaps the seemingly self-evident justice in such wars that accounts for the limited attention given in these plays to the reasons for Spain's fighting.

Spain's entry into the war in Germany by invading the Palatinate in 1620 presented a more complicated problem, one that Lope addresses in *La nueva victoria*:[26] he justifies Spanish intervention as support of an ally whose domain, Bohemia, had been attacked.[27] Conceivably, the war in Germany had something to do with Tirso's criticism of Spanish policy in *La prudencia en la mujer* (c. 1622). In *No hay peor sordo* he seems to favor an invasion of England, justifiable in Spanish theory as a response to the English attack on Cádiz in the autumn of 1625.

Lope wrote more often and more emphatically than the other dramatists in support of Spain's imperial policies. Although the nation's major wars were not, in the opinion of Spanish theologians, undertaken to propagate Catholicism, they acquire in Lope's portrayal of them a religious dimension.

His best and best-known plays are not those about military campaigns (though *El Brasil restituido* has a place on selected lists and *El asalto de Mastrique* merits one). Rather, by critical consensus, his best plays are the tragedy *El caballero de Olmedo* and a group of plays about peasant life such as *Peribáñez y el Comendador de Ocaña* and *Fuenteovejuna*. In plays of this latter kind, Lope portrays men of the lowest social class, peasants, who insist with dignity that they be recognized as men of honor and who, when necessary, avenge affronts to their honor. These plays are unique achievements in Lope's time, unmatched in Spain or even Europe.

Lope's humane clarity of vision enabled him to free himself from habits of perception that were reenforced by literary tra-

---

[26] Ed. Acad., 13:137a.

[27] Luis de Molina, S.J. (1535–1600), one of the influential Spanish theologians, argued that a ruler, for reasons akin to self-defense, could make war in support of an ally who had suffered wrongly. See Bernice Hamilton, *Political Thought in Sixteenth-Century Spain*, p. 140.

dition. The plays reveal a reverence for the institutions of Spain. Yet they reveal as well a respect, even reverence, for men and women in the lowest class.

How could this man, capable of such clarity of perception, write in support of an imperialism that was inescapably militaristic? Lope himself formulated this question in *El asalto de Mastrique*, in the lines he wrote for Alonso García, a common soldier. García's account of the brutality of war culminates in a soliloquy in which he expresses doubt that the capture of Maastricht will be worth the Spanish lives it will cost. The portrayal of his spirited participation in the final attack does not resolve the questions about war he has asked.

El asalto is not representative of Lope's attitude toward Spain's wars. Repeatedly he writes with pride about the nation's military strength and the extent of her empire. As late as 1629 Quevedo includes a passage in *Cómo ha de ser el privado* that gains resonance from its resemblance to passages that had appeared in Lope's plays for thirty and more years. "The realm you inherit is small," the admiral tells the young king of "Naples." "May the limits of your empire reach the other hemisphere";

> *y el sol, que en seguras ruedas*
> *de zafir da vuelta al mundo,*
> *no alumbre reinos extraños.*   (Ed. Blecua 4:151)

and may the sun, which in secure wheels of sapphire circles the world, not shine on foreign realms.

Quevedo's lines turn on images resembling ones Lope had used in *Los españoles en Flandes*. "Su Majestad tiene imperio," Don Juan exclaims, referring to Philip II,

> *Que deste al otro hemisferio*
> *No parte jurisdición.*
>   *Por la tierra de Felipe,*
> *Por islas y mar profundo,*
> *Una vuelta se da al mundo*
> *Sin que de otra participe.*   (Ed. Acad. 12:374b)

His Majesty's rule extends, without intervening jurisdiction, from this to the other hemisphere.

One can travel around the world on possessions of Philip, across islands and the deep sea, without passing over the possessions of another.

Alonso García in *El asalto de Mastrique* refers to Philip II in almost the same way: "that great monarch, on whose sea one can travel around the world without touching foreign land" (Ed. Acad. 12:469b). There are traditional, even formulaic, qualities in the references to the Spanish empire by Lope and other dramatists that gain force from their resemblances to one another.[28]

The dramatists—Lope above all—reveal the grip the imperial ideal had on the Spanish mind. Olivares, J. H. Elliott writes, inherited "the great imperial tradition, which believed firmly in the rightness, and indeed the inevitability, of Spanish, and specifically Castilian, hegemony over the world."[29] Lope too was heir to that tradition, and from the time of his sonnet about the Invincible Armada at anchor in Lisbon harbor before its fateful voyage until that of his long poem about Mary, queen of Scots, *La corona trágica*, in 1627, he gave it eloquent statement. In a poem about Charles V, he describes the inheritance Charles gave his son when he abdicated. Lope makes no clear distinction between the position of the father as emperor and the son as king:

> Al gran Philipo Segundo
> viviendo el mundo dejó;
> fuése a Iuste, y atajó
> la mayor parte del mundo.[30]

[Charles V] while living left the world to the great Philip II. He went to Yuste and partitioned off the larger part of the world.

[28] On the relationships among such passages, see Thomas M. Greene's discussion of intertextuality: *The Light in Troy: Imitation and Discovery in Renaissance Poetry* (New Haven: Yale University Press, 1982), pp. 16–19.

[29] Elliott, *Imperial Spain*, p. 320.

[30] *Obras sueltas*, 4:390.

Lope writes also about Philip III's inheritance: "Because [you are] the Third of such a great Second, you can—as the heir of his sword and sceptre—conquer the world and govern Spain."[31]

Lope's praise of Philip IV is recurrent in *El Brasil restituido*, a play pervaded by the iconography of empire.[32] The personification of Brazil refers to Philip IV (i):

El gran Felipe, mi Rey,
De la católica ley
Y evangélica verdad
   Soberano defensor . . .   (Ed. Acad. 13:84a and b)

The great Philip, my king, sovereign defender of Catholic law and the true gospel,

and when the Monarchy of Spain appears soon after, she is seated on a throne with a globe representing the world at her feet. Fame addresses her (i):

Invicta Monarquía,

. . . .

Cuatro coronas tienes,
Tú en Africa y Europa,
En Asia y en América triunfante.   (Ed. Acad. 13:84b)

Invincible Monarchy, . . . you have four crowns; you [are] triumphant in Africa and Europe, in Asia and in America.

Lope's patriotism had not dimmed with his advancing age.

Olivares' determined though futile effort to achieve what he thought to be Spain's destiny reminds us that Lope's repeated references to it were not isolated expressions of patriotism. Lope could remember, as Tirso and Calderón could not, Spain's triumphant years before 1588; the difference in ages may have contributed to the more critical turn of mind appar-

---

[31] Ibid., 4:287.

[32] For a study of the iconography of Philip IV, see Brown and Elliott, *A Palace for a King.* Note also Graham Parry, "The Iconography of James I," in Parry's *The Golden Age restor'd,* pp. 1–39.

ent in some of the younger men's plays. Even so, both of them write as imperialists when they refer to the events of 1625.

Lope's poetry provides insight into the motives that led Olivares to undertake his anachronistic program. In turn, the successes of Olivares' early years in power assure us that the Englishmen whose fears Middleton expressed in *A Game at Chess* had no phantom enemy in view. The count-duke and the poet, as well as the Black Knight, desired the "possession of the world" for Spain.

Appendix

ENGLISH PLAYS FROM
THE *Comedia*

IN THEIR developments from the religious dramas of the Middle Ages, the English and the Spanish dramas were largely independent of one another. Yet Englishmen in some instances looked to Spanish plays for sources of their own. How early and how often they did so have remained vexed questions.

So eminent a modern historian of English drama as Allardyce Nicoll assumed that the *comedia* was widely influential in Jacobean and Caroline comedy. His reference to the subject appears in a discussion of "The Main Types of Drama, 1600–42":

> The tragi-comedy of a romantic cast had its unquestionable influence on the minds of the comic dramatists, and Spanish intrigue came to usurp more and more attention. The Spanish drama was magnificently fitted to appeal to the ages of James and of Charles. Under Lope de Vega and Calderon it had won a supreme place in the world of art. More and more the Court was looking to Spain, as the old feeling which had risen to white heat in the days of the Armada passed away. The Spanish comic theatre was distinguished by three characteristics: the romantic tone which frequently enveloped the more serious scenes; the insistence upon intrigue, or action, at the expense of the characters; and the air of aristocratic gallantry engendered in a strictly monarchist country amid conventions of a late stage of civilization. All three appealed to the English playwrights and spectators. Here they found the courtly air, the atmosphere of assignations and intrigues, the slight colouring of romantic sentiment, for which they pined. With Fletcher the Iberian comedy was popularized in England, and was destined to run its course well into the eighteenth century.[1]

[1] Nicoll, *British Drama*, 4th edn. (London: Harrop and Co., 1947), pp. 119–20.

Clifford Leech shared Nicoll's opinion on the subject. In 1950 he referred to

Fletcher and some of his contemporaries and successors certainly wrote Iberian comedies of intrigue. But did they turn directly to the *comedia*? Had Tudor dramatists done so earlier?[2]

These questions can be answered. Beginning in 1890 a series of important studies of the relationship between English Renaissance drama and the contemporary Spanish drama has appeared. The studies are to be found in a variety of publications, the most important of them in German. For many years these studies have not been the subject of a systematic review. I attempt to provide such a review. I must emphasize that I give attention not to the many Spanish sources in prose fiction and history used by English dramatists, but solely to the dramatic ones (that is, the sources in the *comedia*).[3]

Early in this century a prominent English historian of Spain, Martin Hume, included in a study of *Spanish Influence on English Literature* (1905) a chapter on "The Spanish Theatre and the English Dramatists." Although his approach is totally different, he is scarcely less restrained in emphasizing the English debt to the *comedia* than Voltaire had been in the eighteenth

---

the Spanish "cloak-and-sword comedy," writing that it "began to affect the development of English drama as early as Fletcher": Leech, *Shakespeare's Tragedies and Other Studies in Seventeenth Century Drama* (London: Chatto and Windus, 1950), p. 224.

[2] In the course of his arraignment of English drama, Stephen Gosson wrote in 1582 that "baudie Comedies in Latine, French, Italian, and Spanish, have been throughly ransackt, to furnish the Playe houses in London," seemingly meaning that early and perhaps lost English plays were based on Spanish ones. Gosson's remark, however, requires careful attention: before 1582—before Lope de Vega and the dramatists of the Valencian School began to write plays—there would have been little published Spanish drama for the English to "ransack." The adjective "baudie" puts us in mind of Fernando de Rojas's novel in dialogue, the *Celestina*, about a Spanish "bawd." A portion of it was translated and adapted, perhaps by John Rastell, as *The Interlude of Calisto and Melebea* (c. 1527). Probabaly Gosson refers solely to the *Celestina*. (See Gosson, *Playes Confuted in five Actions*, Second "Action" [London: 1582], sig. D4. In my discussion of Gosson, I follow A. L. Stiefel, "Die Nachahmung spanischer Komödien in England unter den ersten Stuarts," *Romanische Forschungen* 5 [1890]: 194.)

[3] On the Tudor dramatists' use of Spanish non-dramatic literature, see John Garrett Underhill, *Spanish Literature in the England of the Tudors* (New York: Macmillan, 1899).

century. Hume's casual use of literary evidence results in exaggeration of a kind often found in early considerations of the subject. His book was followed within a year by Rudolph Schevill's "On the Influence of Spanish Literature upon English in the Early 17th Century," an essay notable for close attention to the difficulties inherent in an effort to identify sources in the *comedia*.[4]

Schevill doubted that many existed. He knew of only three English plays that had been traced to Spanish plays: the anonymous *Love's Cure* (of unknown date) and James Shirley's *The Young Admiral* (1633) and *The Opportunity* (1634). Schevill apparently overlooked Massinger's *The Renegado* (1624), which had been shown to have a source in the *comedia*. Yet this is the only English Renaissance play he fails to mention that even now has been convincingly traced to a Spanish one. Schevill doubted that many Englishmen knew Spanish: "How easy it is to exaggerate the extent to which the Spanish language was known and spoken, even among the learned of that age."[5] He is probably right about persons who could speak Spanish, but both previous and subsequent research reveals that a number of prominent Englishmen, including Fletcher as well as Shirley and Massinger, could at least read it.[6]

Arguments have been advanced that other early Stuart plays derive from the *comedia*, but, as I shall explain, I find them unconvincing. G. E. Bentley's judicious review in 1956 of relevant scholarship in volumes 3, 4, and 5 of his *Jacobean and Caroline Stage* simplifies the study of plays later than 1616. I have generally relied upon Bentley, and I have not reviewed arguments he rejects unless I disagree with his conclusions. Nor do I review arguments concerning Shakespeare. The intensive research of the last sixty-four years devoted to Shakespeare's plays has produced nothing to alter the conclusion reached by Henry Thomas, who used the phrase "Much Ado About

---

[4] Schevill, *Romanische Forschungen* 20 (1905–06): 604–34.

[5] Ibid., p. 604.

[6] Gustav Ungerer, *Anglo-Spanish Relations in Tudor Literature*, pp. 43–44; Dale B. J. Randall, *Golden Tapestry*, pp. 231–33. References relevant to the dramatists appear below.

Nothing" to describe earlier efforts to establish Shakespeare's indebtedness to the *comedia*.[7] Seemingly no Tudor and only four early Stuart plays derive from Spanish plays, all of them identified by late nineteenth-century Germans—three by A. L. Stiefel and one by Emil Koeppel. This is curious, given the frequency with which early Stuart dramatists turned to Spanish prose fiction and history, ordinarily but not invariably in English or French translation.

The dramatists obviously found Spanish prose easier to understand and to adapt for their plays than the highly metaphorical, polymetric verse of the *comedia*. Although passages in lines of eleven or more syllables often appear, the short, octosyllabic line, in varying patterns of rhyme or assonance, is predominant; and the English found it an awkward measure to turn into their pentameters. Even in instances in which English dramatists closely follow a distinctive pattern of ideas in a Spanish play—in *Love's Cure*, for example—the phrasing in English is unlikely to approximate a literal translation of the original. In contrast, the English found little difficulty in turning French hexameters into pentameters. Many English plays of the later seventeenth century include passages that are little more than literal translations from French. For this reason, among others, we can more easily identify French than Spanish dramatic sources of English plays.

★

Because most aspects of the relationship between the *comedia* and early Stuart drama remain controversial, it will be useful to review the evidence that Fletcher, Massinger, and Shirley, each in turn chief dramatist of the King's company, could read Spanish. There has been little doubt about Shirley and Massinger. In 1890 A. L. Stiefel revealed that two of Shirley's plays are adaptations from the *comedia*. In 1897 Emil Koeppel traced

---

[7] Thomas, "Shakespeare and Spain": The Taylorian Lecture, 1922, in *Studies in European Literature* (Oxford: 1930).

Hispanists of any nationality are likely to be familiar with Shakespeare's plays and are unlikely to overlook any probable source in the *comedia* used by him.

Massinger's *The Renegado* to a play by Cervantes. In 1923 Maurice Chelli referred to Massinger's mastery of Latin and added that his study of Massinger's sources had convinced him that the dramatist could also read French and Spanish.[8] Massinger's latest editors, Philip Edwards and Colin Gibson, cite Chelli's conclusion with approval.[9]

Fletcher's ability to read Spanish has been the subject of needless controversy. As early as 1899, A. L. Stiefel demonstrated that Fletcher's *The Island Princess* derives from a Spanish work, Bartolomé Leonardo de Argensola's *Conquista de las Islas Malucas*, rather than from a French novel based upon it, the Sieur de Bellan's *Histoire mémorable de Dias espagnol et de Quixaire Princesse des Moluques*. Citing parallel passages, as well as details present in the Spanish and English but not in the French, Stiefel leaves little doubt on the subject.[10] The quality of his evidence will be suggested by the following:

In Fletcher two Portuguese, Pyniero and Christophero, speak (1.i):

CHRISTOPHERO:
. . .
But I wonder much how such poore and base pleasures,
As tugging at an oare, or skill in steerage,
Should become Princes.

PYNIERO:
. . .
They take as much delight in a Baratto,
A little scurvy boate to row her tithly,
And have the art to turne and wind her nimbly,
Thinke it as noble too, though it be slavish,
And a dull labour that declines a Gentleman:
As we Portugalls, or the Spaniards do in riding,
In managing a great horse which is princely.

Neither the reference to a "Baratto" nor that to "princely" custom occurs in the French novel, but both are present in the

---

[8] Chelli, *Le Drame de Massinger* (Lyon: M. Audin, 1923), pp. 42–43.

[9] *Plays and Poems of Massinger*, ed. Edwards and Gibson, 2:2 n. 3.

[10] Stiefel, "Über die Quelle von J. Fletchers 'Island Princess,' " *Archiv* 103 (1899): 277–308.

work of Bartolomé Leonardo de Argensola.[11] Had Stiefel's article not appeared in German, later scholars might have been willing to believe that Fletcher as well as Massinger and Shirley could read Spanish.

Their reluctance to do so[12] prompted Edward M. Wilson to remark with a note of irony in 1948 that "it is simpler to believe that he [Fletcher] read Spanish with some fluency than to postulate undiscovered translations or to invent unwanted collaborators."[13] After reference to Stiefel's discovery, Wilson quotes parallel passages from Fletcher's *The Chances*, from the French translation of Cervantes' novel *La señora Cornelia*, usually assumed to have been the source of Fletcher's main plot, and from the Spanish original. The more convincing of the two parallels isolated by Wilson turns on a passage in *The Chances* in which a young man tells his friend that before going out he has "a few Devotions / To do" (1.i.73–74). For this there is precedent in the Spanish ("el se queria quedar a rezar ciertas deuociones") but not in the French, in which the young man says merely that he has something to do before he can join his friend ("il se vouloit arrester à quelque chose qu'il auoit a faire").[14]

In a separate study of the same year Wilson identifies the source of Fletcher's plot in *Rule a Wife and Have a Wife* as a novel by Alonso Jerónimo de Salas Barbadillo, *El sagaz Estacio, marido examinado*, a work translated neither into English nor French by the time Fletcher wrote his play.[15] Wilson describes in detail the relationship between the two works. A single par-

---

[11] Ibid., pp. 289–91. The quotation is based on *The Dramatic Works in the Beaumont and Fletcher Canon*, gen. ed. Fredson Bowers, 5 (Cambridge: Cambridge University Press, 1982), 553.

[12] Baldwin Maxwell was an exception. In 1939 he wrote that he was "not so certain as some critics have been of Fletcher's small knowledge of Spanish": *Studies in Beaumont, Fletcher, and Massinger* (Chapel Hill, N.C.: University of North Carolina Press, 1939), p. 107.

[13] Edward M. Wilson, "Did John Fletcher Read Spanish?" *PQ* 27 (1948): 190.

[14] Ibid., p. 189.

[15] Edward M. Wilson, "*Rule a Wife and Have a Wife* and *El sagaz Estacio*," *RES* 24 (1948): 189–94.

allel passage, however, should be sufficient to convince doubt-
ers that his argument is sound. Near the end of II.i in the English play the following exchange occurs:

MARGARITA:
Is he so goodly a man doe you say?

[ALTEA]:
        As you shall see Lady,
But to all this is but a trunke.

MARGARITA:
        I would have him so,
I shall adde branches to him to adorne him.

In the Spanish novel, Marcela, a courtesan seeking a husband
to protect her from arrest, speaks: "I am looking for a husband
who will not be a complete one, but a stock, a tree, I mean,
who will shield me from the strength of this sun [that is, of
Justice] with his shadow; for I will fit him for that task by put-
ting branches on his head" (the translation is Wilson's).[16] Wilson comments: "The similarity of the conceits is obvious; perhaps Fletcher really knew a little Spanish."

Yet so eminent an authority as G. E. Bentley is not convinced. "The source of the main plot of the play has not been
certainly identified," he wrote in 1956,

> but Mr. Edward M. Wilson . . . thinks it is *El Sagaz Estacio, Marido
> examinado*, by Salas Barbadillo . . . . As Wilson outlines the Span-
> ish novel, there are clear general resemblances to *Rule a Wife and
> Have a Wife*, but the few common details he cites seem to me suf-
> ficiently obvious developments of the situation to have been due to
> chance.[17]

I can merely say that the shared metaphor of a tree trunk for a
husband whom the wife will equip with branches by making

[16] Ibid., p. 192. In the Spanish: "Por esto busco yo un esposo que no sea
marido entero, sino un leño, un árbol digo, que defienda con su sombra contra
la fuerza deste sol, que yo le habilitaré para ello poniéndole las ramas sobre la
cabeza."

[17] Bentley, *Jacobean and Caroline Stage*, 3:410–11.

a cuckold of him does not seem to me an "obvious" development "of the situation." Bentley's conservatism in acknowl-
edging Spanish sources for early Stuart plays is typical of the
best investigation of the subject in this century. It frequently
results from a realistic assessment of the difficulty in distin-
guishing plays with a common or similar source from those in
which the English derives from the Spanish. Still, in my opinion, Bentley's commendable skepticism becomes excessive in
his response to Wilson's argument about *Rule a Wife and Have
a Wife*.

★

Before turning to the four plays that have been traced to the
comedia, I must consider arguments that two other English
plays were partially based on Spanish ones.

   In 1959 a prominent English Hispanist, Albert E. Sloman,
argued that an underplot of a play sometimes attributed to
Lope de Vega, *La ilustre fregona*,[18] a dramatization of one of
Cervantes' *Novelas ejemplares* of the same title, provided a
source for an underplot of *The Fair Maid of the Inn*.[19] The English play, printed in the Beaumont and Fletcher folio of 1647,
was licensed as Fletcher's in January 1625/6, although its authorship is disputed.[20] Resemblances between a climactic episode in the Spanish novel and the English play—the revelation
of the true identity of the "fair maid"—had previously been
noted.[21] Sloman reveals that there are more extensive resemblances between the Spanish and English plays. Yet he does
not prove, in my opinion, that the dramatic version of
La ilustre fregona should be regarded as a source of *The Fair
Maid of the Inn*.

   [18] Morley and Bruerton do not believe the play is Lope's: *Chronology*, pp.
293–94.
   [19] Sloman, "The Spanish Source of *The Fair Maid of the Inn*," in Frank
Pierce, ed., *Hispanic Studies in Honour of I. González Llubera* (Oxford: Dolphin
Book Co., 1959), pp. 331–41.
   [20] Bentley, *Jacobean and Caroline Stage*, 3:337–38.
   [21] On earlier comment about the relationship of *The Fair Maid of the Inn* to
Cervantes' novel, see ibid., 3:339.

I can be brief in my rebuttal for a reason Sloman himself mentions in his final paragraph: an inconsistency in dates. *The Fair Maid* was licensed January 22, 1625/6; *La ilustre fregona* was mentioned by Alonso de Castillo Solórzano as being acted in Madrid in 1630; the earliest known text of the play was printed in 1641.[22] Sloman writes:

> If, therefore, the Spanish text was available in England, it must have been in a lost *suelta*. There can, I submit, be little doubt that the Cesario-Bianca Clarissa-Mentivole love-affairs and the characters of Forobosco and the Host derive from *La ilustre fregona*, but how this play came to be known to the authors of *The Fair Maid*, and what new light, if any, this fact throws upon the latter's authorship, are matters best left to the English Jacobean scholars.[23]

My admiration for Sloman's other published work notwithstanding, I believe he leaves too much to be determined by "English Jacobean scholars," who customarily regard a sequence of dates such as he describes as precluding Spanish influence on an English play. If, indeed, *The Fair Maid* resembled *La ilustre fregona* as closely, say, as Shirley's *The Young Admiral* resembles Lope de Vega's *Don Lope de Cardona*, we might be driven to the hypothesis of a lost *suelta* (a Spanish approximation of an English quarto), but such is far from the case.

Sloman argues that the Host and Forobosco in *The Fair Maid* derive from the Host and Pepín in *La ilustre fregona*. I can see no distinctive qualities in these two Hosts that differentiate them from the parallel character in Cervantes' novel. All are jovial and yet dignified men who punctiliously fulfill their obligations to their ward, "the fair maid." Forobosco, accurately described in the dramatis personae as "a cheating Mountebank," differs both in his role and in his raucous personality from the quick-witted *gracioso* Pepín, a loyal servant of Don Tomás. The contrast between them is epitomized in their fates at the plays' ends: Forobosco with his accomplice is sent to the galleys; Pepín is given a thousand ducats by his master.

Sloman's case for indebtedness in the English play to the

---

[22] Sloman, "Spanish Source of *The Fair Maid of the Inn*," p. 341.
[23] Ibid.

Spanish one rests primarily on the similarity between the family relationships of the two pairs of young lovers. In his words:

> In both [plays], a lady of the same name (Clara, Clarissa) has a secret love-affair with the son of her father's friend (Diego, Mentivole), and her brother (Pedro, Cesario) makes advances to an inn-girl (Costanza, Bianca); and in both it transpires that the inn-girl is the half-sister of Diego/Mentivole, who has been left by her mother to be brought up by the keeper of an inn.[24]

In isolation from the plays in which they appear, these relationships may seem to provide impressive evidence. Even so, we note that the relationships are merely such as to make possible double marriages between two families, an especially useful arrangement of characters in *The Fair Maid of the Inn*, in which the double marriages can terminate a feud between the two families. Apart from the episode revealing the identity of the maid—an episode present in Cervantes' novel—the Spanish and English plays are very different from one another: *La ilustre fregona*, a light-hearted comedy of love intrigue; *The Fair Maid*, a tragicomedy of dark emotions in which the love affairs are, until the denouement, subordinate to events related to the feud separating the two families.[25]

In *The Demetrius Legend* Ervin C. Brody asserts that Lope de Vega's *El Gran Duque de Moscovia* and *El Duque de Viseo* are among the sources of Fletcher's *The Loyal Subject* (1618).[26] Again I can be brief in offering rebuttal: Brody's phrasing suggests that he is not fully convinced by his own argument; furthermore, relevant dates, though not totally incompatible, pose difficulties.

After citing several historical works, including one by the dramatist's uncle, Dr. Giles Fletcher's *Of the Russe Commonwealth* (1591), Brody adds that "The main literary sources of

---

[24] Ibid., p. 334.

[25] The main plot of the English play derives from the Neri-Bianchi feud in Florence: Baldwin Maxwell, "The Source of the Principal Plot of *The Fair Maid of the Inn*," *MLN* 59 (1944): 122–27.

[26] Brody, *The Demetrius Legend and Its Literary Treatment in the Age of the Baroque* (Rutherford, N.J.: Fairleigh Dickinson University Press, 1972).

the play" are the two plays by Lope "and Thomas Heywood's
The Royal King and the Loyal Subject."[27] Heywood's play has
long been considered a probable source for Fletcher's. Of the
two Spanish plays, Brody devotes much the larger share of attention to *El Gran Duque de Moscovia*. His phrasing requires attention. Writing about Fletcher's character Theodore, a colonel who is the son of Archas (the "loyal subject"), Brody
remarks that "In looking for a prototype, Fletcher *apparently*
[my emphasis] decided to borrow from Lope's treasure house,
and he chose Teodoro from *El Gran Duque de Moscovia,* who
came close to his imagination, transforming the latter's trait of
passive resistance into the rebellious nature of his own hero."[28]
In reality, the two characters have nothing in common except
the similarity of their names and their nationality. Teodoro is
incompetent, even feeble-minded; Theodore is a decisive
leader of men.

Most of Brody's argument turns on Fletcher's alleged use of
"the Demetrius legend": the mélange of deception, specula-
tion, and historical fact surrounding the presumed death in
1591 of the nine-year-old Demetrius, son of Tsar Ivan the Ter-
rible; the appearance in Poland about 1603 of a man claiming
to be Demetrius; the coronation of that man as Tsar in July
1605; and his assassination in May 1606. Lope's play, published
in 1617 although written earlier,[29] depicts the "pseudo" Demetrius as the true heir to the Russian throne. After showing
him as boy and man driven from place to place in his effort to
escape assassins employed by Tsar Boris Godunov, Lope concludes with Demetrius triumphant, recognized as the legitimate Tsar. Fletcher's play could scarcely be more different
from Lope's. Brody isolates a thin subplot in *The Loyal Subject*, in which the younger son of the "loyal" general Archas,
watched over by Archas's brother Briskie, assumes the dress of
a young woman as protection from the Great Duke of Moscovia, believed to represent a threat not only to Archas but to

[27] Ibid., p. 166.
[28] Ibid., p. 174.
[29] Morley and Bruerton believe that it was written not later than 1613: *Chronology*, p. 39.

all his family. The only significant resemblance between the young Archas and Lope's Demetrio is their common need to disguise themselves for protection against the Great Duke of Moscovia and their common wanderings in company with a loyal protector.[30]

In asserting that Fletcher made use of Lope de Vega's *El Duque de Viseo* in writing *The Loyal Subject*, Brody follows J. K. Klein, who referred to resemblances between the plays in his *Geschichte des spanischen Dramas* (10: 490) of 1872–1875. As Brody writes, both A. W. Ward and R. Warwick Bond considered Klein's reference and disregarded it. Brody describes resemblances between the plays that are impressive only in isolation from the plays in their entirety. In fact, almost all the similarities between Fletcher and Lope that Brody isolates exist also in Heywood. Furthermore, despite their common theme of a subject's duty of passive obedience to his sovereign, *El Duque de Viseo* and *The Loyal Subject* are in their preoccupations and plots very different.

★

In considering the relationship of English drama to the *comedia*, we must distinguish between what is demonstrable and what is merely probable or possible. In addition to four instances in which a Spanish play can be shown to be a major source of an English one, it is likely that certain scenes or striking episodes in the *comedia* provided suggestions for passages in English plays. Englishmen of literary interests and aptitudes such as Endymion Porter, Kenelm Digby, and Richard Fan-

---

[30] Brody seems to be aware of the uncertainty inherent in his argument. "I cannot even be sure," he writes, "whether Fletcher intended the inclusion of this Demetrius fragment to excite the curiosity of his spectators, or whether this episode was only the unconscious reflex of a sensitive dramatist, who, accustomed to listening so often to the events of Russian history at the end of the sixteenth century, could not help utilizing motifs from this fascinating tale" (*Demetrius Legend*, p. 187). Surely such an admission comes very close to an acknowledgment that he has not proved Fletcher's indebtedness to a Spanish play which was published in Madrid just one year before *The Loyal Subject* was licensed for production in London (Bentley, *Jacobean and Caroline Stage*, 3:370).

shawe travelled in Spain in the early seventeenth century, and presumably some of them attended the theatre and after returning to England talked about what they had seen. Oral reports must at times have reached dramatists and influenced their work. Conceivably, the appearance in both Lope de Vega's *El mayordomo de la Duquesa de Amalfi* and Webster's *The Duchess of Malfi* of the striking episode in which the duchess views, either in reality or in waxen counterfeit, the mangled bodies of her husband and two of her children might be the result of Webster's having heard a traveller describe a performance of Lope's play. The episode is not present in the novel of Bandello that is their common source; *El mayordomo* was not printed early enough for Webster to have made use of it. Yet this kind of influence on English plays is difficult to establish.

A more probable instance of Spanish influence has been described by Robert Davril, who calls attention to the resemblance between John Ford's final scene in *The Broken Heart* and that in Mexia de la Cerda's *Doña Inés de Castro*,[31] a play based on the Portuguese legend about the lady of that name. In both plays a sovereign (a male in the Spanish play, a female in the English) succeeds to the throne and symbolically marries the dead body of his or her beloved, who had been killed before the sovereign attained supreme rank. Perhaps Ford saw a printed copy of the play; perhaps he heard about it or about the Portuguese legend on which it is based from a traveller. We must be content with uncertainty in this as in other aspects of the relationship between these two national dramas of the Renaissance.

★

All four English plays based on the *comedia* follow Prince Charles's journey to Madrid in 1623 to court the sister of Philip IV. Although the journey ended in diplomatic disaster, with Charles and his companion the duke of Buckingham urg-

---

[31] *Le Drame de John Ford* (Paris: Marcel Didier, 1954), pp. 176–78. Very little is known about La Cerda, whose only play is *Doña Inés de Castro*. It is included in B.A.E., 45: *Dramáticos Contemporaneos de Lope de Vega*, I (Madrid, 1881).

ing Parliament to vote supplies for a war against Spain, it resulted in an intensified interest in the country and its literature among gentlemen of rank. A number of them had joined the prince in Madrid, and while they were there some had seen both secular and religious plays. Earlier, English dramatists had often turned to Spanish prose fiction, usually in translation, for their sources. Possibly accounts they heard from Prince Charles's attendants of performances in Madrid led a few dramatists to adapt Spanish plays.

The dates of first performance of three of the plays are known: Massinger's in 1624, just before a war with Spain, and Shirley's in 1633 and 1634, not long after peace had been concluded. In March 1624, Parliament responded to Prince Charles's and Buckingham's recommendations by voting supplies for a war; and by the end of the year an army of 12,000 men had been organized to be sent to the Continent.

The Master of the Revels licensed Massinger's *The Renegado, or the Gentleman of Venice* on April 17, 1624,[32] and presumably it was performed not long after. Massinger's first title is a Spanish word, but the protagonist, as the second title emphasizes, is not Spanish or from a state under Spanish rule. Although the locale of the play is Moorish North Africa, all the European characters are natives of the independent republic of Venice. Surprisingly, this play, performed at a time when England was preparing for war with the principal Catholic power, reveals, as I have explained, a marked sympathy, even admiration, for Catholicism.

Shirley's plays were performed at a less sensitive time in Anglo-Spanish relations. The war, not prosecuted vigorously by either nation, was terminated in 1630. In the decade that followed, as indeed throughout most years of the reigns of James I and Charles I, the crown's pro-Spanish policy occasioned frequent criticism, some of it expressed cautiously in drama. Perhaps to avoid controversy, perhaps merely out of dramatic expediency, Shirley took care that neither of his plays revealed its Spanish origin.

[32] *Plays and Poems of Massinger*, ed. Edwards and Gibson, 2:1.

Rather than consider the four plays known to be based on the *comedia* in chronological order, I shall approach them in the descending order of their closeness to their Spanish originals.

As already noted, A. L. Stiefel identified sources in the *comedia* for Shirley's *The Young Admiral* (1633) and *The Opportunity* (1634): respectively, Lope's *Don Lope de Cardona* and Tirso's *El castigo del penséque.* [33]

Both *The Young Admiral* and *The Opportunity* have Italian locales, as have many English Renaissance plays. However, the two plays are fundamentally different: *The Young Admiral,* a tragicomedy of wartime adventure; *The Opportunity,* a witty comedy of courtship, turning on mistaken identity.

The Young Admiral resembles *Don Lope de Cardona* so closely in its plot that there can be no reasonable doubt about their relationship. The plays nevertheless illustrate the difficulty in identifying Spanish sources: the discovery of the relationship depended upon a man's familiarity with two infrequently read plays that superficially reveal few similarities. Only two of the characters' names are identical, and only one, Cassandra, applies to a character in a parallel role. The locales are different: Aragón and Sicily in the Spanish; Naples in the English.

To read the two plays in succession is to be reminded that Lope is a European dramatist of major stature capable of work beyond the reach of Shirley. *The Young Admiral* may be described as a simplified adaptation of *Don Lope de Cardona*; it

---

[33] Stiefel, "Die Nachahmung spanischer Komödien in England unter den ersten Stuarts," *Romanische Forschungen* 5 (1890): 193–220. In this study he provided a detailed account of Shirley's indebtedness to Tirso. Not until 1908 did he do so for the indebtedness to Lope: Stiefel, "Die Nachahmung spanischer Komödien in England unter den ersten Stuarts, III," *Archiv* 119 (1907–08): 309–50.

In an intriguing and yet frustrating footnote to his study of 1890, Stiefel asserts that Shirley's *The Wedding, The Humorous Courtier, The Example,* and *The Royal Master* have Spanish origins (*RF* 5 [1890]: 196 n. 1). He provides no further information about those origins, leaving us in doubt not only about which Spanish works he had in mind but even whether they are dramatic or nondramatic. Subsequent research has provided no elucidation (see Ruth K. Zimmer, *James Shirley: A Reference Guide* [Boston: Hall, 1980]). Yet a statement by Stiefel is not to be taken lightly.

follows the Spanish plot with moderate fidelity, although with omissions. Comparison of the plays illustrates the rapidity of movement of which Lope was capable: the introduction and assimilation without digression of more episodes than we are accustomed to encounter in English drama. Shirley compensates for his omissions by introducing comic characters and scenes, as well as by adding conversations by the major characters about moral dilemmas that confront them.

The dilemmas arise from the obligation felt by the protagonists to serve their princes loyally despite outrageous affronts from them. Despite all provocation they resist opportunities to rebel. Don Lope and Vittori, the Spanish and English protagonists, return as victorious admirals from sea battles with the Sicilian fleet. Hostilities had arisen because of the behavior of the Aragonian-Neapolitan prince in Sicily, where he had gone to court the Sicilian princess. He had given affront by rejecting the princess, as well as by engaging in a duel. In Lope the opponent was the king's son, whom the Aragonian prince killed; in Shirley, the opponent was a nobleman, whom the Neapolitan prince merely wounded. In both plays the admirals return expecting heroes' welcomes. Instead, they find the cities' gates barred against them. The women they love, the two Cassandras, explain the reason for the hostile reception. (Don Lope is already married; Vittori, betrothed.) The princes have tried to seduce the Cassandras. Don Lope's father, attempting to protect his daughter-in-law, has inflicted a minor wound on the prince, spilling a few drops of royal blood, a grave offense for which he has been imprisoned; Vittori's father has admonished the prince, who in return has accused him of treason and has imprisoned him.

Lope de Vega's prince, Don Pedro, whose villainy is the more fully revealed, prides himself on his name and his cruelty, associating himself with the Castillian and Portuguese Pedros the Cruel. Such an allusion to Spain's history, which gives resonance to Lope's play, was of course impossible for Shirley.

Lope's superiority to Shirley appears in his greater subtlety in depicting his wicked prince's reformation as preliminary to his union with the princess. In both plays the rapid transformation of the prince from an unprincipled young man, unjustly harming others, into an individual worthy to marry an admirable princess remains improbable. To be sure, having been captured by the Sicilians, the prince undergoes his transformation under the emotional stress of imprisonment and anticipated execution. He is provided with the example of the princess, who loves him and has willingly made herself a hostage to save his life. Yet Lope goes further. A musician sings about the three Don Pedros, the third the prince himself. And the musician concludes with a reference to the Sicilian princess that leads Don Pedro to a belated awareness of her worth and her love for him. He can then more plausibly undergo a change of character.

Although *The Opportunity*, like *The Young Admiral*, resembles its source play closely enough to be regarded as an adaptation of it, Shirley reveals more independence in his reworking of the Spanish material. Perhaps for this reason, more probably because the nature of his source, *El castigo del penséque*, permitted him to exploit his abilities as a writer of witty social comedy, he produced a better play than *The Young Admiral*. But his success owes much to the clever dramatic situations devised by Tirso.

In both *El castigo* and *The Opportunity*, the action turns on an improbability that we accept as a stage convention: a young man, just arrived in a strange town, is regarded by everyone, including his putative father and sister, as a native of the town who has been absent for several years. In Tirso, the man, Don Rodrigo Girón, accompanied by his servant, a *gracioso*, arrives in a town in Flanders without money, needing food and shelter. In Shirley, two young gentlemen, Aurelio Andreozzi, the protagonist, and a friend accompanied by Aurelio's servant, arrive in Urbino from Milan on a journey to the war in Germany. In both plays the confusion of identities at first occasions humorous situations, until the young men perceive the cause of the confusion and decide to accept the roles thrust upon them. In Tirso, Don Rodrigo has the spur of poverty for doing so, to which is soon added an interest not in one but in two women: one, assumed by others to be his sister; the other, the sovereign countess of the state, a young widow. In Shirley, Aurelio, attracted by the wealth of the man who believes himself to be his father, soon is similarly interested in his so-called sister and in the young widowed sovereign, the duchess of Urbino.

In his depiction of the countess, Tirso reveals his skill in portraying female characters. Early in the play the countess rejects the proposal of a social equal, Count Casimiro, who has come to her court bringing letters in support of his suit from her brother, the duke Arnesto. She rejects him, expressing uncertainty about her willingness to remarry. Rather than accept her refusal, Casimiro employs an armed force to besiege the town. At this juncture, the countess makes the acquaintance of Don Rodrigo and, in compliance with a promise she has made to his supposed father, she appoints him her secretary. Recognizing the military crisis of the moment, Rodrigo, known as Otón, requests that he be permitted to join the force defending the town. The countess makes him captain of her troops. He promptly leads them to victory, routing the troops of Casimiro. This brief military interlude, for which Shirley provides no parallel, lends credibility to the noblewoman's sudden infatuation (in the English as well as the Spanish play) with the newcomer, who is merely a gentleman in rank.

In each play the gentleman's aspiration to marry the noblewoman ends in frustration, not so intense, however, as to prevent him from turning at once to an attractive alternative—his supposed sister, who has shown an unsisterly interest in him. In Tirso, the newcomer, his true identity revealed, succeeds, winning an attractive wife of his own rank. In Shirley, he does not—and with his companion and servant he resumes his journey to the war. This difference in the plays is fitting. Shirley's Aurelio is an adventurer, less engaged emotionally in his intrigues than Tirso's Don Rodrigo.

★

Writing in 1956 about scholarship devoted to *Love's Cure, or The Martial Maid*, G. E. Bentley remarked that "nearly everything about the play is in a state of confusion."[34] After considering arguments about its date, authorship, and inclusion in the Beaumont and Fletcher folio of 1647, he continues:

> The discussions of the source of *Love's Cure* are also contradictory. Stiefel[35] . . . thought that the source was *La Fuerza de la Costumbre* of Guillen de Castro, and [R. Warwick] Bond (*R.E.S.* xi. 262–6) develops the relationship at length, but [G. E.] Macaulay (*C.H.E.L.* vi. 140) denied it. The Spanish play was published in a volume not licensed until February 1624/5 . . . , and such a date would seem to make it rather improbable that Fletcher exploited the new Spanish piece before his death in August. Bond also contends that part of the play is derived from [Céspedes y Meneses's] *Gerardo*, which was translated by Leonard Digges in 1622. (Op. cit., pp. 266–7.) . . . If the relationship of *Love's Cure* to the Spanish play and the romance is as close as Bond thinks, it seems unlikely that they would have been sources for the reviser only. Perhaps a more detailed examination of the relationship between *Love's Cure* and *La Fuerza de la Costumbre* and *Gerardo* would be illuminating.[36]

I shall attempt to provide that examination.

Love's Cure follows Castro only in its main plot—much the larger part of the play—in which the resemblances to *La fuerza de la costumbre* in theme, in situations, and at times even in dialogue, are striking. The theme epitomized in Castro's title, "The power of custom (or habit)"—in this instance its power to give a woman the attributes of a man and to give a man the attributes of a woman—provides the principal complication in the action of each play. In addition to the customary use of the title phrase in the curtain speech of *La fuerza*, it is spoken in dialogue four times earlier. In the English play the idea conveyed by the Spanish phrase is expressed at least five times.

[34] Bentley, *Jacobean and Caroline Stage*, 3:364.

[35] Stiefel, "Die Nachahmung," *Archiv* 99 (1897): 271–310.

[36] Bentley, *Jacobean and Caroline Stage*, 3:366.

The voluminous body of writing devoted to investigating the sources of *Love's Cure* is well described by Martin E. Erickson, "A Review of Scholarship Dealing with the Problem of a Spanish Source for *Love's Cure*," in *Studies in Comparative Literature*, ed. Waldo F. McNeir (Baton Rouge, Louisiana: State University Press, 1962), pp. 102–19.

Both plays emphasize the corollary theme, the power of human nature—specifically love—to reassert itself over the crippling power of habit.

The plays resemble one another even more closely in their plots. In both first acts a mother, accompanied by a twenty-year-old son, joyously prepares to welcome her husband home from an exile that began before the son's birth. In each instance the father, accompanied by a daughter who had been a small child when they left home, has spent the years of his exile fighting for his king in Flanders, and has raised his daughter like a son. Recent events, different in the two plays, have enabled the father to return to Spain. The mother in each play has symbols of mourning taken down and replaced by signs of joy. Fearful lest their sons be wounded or killed in duels, the mothers have reared them as though they were girls, teaching them accomplishments befitting girls, and bringing them up to fear fighting. Both wives receive their husbands with such joy they cannot speak for a moment but soon pour out their emotions.[37]

Although the underplot of *Love's Cure* obscures the closeness of the relationship between the two plays, the parallels between the main plots continue almost to the end. In both plays brothers and sisters, moved by love for sisters and brothers of families introduced in the first act, as well as by parental instruction, gradually acquire the characteristics appropriate to their sexes.[38] The brothers learn manly assertiveness; the sisters lose their pugnacity and become receptive to their lovers.

As I have said, the underplot of *Love's Cure* has no precedent

---

[37] Stiefel, "Die Nachahmung," *Archiv* 99 (1897): 293.

[38] The experiences of the brothers should be sufficient to reveal the relationship between the plays. In each instance the brother falls in love with the sister of his own sister's beloved and his passion is reciprocated. The young woman gives her suitor a glove as a symbol of her affection. A rival suitor takes the glove from him in the woman's presence and he fails to offer resistance. Repelled by his cowardice, the woman rejects him. However, stung by humiliation and the loss of his beloved, he seeks and finds the rival, overcomes him in a duel, spares his life but regains the glove, which he promptly returns to his beloved. She accepts the proof of his courage and accepts him as her future husband.

in *La fuerza de la costumbre*. It is markedly different in tone not only from the Spanish play but from the main plot of the English one: coarse in its preoccupation with illicit sexual relations, reminiscent of Ben Jonson in its focus on the misdeeds of depraved characters. Bond believed that the English dramatists took suggestions for episodes in the underplot from Leonard Digges's translation (1622) of Gonzalo de Céspedes y Meneses' *Gerardo*—in its descriptive English title, *Gerardo the Unfortunate Spaniard. Or a Patterne for Lascivious Lovers. Containing severall strange miseries of loose Affection.*[39] Bond's argument is plausible, and yet I can see no way to verify it. There are resemblances between the romance and the play, but not close and circumstantial ones such as exist between the Spanish play and the main plot of the English one. Furthermore, the resemblances are so conventional that they render a search for sources almost gratuitous. Fletcher and Massinger had each previously drawn on *Gerardo* in writing plays,[40] and perhaps one or both of them did so in writing *Love's Cure*; but I would regard Bond's argument as not proved.

The presence of the underplot of *Love's Cure*, with its coarse sensuality and greedy rogues, provides the most conspicuous difference between the English play and its Spanish source. But other differences—suggestive of differences between the two national dramas—should be mentioned. In *La fuerza de la costumbre*, for example, the stern Spanish sense of honor, personified in the father, is more prominent than in the English play. Furthermore, the son's progress toward an acceptance of family obligations comprises a major strand in *La fuerza de la costumbre*. So also Castro's play, far more than the English one, conveys the romance of temperate Spanish nights with gallants courting their mistresses beneath balconies. This is the romance of the cape-and-sword play, absent in *Love's Cure* despite its Spanish setting, incompatible with the schemes and

[39] R. Warwick Bond, "On Six Plays in *Beaumont and Fletcher, 1679*," *RES* 11 (1935): 266–67.

[40] Ibid., p. 266.

counter-schemes of the unprincipled although high-spirited characters of the underplot.

There can be no reasonable doubt that the main plot of *Love's Cure* is based on *La fuerza de la costumbre*. The related problems of authorship and date are not so easily resolved. Edwards and Gibson, Massinger's latest editors, attribute it "on the internal evidence of style" to Fletcher and Massinger.[41] Yet the volume of Castro's plays including *La fuerza* was not licensed until February 1624/5 and Fletcher died in August. Martin E. Erickson makes two suggestions, either of which could account for Fletcher's hand in the play—and thus its presence in the folio of 1647. It is possible, he writes, that *La fuerza de la costumbre* had been printed before 1625.[42] Alternatively, he adds, "it was quite possible for Massinger to have written a play around bits of an old Beaumont and Fletcher play."[43]

★

I have referred earlier to Massinger's *The Renegado, or The Gentleman of Venice*, an expertly constructed tragicomedy about the experiences of some Christians held captive as slaves in Moorish North Africa. Massinger based it primarily on Cervantes' autobiographical writings about his five years of servitude after he was captured in 1575, although he also read widely in accounts of Turkey and Turkish life to achieve a measure of authenticity in depicting the customs of the Moors.[44] "The general impression made by *The Renegado*," Samuel C. Chew comments, "is of a romantic and picturesque yet, generally speaking, accurate and realistic orientalism unmatched elsewhere in the imaginative literature of Renaissance England."[45]

[41] *Plays and Poems of Massinger*, ed. Edwards and Gibson, 1:xx–xxi.

[42] Erickson, "Review of Scholarship," in *Studies in Comparative Literature*, ed. McNeir, p. 106.

[43] Ibid., p. 115.

[44] Warner G. Rice, "The Sources of Massinger's *The Renegado*," PQ 11 (1932): 65–75.

[45] Chew, *The Crescent and the Rose: Islam and England during the Renaissance*

Cervantes turned repeatedly to his experience as a slave in his subsequent writings: in, among others, the "Historia del cautivo," one of the intercalated stories in the first part of *Don Quijote*, published in 1605 and translated into English by Thomas Shelton in 1612; and in a *comedia, Los baños de Argel*, published in 1615 and never translated. *The Renegado* resembles this latter play more closely than any other of Cervantes' writings about the experiences of Christians while enslaved by the Moslems.[46] Yet if *Los baños de Argel* may be regarded as Massinger's "source" play, he probably took suggestions from Cervantes' other writings on the subject, which indeed bear a strong resemblance to one another. In particular, the "Historia del cautivo" in *Don Quijote* anticipates much that is in *The Renegado*. It would be a reasonable guess that Massinger first became aware of the subject's possibilities by reading the story in a readily available English translation, and that he then read more widely and found in the untranslated play more comprehensive suggestions for his own play.

Although the parallels between *Los baños de Argel* and *The Renegado* are sufficiently particularized for us to be confident that Massinger made use of the Spanish play, he cannot be said to have written an adaptation of it. He altered the locale from Algiers to Tunis, and the nationality of his principal Christian characters from Spanish to Venetian. Cervantes includes vivid scenes depicting the cruelty of the Moslems that were irrelevant to Massinger's purpose and find no reflection in his play. Massinger reworked extensively those portions of *Los baños de Argel* on which he drew; some of his best scenes have no Spanish precedent, and he achieves a coherence and intensity of focus absent in Cervantes.

(New York: Oxford University Press, 1937), p. 536. Chew notes that "the renegado is a stereotyped figure" in "the Spanish pirate-romances" (p. 534).

[46] Emil Koeppel identified *Los baños de Argel* as Massinger's primary source: *Quellen-Studien zu den Dramen George Chapman's, Philip Massinger's und John Ford's* (Strassburg: Karl J. Trübner, (1897), pp. 97–103. The relationship between the plays is examined by Theodor Heckmann in *Massinger's "The Renegado" und seine spanischen Quellen* (Halle: 1905). Edwards and Gibson provide a compact account of Massinger's sources: *Plays and Poems of Massinger*, 2:2–4.

Massinger opens his play in the marketplace at Tunis, to which foreigners are allowed to come at market time. The protagonist, Vitelli, a Venetian gentleman disguised as a merchant, displays his wares for sale to the Moors. He has actually come to rescue his sister Paulina, who was seized in Venice by a renegade Venetian pirate, Antonio Grimaldi, and brought to Tunis. His task will not be easy, a Jesuit priest named Francisco cautions him. Grimaldi has sold Paulina to the viceroy, Asambeg,[47] who is infatuated with her. When Vitelli expresses fear both for her chastity and for her religious faith, the priest comforts him, telling him that he has given Paulina a sacred relic that will keep her from violence if she continues her prayers and does not yield of her own consent.

Cervantes opens his play at an earlier stage in the action, depicting a Moorish raid on a coastal town in Spain. As in Massinger, a renegade native of the place is a leader of the raiding party. Among those captured are a young married couple, Don Fernando and Constanza, and a young bachelor, Don Lope. In Algiers, Lope is placed in the sultan's prison and Fernando and Constanza, not known to be married, become the property of Caurali, the captain of Algiers. Fernando confronts a problem similar to that of Massinger's Vitelli when their master falls in love with Constanza, while he must tactfully repulse the advances of Caurali's wife.

Like Lope, Massinger's Vitelli attracts the love of a highborn Moorish lady, in this instance Donusa, a princess and the niece of the sultan himself. As Edwards and Gibson note, Donusa represents two of Cervantes' characters, Halima, the wife of Caurali, and Zara, the beautiful daughter of a rich Moor.[48] Although sought in marriage by the king of Fez, Zara, who has been converted to Christianity by a slave woman, sees Lope in his prison cell and falls in love with him. Attracted not only by Lope's appearance but also by the hope he can offer of escape to Spain, where she could practice her new religion, she con-

[47] On possible sources for this name in histories of Turkey, see Rice, "Sources of Massinger's *The Renegado* 11:73 n. 11.

[48] *Plays and Poems of Massinger*, ed. Edwards and Gibson, 2:3.

veys a large sum of money to him with which he purchases freedom for himself and his cellmate. He subsequently makes his way to Mallorca, where he buys a ship in which he returns at once to a prearranged place near Algiers and rescues Zara, Fernando, Constanza, and other Christians. In *The Renegado*, the principal characters similarly escape in a flight by sea, this one carefully planned by Francisco, who combines skill in practical affairs with a saintly power over those around him.

Although Cervantes' power as a writer appears intermittently in *Los baños de Argel*, which is more impressive in isolated scenes than in its entirety, his play must be regarded as inferior to *The Renegado*. Yet it should be counted among Cervantes' accomplishments that, in turning his five years of bitter captivity into writings about Christians in Moslem servitude, he provided materials that Massinger could rework into an important play. But *The Renegado* is emphatically Massinger's own. The striking portrayals of individuals undergoing transformations of character are Massinger's. So, too, is his moral earnestness. This is a striking instance of English drama enriched by the *comedia*.

★

Even so small a sample as four plays permits a few observations to be made about differences between the sources and their English progeny. In all instances except that of *The Renegado*, the English play is inferior. The inferiority appears most patently in *The Young Admiral*. Shirley could not be expected to rival Lope. But more than their respective abilities is at issue, since Lope could add a dimension to his play, as Shirley could not, by alluding to Spanish history and legend. Except in the instance of *Los baños de Argel*, the Spanish plays are more neatly ordered than the English. Coming to *Love's Cure* after a reading of *La fuerza de la costumbre*, one is repelled by an intrusive underplot scarcely in harmony with the romance of young love. The dialogue of the Spanish plays is consistently more chaste than that of the English. No one of the four English plays captures the spirit of the Spanish cape and sword play, the form in which several Restoration dramatists succeeded. Only one of them, *Love's Cure*, has Spanish characters and a Spanish setting. This play and *The Opportunity* have resemblances to the cape and sword play, although only the former reveals, even in weakened form, something of the code of honor that animates what Dryden later called "the Spanish plot."[49]

After the Restoration, the "Spanish plots" comprised the earliest distinctive sub-genre to appear. However, the impetus that established them in the 1660s was provided not by English Renaissance plays—either the adaptations from the *comedia* or the intrigue plays based on Spanish fiction—but by the experiences of Cavaliers during the Interregnum, some of whom (including Charles II himself) had spent years of the royal exile in the Spanish Netherlands. On the king's suggestion, Sir Samuel Tuke wrote an adaptation of Antonio Coello's *Los empeños de seis horas* (then thought to have been written by Calderón), the successful and influential *The Adventures of Five Hours* (1663). George Digby, second earl of Bristol, who had been born in Madrid when his father was ambassador there, adapted three of Calderón's cape and sword plays. These and other adaptations provided the formal model for the "Spanish plot," a model employed by some dramatists even when they wrote plays based on French or English sources.[50]

Although additional Renaissance plays may be traced to Spanish plays, there are good reasons to assume the discoveries will be too few to alter the pattern of relationship of English drama to the *comedia* that has already emerged. For one thing, although only four Spanish plays have been identified as sources, one of them, *La fuerza de la costumbre*, has been independently identified by three different scholars. I have referred to Stiefel's original discovery of 1897 and to Bond's essay of 1935. Bond states that he identified the Spanish source in the first decade of this century, only to be told that his discovery

[49] *Love's Cure* would not have provoked the complaint spoken by a character in the final act (v.i) of Dryden's *An Evening's Love* (1668), "I hate your *Spanish* honor ever since it spoyl'd our *English* Playes." Quoted from Loftis, *Spanish Plays of Neoclassical England*, p. 97.

[50] Ibid., pp. 64–96.

had been anticipated by Stiefel. In addition, we learn from Felix E. Schelling's *Elizabethan Drama* (1908) that Schelling's former student, A.S.W. Rosenbach, had discovered the source and reported it in his unpublished dissertation.[51] Such duplication implies that further search for sources in the *comedia* is unlikely to yield fruitful results.

An even stronger reason for believing that few sources in the *comedia* await identification is the striking fact that the last convincing discovery was made in 1897, eighty-nine years ago. To be sure, since the Second World War source-hunting has not been a favored occupation among literary scholars. Yet editors of plays are perforce source hunters, and many notable editions of Renaissance plays continue to appear. The failure to find additional sources in the *comedia* may be attributed more plausibly to the absence of them than to scholarly indolence. We may safely conclude, I believe, that the many similarities between the Renaissance English and Spanish dramas are the result of parallel but independent development from the medieval dramas of the two nations.

The negative results yielded by twentieth-century attempts to find sources in the *comedia* for Tudor and early Stuart plays should stimulate rather than discourage the comparative study of the two national dramas. Knowing that the "influence" of Spanish upon English drama was negligible, we can leave the search for sources and turn our attention to the far more rewarding study of the striking similarities amid differences in the two dramas. Voltaire in the eighteenth century and Allardyce Nicoll in the twentieth would not have mistakenly assumed that English dramatists frequently drew on Spanish plays had they not perceived important resemblances between the two dramas. Let us direct our attention to the resemblances and also the differences: for example, to the respective relationships of the plays to classical drama, classical literary criticism, and Renaissance commentary; to the conceptions of tragedy in the two countries; to the nature of Lope de Vega's and Shakespeare's history plays; to the relationships, respec-

---

[51] Schelling, *Elizabethan Drama*, 1:401–02; 2:214–15.

tively, of Lope and Shakespeare to the dramatists who were their predecessors, their contemporaries, and their seventeenth-century successors; to Lope's and Shakespeare's reputations in that century; to differences in the portrayal of social class relationships in Spanish and English comedy; to the conventions controlling Spanish and English dramatic dialogue; to the uses made of Italian prose fiction in the two dramas; to the levels of freedom permitted by government censorship in the two countries, as well as to emphases in the censorship; to the differences in the dramas, if any, that can be attributed to the Spanish employment of actresses and the English employment of boys for women's roles. Such subjects will be more rewarding than source-hunting.

Index

Aerschot, Philippe de Croy, duke of, 49; in Lope, 31, 48–49
Alagón, Enrique de: in Lope, 206
Alba, Antonio Alvarez de Toledo, 5th duke of: in Calderón, 190
Alba, Fernando Alvarez de Toledo, 3rd duke of, 35–38, 45, 72, 82, 83, 219; in *La aldehuela*, 38n; in *A Larum for London*, 218–19
Albert of Austria, archduke, 94, 94n, 120, 145, 166n
Alcacer-el-Kebir, Battle of, 171, 172
Alfonso VIII of Castile, 73
Almansa y Mendoza, Andrés de, 210n
Alvise, Contarini, Venetian ambassador to the Netherlands, 193–94
Anjou, duke of. *See* Henry III, king of France
Anjou, Hercules Francis, duke of, 34
Anne of Austria, queen of France, 127
Antiochus of Syria: in Massinger, 172–73
Antwerp: in *A Larum for London*, 218–19; sack of (1576), 48, 218, 219, 219n; siege of (1585), 58, 188; and Spanish books, 108n; as trade center, 36, 38
Aristotle, 19, 62
Armada, Invincible (1588), 34, 45, 60, 61, 63–64, 111, 204, 221; Lope de Vega's service in, 62; in Marlowe, 86–87; in Shakespeare, 81; in Spanish nondramatic poetry, 62, 63, 232
Armada, second (1596), 27, 63
Arminianism, 134–35, 137
Arthur, duke of Brittany, 73; in Shakespeare, 22, 74–76

Aston, Sir Walter, English ambassador to Madrid, 122, 162
autos sacramentales, 112
Auvergne, Charles de Valois, count of, 99–100, 99n; in Chapman, 98, 99, 100, 100n, 101
Avila, Sancho de, 219; in *A Larum for London*, 218

Bacon, Francis, xiii, 20, 121; on menace of Spain, 6, 71, 139–40, 184–85
Baden-Durlach, margrave of, 124, 128
Bahía de Todos Santos, Brazil: Dutch capture and Spanish recapture of, 189, 199–200, 205, 206, 206n, 208, 208n, 222; in Quevedo, 214. *See also* Vega Carpio, Lope de: *El Brasil restituido*
Bale, John, *King Johan*, 78, 78n
ballads, folk: as source of history plays, 5, 224
Balzac. *See* Entragues
Bances Candamo, Francisco Antonio de: on Coello, 62n
Bandello, Matteo, 247
Beaumont, Francis: and authorship of *Love's Cure*, 256
Bedford, William Russell, 7th earl of, 108
Bellan, Sieur de, *Histoire mémorable de Dias espagnol*, 239
Bellièvre, Pomponne de, chancellor: in Chapman, 102
Bergen-op-Zoom: siege of, 130, 130n, 188, 222
Berkeley of Stratton, John Berkeley, 1st baron, 109
Berlaymont, Charles, count of: in Lope, 49, 51

180, 181n, 227–28; and French history plays, 85n, 227; and Spanish history plays, 40, 42–45, 85; and Spanish nondramatic poetry, 42, 60

Dekker, Thomas, 46n; *The Virgin Martyr* (with Massinger), 169

Demetrius legend, 245–46, 245–46n

Digby, Kenelm, 246

Digby, Sir John: and Anglo-Spanish marriage alliance, 113–15, 113–15n, 118–19, 225; on Gondomar, 122–23. *See also* Bristol, John Digby

Digges, Leonard: translation of Céspedes y Meneses' *Gerardo*, 253, 255

Doleman, R. (probably pseud. of Robert Parsons), *A Conference about the Next Succession to the Crowne of Ingland*, 72–74, 81, 90, 105

Dominis, Marco Antonio de, 175

Don Juan of Austria. *See* Juan of Austria, Don

Donne, John, 159n

Dorset, Thomas Sackville, 1st earl of, *Gorboduc* (with Thomas Norton), 20

drama, English Renaissance, xi; relationship to French drama, 238; relationship to medieval religious drama, 155, 235, 261; relationship to Spanish Renaissance drama, 3–4, 5, 6–7, 235–61 *passim*, 236n; traditions of, 5, 9–10n; Voltaire on, 3–4. *See also* history plays, English

drama, English Restoration: and Spanish plots, 259–60, 259–60n

drama, French neoclassical, 5n, 238

drama, neoclassical theory of: and Renaissance dramatists, 3, 4–6, 19–20. *See also* decorum in characterization, principle of

drama, Spanish Renaissance, xi; performances of for Englishmen in Spain, 112, 112n, 154–55, 154n, 247, 248; performances of in Amsterdam, 4; publication of before 1582, 236n; relationship to English Renaissance drama, 3–4, 5, 6–7, 235–61 *passim*; relationship to medieval religious drama, 155, 235, 261; Voltaire on, 3–4. *See also comedia*; history plays, Spanish

Drew, Thomas, possible author of *The Duchess of Suffolk*, 167

Dryden, John, 43, 43n, 260n; *Don Sebastian*, 171

Durlán: relief of, 66

Dutch expeditionary force: capture and surrender of Bahía de Todos Santos, Brazil, 189, 199–200

Dutch Republic: and the Palatinate, 121, 123–24, 126

Dutch wars. *See* Netherlands: and Eighty Years' War with Spain

Dutch West India Company: and Brazil, 199, 208

Effingham, Lord Howard of. *See* Nottingham, Charles Howard, 1st earl of

Eleanor, elder sister of John of England, wife of Alfonso VIII of Castile, 73

Eleanor of Aquitaine: in Shakespeare, 75

Elizabeth I, queen of England, 14, 21, 22, 23, 71, 85n, 108, 141, 226, 227, 228; alliance with Henry IV of France, 64–65, 64n, 85, 87, 92–93; attempts on life of, 35–36, 79, 79n, 81–82; in English history plays, 22, 23, 24, 93, 96, 104, 136; and Don Juan of Austria, 52, 52n; and Essex, 62, 90; in French history plays, 85n, 227; marriage proposal from Philip II, 24–25, 35; and Mary, queen of Scots, 81–

Library of Congress Cataloging-in-Publication Data

LOFTIS, JOHN CLYDE, 1919–
RENAISSANCE DRAMA IN ENGLAND & SPAIN.

INCLUDES INDEX.

I. ENGLISH DRAMA—EARLY MODERN AND ELIZABETHAN,
1500–1600—HISTORY AND CRITICISM. 2. ENGLISH
DRAMA—17TH CENTURY—HISTORY AND CRITICISM.
3. SPANISH DRAMA—CLASSICAL PERIOD, 1500–1700—HISTORY
AND CRITICISM. 4. GREAT BRITAIN—RELATIONS—SPAIN. 5. SPAIN—
RELATIONS—GREAT BRITAIN. 6. LITERATURE, COMPARATIVE—
SPANISH AND ENGLISH. 7. LITERATURE, COMPARATIVE—
ENGLISH AND SPANISH. 8. HISTORY IN LITERATURE.
I. TITLE.

PR655.L64 1987   823'.3'09358   86–25431
ISBN 0–691–06706–6